Peace!
Carol Maste
3/10/12

You Can't Do That!

You Can't Do That!

Marv Davidov,
Nonviolent Revolutionary

Carol Masters
and Marv Davidov

NODIN PRESS

ISBN: 978-1-932472-89-9

Library of Congress Cataloging-in-Publication Data

Masters, Carol.
  You can't do that! : Marv Davidov, nonviolent revolutionary / Carol Masters, Marv Davidov.
      p. cm.
  ISBN 978-1-932472-89-9
  1. Davidov, Marv. 2. Political activists--United States--Biography. 3. Pacifists--United States--Biography.
4. Environmentalists--United States--Biography. 5. Peace movements--United States. 6. Social justice--United States.
7. Nonviolence--United States. 8. Antinuclear movement--United States. I. Davidov, Marv. II. Title.
  CT275.D237433M37 2009
  324'.40973--dc22
                                    2009040451

design and layout: John Toren

Nodin Press, LLC
530 N. Third Street,
Suite 120
Minneapolis, MN
55401

"Never doubt that a small group of thoughtful, committed citizens can change the world. Indeed, it is the only thing that ever has."

– Margaret Mead

ACKNOWLEDGEMENTS

Marv and the beloved communities make change possible. My personal beloveds ease the loneliness of writing and made this book happen:

The writing workshop Onionskins, especially patience and critique from friends and poets Pat Barone, Sharon Chmielarz, Kate Dayton, Martha Meek, Nancy Raeburn, Mary Kay Rummel, Cary Waterman.

Women of WAMM, especially Polly Mann, Mary Beaudoin, Sarah Martin, Sue Ann Martinson, Lucia Wilkes Smith, Vicky Brockman, coordinators Roxanne Abbas, Betty McKenzie, Sue Welna, Ann Galloway; and people of PAMM, Greg and Nancy McDaniels, Mark and Abby Jensen, Steve McKeown and Joan Johnson, Mary Ellen Halvorson, Anne Newhart, Sue Ann again; and congregations of the Community of St. Martin and Holy Trinity.

Many thanks to Movement photographers Mark Jensen, Gregory McDaniels, and Michael Bayly, and to John Toren for exemplary and patient editing.

And a special word of thanks to my family, especially Ken.

– Carol Masters

Contents

1

Who will speak if we don't?

The Park Avenue Dialysis Clinic is a yellow brick two-story building with a modest sign beside the glass double door. On this day in early November 2004, the weather is dreary, the sky lead-colored and low. I'm here to tape Marv's stories and ask questions, but mostly to listen. Marv has kidney failure and undergoes dialysis three times a week on a machine that looks like a tall automated bank teller. During these three-hour sessions his blood is cleansed and wastes removed through tubes strung like decorative streamers to and from the machine.

He makes use of the time by telling stories about the Movement. To him, it's all one movement: the nonviolent peace, antinuclear, anti-weapons campaigns, anti-racism, and civil rights movements. He's been there, a full-voiced participant in many people's struggles, from the Freedom Rides in 1961 to the Canada to Cuba Peace Walk in 1963, to Vietnam era activism, the Minnesota farmers' power line struggle (which Marv calls the World Series of Civil Disobedience), to the anti-weapons campaigns of the Honeywell Project and Alliant Action, to current antiwar protests.

Over the next year, as I ask questions and listen, Marv's voice gains in strength. His rage for justice takes him off the dialysis couch and back into classrooms and on the streets, back home: in the "circle" protesting Alliant TechSystems, maker of nuclear and "conventional" weapons of mass destruction, or on the Lake Street bridge and in Washington, DC protesting the war in Iraq, or before the gates at Fort Benning, Georgia.

I suspect that Marv's voice is one of the things that drew some people to the peace movement in the first place. Its physical timbre is not impressive—a flat Midwestern sound, sometimes harsh, with broad drawn-out vowels that seem to mock the outrage—but the stories that it conveys draw us in, making us question what's right and what's wrong. Maybe we hope it can be our own moral story. I've been listening for twenty-five years, at first from a distance, at the edge of a crowd, then more closely in his office or at meetings, in small circles, and over meals. Always there are meals, after vigils, demonstrations, or actions.

"We have to make the connections between issues," he says. "Every particular struggle exposes one more aspect of the United States' military, capitalist system." He knows—and his stories begin in childhood—that the U.S. is not a classless society. "It's all class-based ... there's the ruling class, and the rest of us." His gesture sweeps in the nurses and technicians and the patients on their blue couches lining three walls of the long room—a dozen middle-aged to elderly men and women of different races. They do not look gravely ill but seem tired, dozing or reading to pass the hours.

Are the workers reasonably paid? he wonders. They are professionals. And these patients must have insurance, they must be lucky enough, or sick and poor enough to have their dialysis covered. Still, they are clearly not among the 1 percent of American people who control 40 percent of the wealth, nor among the 5 percent who control 60 percent. "Another reality," Marv continues, "is that whoever owns it, runs it. The economic system is run in their interest; no matter what the struggle is, we always come up against that."

He looks around at his tethered companions. In the next chair a stocky black man, eyes closed, mutters something, a curse; across the room a cocoa-skinned Latina listens through ear-plugs to a radio, her mouth drawn down in discomfort or annoyance at whatever truth or lie is on the market today. Marv shifts his shoulders, less a shrug than a weariness. "Racism is used to exploit people and divide poor whites against blacks." This is not a change of subject....

2

"I had these rules"

The injustice of prejudice came early to Marv's awareness. He was about eight at the time.

In the early 1940s Gerty and Louie Davidov and their two sons, Marv and his younger brother Jerry, lived in a fourplex on Detroit's East Side, near the outskirts of Grosse Point, a community of large wooded estates, sweeping lawns, and views of Lake St. Clair. At the time a system of housing "points" determined who could live in Grosse Point. "We didn't have those points, like most blacks or Jews at that time and place," Marv said.

Although many of Detroit's Jews had achieved a measure of affluence as early as the 1930s, they were barred from living in suburbs such as Dearborn and Grosse Pointe as well as from some Detroit neighborhoods. In Detroit, department stores advertised that "Hebrews need not apply" for sales positions, and Jews were restricted from working in supervisory or executive levels of the automobile industry. Resorts around Detroit advertised that they had "no Hebrew patronage."

But the kids in Marv's neighborhood, Jew and non-Jew, played together in the alleys, streets, and schoolyard. They played baseball—even with Marv's mom, Gerty, who could hit better than anyone. Marv was skillful and fast and did well at games, excelling at Knock the Can: one kid would place a can on a rock and run like hell to avoid rocks hurled to knock it off. They played war games as news of World War II battles filled the airwaves.

Marv found school interesting; he began a lifelong habit of reading omnivorously. He had lots of friends and thought of himself as a popular, well-rounded kid. His family, he knew, was not as wealthy as some;

in fact he was acutely aware of his parents' conflicts around money. But he had what he needed.

Then something changed. "I was in third or fourth grade; One of my friends, who came from a very wealthy family, invited me to his party. There would be horse-drawn sleighs across the family estate. I was *very* glad to be invited."

But Marv's happiness was short lived. The boy came to school a couple of days later and was very sad. His grandmother had told him, Marv says, mimicking the young, puzzled query in a soft voice, "You can't come to my party because you're a dirty Jew."

"What's that?" Marv asked, and his friend said, "I don't know." He ran home crying and told his mother the story, asking her, "How could I be dirty when I have to take a bath every night?"

However, the morning of the party a chauffeur-driven car pulled up and Marv's friend got out along with his mother. She explained to the whole family, "My mother's a bigot, I'm not. My child is crying and we've come to take you to the party!" Marv followed them out, his distress gone—for a while. "I learned something, that not all rich people are bigots. Just some of them. But that whole incident was painful—no child should ever experience that." He made a decision that day that when he was old enough he would do something about such invidious bigotry—something serious.

"As a child I had these rules, you know? I don't know where the hell they came from." For example, in third and fourth grade, even before the incident of the birthday party, Marv determined that he ought to dance with the girls that no one else asked during his grammar school dances. He thought, "These girls are gonna be very sad if no one wants to dance with them. That was a beginning somehow. I understood people were hurting, therefore I had to do something." It became a rule.

Marv's parents were good, hard-working people, but looking back on his childhood years, he doesn't see their influence as the source of his growing commitment to battling hurt and injustice. All the same, Marv loves to tell stories about his mother. "You know, Gerty told me I was a breech birth. Maybe that's why... I knew you had to jump."

According to Gerty, Marv's first act was to piss in the doctor's eye. "My humor tells me he belonged to the conservative AMA so maybe I

Marv's grade school class, 1937. Marv is second child from the left.

better piss in his eye ... my first human act." Marv's mother had a caustic humor that still intrigues and delights him and may have influenced him more than he admits.

Gerty and Louie were immigrants; Louie's family came from Minsk and spoke Yiddish and Polish or Russian. Gerty's family origins were in northwestern Romania. Both families came to this country around the time of World War I, chased by pogroms during which Jews were rounded up, arrested, and often killed. Louie's family wound up in Detroit, Gerty's in North Dakota and then in the Twin Cities. "They were all hard-working people, working class. They spoke fluent English by the time Jerry and I were born, and a little Yiddish. I'm a one-language person, unfortunately. Language is hard for me."

A second seminal event that shaped Marv's world-view took place in the summer of 1943, when Marv was about twelve. The family had moved from the east to the west side of Detroit in 1941, and Marv and his brother Jerry were attending school in a compound campus that included Roosevelt, Durfee and Central schools—elementary, middle and high school. The student body was 90% Jewish. One morning the students were surprised to see National Guard trucks pulling up in front of their campus. Teachers had a hard time curbing the students' curiosity as the Guard proceeded to set up camp on their school grounds.

The Guard had been called to quell race riots. In the years before and during World War II, hundreds of thousands of people, black and white, had migrated north, many to work in the auto industry.

On June 20, rioting broke out on Belle Isle, a recreational area used predominately by blacks. Fistfights escalated into city-wide violence in some areas, though not in Marv's neighborhood. White mobs attacked blacks downtown and drove into black neighborhoods where they were met by snipers. Cars were overturned and set on fire. By the time federal troops arrived to halt the riots, twenty-five blacks and nine whites had been killed and property damage exceeded two million dollars.

Gerty as a young woman

Both Marv and his brother Jerry talk about the constant wrangling of his parents about money. "At home, it was a war zone most of the time; maybe that's why I'm attracted to nonviolent solutions," Marv says. As opposed to his flamboyant and talkative mother, Louie was more reticent. Jerry says that he, at least, called Louie "the silent man." Marv describes Louie as an industrious auto worker and later, once the family had moved the Minneapolis, a salesman at Nate's Department Store. At noisy family gatherings and at home, he did not have much to say. The orders and the discipline came mainly from Gerty.

Later, Marv says, he came to treasure growing up in a working class family. "We always went to public schools. We couldn't afford anything else. There was a great deal of conflict in our house about money. We never were starving, we always had clothing that was presentable. But Jerry and I got very little allowance money—we had to work."

Marv had a paper route in grade school and during high school he drove a lumber truck for a company owned by a neighbor. He enjoyed being around "working-class guys" at the lumber company. "I was class conscious. In grade school and high school most of my fellow students came from middle- or upper-class families."

Yet Marv insists that even as a young boy, his understanding of injustice had less to do with economic inequities than with human dignity. As far as he can remember, he had a feel for fair play which later turned into a "hunger" to see justice done. "As I learned more, and grew, that feeling of wanting fair play for everybody got systematized into a political vision of justice. You must struggle for justice. It must be done. And I don't know where the hell it came from. Scripture? Not with me. Mm-mm. I didn't pay too much attention to the Hebrew teaching. I was more interested in baseball. You know, in sports you have to play fair, too. It's no fun, otherwise."

When Marv was in seventh grade, a woman from Columbia University came to speak to the school assembly. In the course of her presentation, she told her young audience that black people were *not* biologically or genetically inferior to white people. Marv ran home. "I was so excited. 'Gerty!' I yelled, before she could even open the door, I was shouting, 'I knew it I knew it!' I learned how influential one teacher can be. With one talk. It blew my mind. I *knew* that, and here was a scholar, an important professor from Columbia, who spoke to all of us." Marv wanted to play that role. He wanted to tell truths like that.

Thanksgiving, 2005. Marv and his brother Jerry are together with friends from Marv's building. Barb Mishler, antiwar activist and coordinator at a Southwest Minneapolis Loaves and Fishes, has invited all of us for a feast. Grace before the meal circles the table, guests taking turns expressing their thanks and good wishes. But minor keys are struck in our prayers, talk about Iraq and Afghanistan and harsh words about our president, vicious U.S. foreign policy, profit-seeking corporate killers, cowardly Congress, and so on. Marv holds up Native Americans, especially on this day, as early and continuing victims of U.S. oppression.

Racism as it affects indigenous people is an important part of Marv's awareness. His extended family in Detroit, Louie's family, encouraged him to read, and he did, as furiously as he played. Louie's sister Mildred was married to a wealthy lawyer who had an extensive library, and they were always encouraging Marv to borrow books. "I borrowed everything I could get my hands on to read. I read all the time, profusely, *especially* about Native people. Like other kids, reading under the covers at night, I didn't want to go to bed, I wanted to go on adventures in the books."

He could see from both fiction and historical works how repressed and battered American Indians were. "But they fought back! and I al-ways admired that, and I said one day maybe I would work with Indians. I was absolutely fascinated. Years later I worked intimately and closely with people in the American Indian Movement including the founders, Clyde and Vernon Bellecourt."

Marv was a good student, and his brother Jerry laments coming up "be-hind" Marv through grade school and junior high. "Oh, the teacher would say, Davidov? I expect a lot from you." He shakes his head, laughing

Marv's graduation photo

ruefully. "Too bad for them." School was apparently a happier place for Marv than Jerry, but both were more interested in what was going on outside than in the classroom.

The boys enjoyed each other's company then as now, though there were years of separation—Jerry went into the Navy, Marv into the Army. Jerry enjoyed and learned from the experience, he says. Marv, too, learned a great deal, but enjoyment was another question.

3

Learning Nonviolence in the Army

In 1949, at the age of 18, Marv said goodbye to his Detroit friends and left for a new home in St. Paul, Minnesota, where his uncles Max and Adolph Nachman lived. He had never considered going to college, since the family could not afford it, but his uncles offered to pay his tuition to the University of Minnesota in return for a few days of work each week in their Midway department store. Home became an apartment in a fourplex on Goodrich Avenue that his uncles owned, and except for a stint in the Army and time spent working for the Movement on the west coast, Marv has lived in the Twin Cities ever since.

Gerty's health had been deteriorating, however, and one day a few months before Marv left Detroit, she collapsed with a severe attack of ulcerative colitis, bleeding from the mouth. Fortunately, Marv was home from classes at the time and called an ambulance. Gerty was rushed to the hospital and had soon regained her usual robust health (she lived to the age of 100). The following year Gerty, Louie, and Jerry joined Marv in the Twin Cities. Gerty wanted to be closer to her brothers and sister Bea, and Louie, too, was ready for a change. He planned to work in the retail business with his relatives.

Marv found life with his mother's relations to be noisy and full. He describes his uncles as outgoing and generous men, pillars of the Jewish community. They were athletes, fishermen, and warm family men. His uncle Sam was a locally famous boxer during the 1930s, at a time when boxing still had a wide following. Uncle Jack had served some years in the military then returned to help Adolph and Max in the department store.

The store in the Midway area was an old-fashioned neighborhood business serving a clientele of working class people. "I loved working in the store. I can still smell the resin. I'd sweep the sawdust off the floor with my Uncle Jack, then check the new merchandise and ticket it all. They taught me how to sell and treat everyone with respect. I especially liked fitting the small kids with Red Goose shoes." He remembers walking home most winter evenings with Adolph, several blocks down University Avenue and along the quieter streets of 1930s and 40s bungalows and small apartment buildings, the neighborhood hushed with falling snow. Minnesota winters in the early 1950s were memorable for the snowfalls: Marv and Jerry would climb up on their garage roof and jump into tall drifts in the back yard. They ice-fished along with thousands of other Minnesota fishermen—almost as many in the winter as in the summer.

The family now had an apartment at a reduced rent in the fourplex. Gerty's brothers Adolph and Max, who owned the building, occupied two of the other units with their families, along with sister Bea, her husband Ben and Grandpa; another Jewish family rented out the fourth unit. Later Bea's daughter Rita, her husband Benny, and four children lived at the fourplex. Family gatherings were frequent and almost invariably laden with food. At Christmastime corned beef was often served with pickles and onion buns, cole slaw and brandy. On most Friday nights, sumptuous dinners of steak, salad, potatoes, mushrooms, chicken soup and dessert were a regular occurrence. After dinner everyone would crowd around the new-fangled TV to watch the fights, and cheer on their favorite boxers Del and Glen, the 'fighting Flannigan brothers,' who they knew by sight because the pugilists shopped at their Midway department store.

Marv's academic career got off to a rocky start. Though he had been an excellent student in high school, the University of Minnesota rejected him because he scored poorly on the entrance exam. This was an unexpected blow, and it disappointed him profoundly, but he was encouraged by a friend of his uncles to apply to Macalester. He passed the exams and was admitted in 1950.

Macalester was a welcoming community. Classes and student activities engrossed him. He was on the track team and enjoyed athletic training. He studied hard, choosing history and political science as his major fields, and also jumped into politics with Students for Democratic Action (the student wing of Americans for Democratic Action) and worked in precinct caucuses. Professors Theodore Mitau, German Jewish refugee Dorothy Jacobson, Evelyn Albinson, and his advisor Dr. Lichtenstein, also a Jewish refugee from Germany, were seminal influences. In retrospect these college years, full of stimulating ideas and passionate discussion with the support of his extended family, seemed idyllic.

In 1953, Marv joined Military Intelligence Reserve at Fort Snelling, having passed the college qualification draft test in his senior year at Macalester. But that same year he suffered the first of what were to become periodic depressions accompanied by incapacitating anxiety.

Marv doesn't know what brought on the bout of depression he experienced in 1953, but he spent four months isolating himself at home where he watched a lot of television. Before he could climb out of it he was drafted. He went gladly, which may seem mystifying until we recall the political climate of the times. Senator Joseph McCarthy's charges of "communist influences" within the government had helped the Republican Party in the 1952 elections, and by 1953, McCarthy himself, as chairman of the Senate Permanent Subcommittee on Investigations, held scores of hearings on "communist subversion." Those who refused to name names were cited for contempt of Congress and jailed. Blacklists were created against Hollywood actors, directors, and workers in the filmmaking industry. Red scares forced many militant workers out of factories.

Though Marv thought of himself as a liberal and was active in DFL precinct politics, he had no doubt that in such a poisonous political environment his own belief system was under attack. A countervailing voice was offered by Edward R. Murrow on his television news magazine *See It Now*, which became the most influential news program on television. In a society gripped by anti-communist hysteria, Marv came to see that the battle between liberal ideals and high-handed political persecution could have life and death implications.

The trial and execution of Ethel and Julius Rosenberg also affected him profoundly. To Marv, the case seemed to be part and parcel of the hysteria-prone and violent society that had developed in the United

States following World War II, and reflections on state-sponsored violence were never far from his thoughts during the summer of 1953, when he was in basic training at Fort Riley, Kansas.

Fort Riley prided itself on its heritage, and happened to be celebrating its hundredth anniversary in 1953 when Marv was there. He did his physical training in the stables from which General Custer led his cavalry off to the Indian Wars. Marv had long since familiarized himself with the history of American westward expansion, and he had come to view those events from a perspective quite different from that of the commemorative plaques surrounding him on the base. But he was invigorated by the physical challenges of basic training and impressed by the prairie landscape. It wasn't until his second month in basic training that an event occurred that shaped his response to confrontation and changed his life.

As Marv tells the story: "The Korean War had ended the week before I got drafted. One day, the sergeant in charge of our platoon, guy named Kemmett, gets our platoon off to the side and he says to us, 'we're sending a guy named Anderson into your platoon. He jumped the boat and missed fighting the gooks in Korea. So I want you to beat the shit out of him tonight... I can assure you nothing will happen to you.'"

When the sergeant said *gooks*, Marv's hackles rose. "I thought, *He must look on black people, Negro people, as niggers. Puerto Ricans and Mexican people as Spics, and me as a Kike.*

"So right away I knew this guy was a bigot. I went back to the barracks... everybody came up and talked about it and everybody said, Let's go. Give this kid Anderson a 'blanket party.' Being one of those *liberals*, I looked around, to see if anybody would say or do anything."

Marv decided he had to say something. Anderson, he thought, most likely was not going to be in the company very long, and if he'd done what the sergeant said, he'd probably been in prison, he'd probably been punished already for what he did. "I don't remember what the hell I said exactly, but I remember I asked, are you going to let this sergeant make an unthinking mob of us?"

Most of the guys in that unit were eighteen or nineteen—tough kids from Chicago, for instance, who'd been given a choice by a juvenile judge, *Reform School or Army*, so they chose the army.

"'No, no,' they said, 'we've got to go give him a blanket party.'"

Marv had to try one more time, so he said, "You remember when we were in the post theater, and the general in charge of our training division said to us, 'We're going to make you trained killers! You will obey every order, without thinking.'?"

"Well, *Not me!*" He told the new soldiers he didn't think they should do it. He said, proudly, "I'm Jewish, and 6 million of our people went to the gas chambers, and so many gypsies, communists, socialists...because of such unthinking behavior. "

"'So I don't think you should do this,' I said. But I just didn't get to them. Didn't reach them. They all went downstairs and they put a blanket on Anderson's head, and they shoved him down a gauntlet, and those who wanted to kick him or punch him did so, and then they took the GI brushes, which we used to scrape the floor clean for Saturday morning inspection, and bloodied up his skin."

The victim couldn't see who was doing the beating. They left him on the floor sweating and crying in the suffocating heat of the Kansas night. "Beat up. Alone. A good friend, Tom, told me what they had done. Tom went down, but didn't take part in the beating. But he was there. Everybody went downstairs except me."

Marv couldn't sleep all night. "In the morning we were changing our sheets, before going out to training. I look at the guys on my floor in the barracks and I say, 'You're a bunch of stupid cowards. Don't you know what you've done to yourselves! I'm ashamed of myself I didn't go downstairs and stand next to him!"

Then he turned around to fix his bunk. The next thing he knew he had a blanket over his head and the blows rained down. Two of the men were holding him down and punching him in the face. Marv now punches his fist in his palm—there is no sound like it.

"Then they walked away. Someone pulled the blanket off. And I was *fine*, you know, except for the humiliation, not the pain; and everyone took off, except one guy at the end of the barracks, standing by his bunk to see what my reaction's going to be... so I felt what Anderson must have felt—lone in the world, in that moment."

He stormed across the street to the orderly room, where his

sergeant was preparing for the drill to take place in a few minutes, too furious to care what the sergeant's response would be. "I told the sergeant, 'This is what you set up, man! What the hell's wrong with you? And they did it to me, too!'"

The sergeant replied, "Well, I'm on your case, Davidov. And we think you're a Commie."

"Commie?" Marv exclaims. "I couldn't believe the guy! I told him I never met one!"

Marv laughs, a head-back bark of laughter at the absurdity of life and his wonder at it.

Marv had studied Russian history, language and literature at Macalester, he tells his students. He even brought his textbooks and stowed them in his footlocker. When he was drafted, he didn't think anyone would stop him from reading or thinking. His outspoken behavior and opinions had already attracted attention. This outburst added to it.

The next piece of his education came when he went to the Jewish chaplain, a rabbi from New York. In the first months of basic training, he had developed a habit of attending services on Friday nights. He wasn't particularly religious, but "in a way, I wanted to get away from the training, be with people, drink a little wine." The services helped the loneliness. But the rabbi's response to Marv's defense of the deserter surprised him: he didn't commend Marv's moral courage in standing up for Anderson, but rather, accused him of rocking the boat. The chaplain also suggested a transfer, which he said he could arrange.

Marv was bewildered. He didn't want to be transferred. He wouldn't run away from the situation, from what he saw as systemic injustice. Nothing in his nature supported the rabbi's advice to lay low and keep his mouth shut, or leave. "From then on, whenever I was in a class and an officer would say something I thought was *really* wrong, I raised my hand and said, 'That's a lie.' And they don't like that kind of behavior in anybody's army."

Shortly after the 'blanket' episode, Marv saw the film *From Here to Eternity* at the post theater, and he identified strongly with the persecuted Robert E. Lee Prewitt (played by Montgomery Clift) who tried to maintain his integrity through a campaign of official harassment.

"I was sitting there in the post theater watching," Marv recalls, "and I thought to myself, *That's me.*"

Many years later, in 1982, the University Film Society held its first Rivertown International Film Festival in a barn in Stillwater. As part of the event it ran a documentary on Montgomery Clift. Marv, a film buff, attended. His friend Al Milgrom, who founded the Society, brought in Clift's brother Brooks to introduce the film. Marv spotted Brooks, smoking and drinking outside the huge barn, and went up to him. "I got a story for you," he proposed, "about your brother, if you have 15-20 minutes."

Brooks said, "Yeah."

"The only thing that kept me going when I was in the Army and feeling alone," Marv continued, "was your brother's character Prewitt in the movie *From Here to Eternity.*" And he told Brooks the story of Anderson and the blanket party, 'the treatment,' and being called a commie.

Brooks said, "Marv, if Monty were alive he would have *loved* that story. To think a role he played in a film kept you going."

A half century later, teaching his class on Active Nonviolence at St. Thomas University, Marv incorporates what he learned that day in basic training into his discussion of the role that small acts of civil disobedience play in bringing attention to pervasive acts of injustice. The course, which he team-teaches with Jack Nelson-Pallmeyer, has not attracted great numbers, but the students who do attend are bright and articulate. They discuss a central text of the course, the third of Gene Sharp's three-volume *The Politics of Nonviolent Action: The Dynamics of Nonviolent Action.* Sharp sees nonviolent action as the *most* effective form of resistance to oppression.

Jack and Marv challenge those students who did not take part in a recent peace conference on campus, a "peace convergence," or the civil disobedience action that took place later at the weapons maker Alliant TechSystems, to explain in writing why they chose not to participate. Were they nervous about the judgment of others, or their place in school, or the reactions of their friends? Were they convinced that such actions were useless—a waste of precious time?

One of the problems these days, Marv suggests to the class, is that many activists have come to see nonviolent action as a merely *symbolic* statement: It seems less important to them that the action has any practical effect. "It's very easy, in the context of our country," Jack emphasizes, "where people committed to nonviolence are a small minority, to fall into a kind of *closed circle*, in which you carry out small nonviolent actions which very few people pay any attention to."

The students nod, looking worried. "So there are a couple of conclusions you can come to. Maybe what we're doing isn't very effective and we'd better revisit it. But sometimes we interpret the lack of attention as a confirmation that we're prophetic, and morally right," Jack says. "That people *aren't* paying attention is a confirmation of our rightness. Sharp's corrective is that symbolic actions can be an important part of nonviolent movements, but *only* if they in fact lead to successful nonviolent movements." Marv agrees emphatically. His experience in the Army underscored for him the importance of going beyond symbolic gestures to acts that carry greater impact.

4

The Good of the Service

A quiet fury drove Marv for the next ten weeks of basic training. His awareness of the army's injustice was rekindled by the way almost everyone had mistreated Anderson—and then mistreated Marv for defending him! His anger was compounded by the disillusionment he felt at the rabbi's words. Where was the spiritual wisdom, the morality? 'Don't rock the boat? Be transferred?'

Marv felt alone. But he was not a quitter. So in the following weeks of Army indoctrination, whenever he heard something he thought was untrue, he would raise his hand and say, "That is a lie."

His attendance at Friday services continued, and his relations with his unit, at least the enlisted men and draftees, improved. Matters came to a head two weeks before Christmas, when the unit was to go out on bivouac, orienteering in the windy and desolate Flint Hills. There was no snow, but the dry cold wind blew all day and at night hardly ceased. In the pup tents, the men slept as they could until dawn, too tired to complain. The first Friday on bivouac Marv went into the captain's tent and asked permission to attend services. The company basketball team was going back to the base for practice—maybe he could hitch a ride. The captain replied that "we" were running a mandatory compass problem and Marv had to participate. Marv argued, wasn't religion as important as basketball? The captain told him *he* had to do the orienteering problem. Respectfully, Marv saluted with the three-fingered Boy Scout salute and walked out of the tent, saying he would do it on his way to services.

He lined up in the rear as the unit marched off into the wintery darkness. As the men strung out along the poorly lit county road, Marv peeled off and walked briskly in the opposite direction, marching the fourteen miles back to base camp. Services were over when he arrived, but the rabbi had stayed around to let him know that Sergeant Kemmett was waiting for him in the company orderly room. He was busted, though not quite the way he had expected.

CIC officers had come out to the bivouac area to tell him he had passed the counterintelligence tests and would be going to Fort Holabird, Maryland, after basic training. Then they found out he had walked back into camp.

Kemmett told him he'd be staying in camp during Christmas leave, doing dishes for the skeleton staff. He nodded, not arguing now, aware that the harassment was getting to him—he really needed that leave. He gloomily watched the others pack to go home. Late that night, a reprieve came: the company captain called him into his office, said "Good thing for you they found you at services!" and gave him his leave papers. Marv figured it wasn't the time to ask questions.

Despite a pre-graduation party with his sergeant and the unit, during which Marv and Kemmett got falling-down drunk together, walking arm-in-arm and singing, Kemmett still seemed to have it in for the troublemaker. In time the men in his unit became closer to one another, some of the guys even beginning to question authority as Marv had. But when a group of friends made plans to go into Kemmett's room the night before graduation and beat the shit out of him, Marv persuaded them not to do it. That same night the men in his barracks readied themselves for final inspection, in high spirits, and looked Marv over at his request. They concluded he was ready for inspection, his uniform and gear neat and polished. But the next morning at 6:00 as the men lined up on the street ("It was so dark you couldn't see the guy next to you,") Kemmett came up behind him and bawled, "Davidov, fall out!" He was to go to the supply room and clean weapons while everyone else attended graduation. With great trepidation—taking the guns apart was no problem, but putting them back together was a nightmare—he did as he was ordered.

The sergeant returned, hours later, to find Marv on the floor surrounded by parts of machine guns, bazookas, and mortars, all spic and span. But the young draftee was in a frenzy, trying to put the pieces back together. "Davidov," he groaned, "you've destroyed this outfit."

Marv wasn't sure whether he meant the gear or the unit—probably both, but he agreed. "My dad never taught me how to fix things."

Kemmett shook his head, but he sat down with Marv to have what could have been a mature conversation. "I tried to break your spirit," the sergeant admitted. "I still think you'll never make it in the Army."

"Sergeant," Marv answered, his spirits unaccountably light as the oily weapons fragments lay strewn at his feet, "You may be right."

He graduated *in absentia* and headed home for two weeks' welcome leave before continuing on to the Counterintelligence Corps training in Baltimore, Maryland.

Camp Holabird was located in a congested, blighted area of Baltimore. It operated as a center for motor transport and repair until the early 1970s, when it was finally shut down, and it was also home to another Army specialization—counterintelligence.

The Central Intelligence Agency (CIA), newly-established under the National Security Act of 1947, had its own budget and could gather and produce intelligence at its own discretion. Fort Holabird was the training ground for the military-based agents of its Counter Intelligence Corps (CIC), which attracted college-trained men who wanted to fulfill their service obligation in civilian clothes, but did not intend to make intelligence work a career. Many, like Marv, looked forward to having their education enhanced by foreign policy study.

In the first week, Marv was brought before two officers for an oral exam to test "spontaneous reasoning." His predecessors in the examination room had shared a few of the standard questions with him, so Marv knew the capital of Tasmania. He remained cool when, after determining Marv was from Minnesota, the examiners made disparaging remarks about the state, its "liberal" climate, and Hubert Humphrey. His radar picked up animosity, whether genuine or manufactured for the test purposes, and he grew nervous. He nearly made the mistake of laughing when an officer asked, "If I ordered you to jump out a fifth story window, would you do it?" Marv shot back, "No way."

His 'spontaneous' responses must have been reasonable enough, because he was assigned to Intelligence Analyst School as a group leader. This distinction meant that he would march the men to classes and make sure the barracks would pass weekly inspection. With this assignment, and impelled by some combination of idealism, stubbornness, and new confidence, Marv re-enlisted, now to serve three years instead of two.

He hadn't grasped the sort of intellectual exercise this would be, or the depths to which it would take him. Cold war propaganda was a staple of formal classes and discussion, and Marv felt his recurring depression overtaking him. He remembers that in about the fourth week, a civilian teacher from Johns Hopkins held a class in which he informed the group that Edward R. Murrow was a 'pinko' because he narrated films on the battle of Stalingrad in a manner sympathetic to the Communists. The teacher castigated Ed Sullivan as a leftist who regularly had Reds or Communist Front guests on his show. It didn't seem possible to raise his hand and question these esteemed professors. If he were to serve on the course set for him, he'd need to participate in his own indoctrination. He felt more and more alienated from Army culture and also from the accepted "truths" of mainstream American society. He was beginning to feel that he was on the wrong side of history; his discouragement deepened, and he resigned from the CIC.

After two weeks in a South Carolina reassignment camp, he was sent to Fort Campbell, Kentucky, home of the 11th Airborne Division. A captain there, who thought he looked "tough and wiry" enough to be a paratrooper candidate, tried to persuade him to follow that track. Marv insisted he was "not crazy enough to jump out of a plane, unless there was no other way." He ended up in a non-jumping battalion and learned the new trade of loading a 155-millimeter cannon.

Then, while substituting for a day room leader on leave, he became engaged with helping battalion members with schooling. He discovered that many of the young men had not even graduated from eighth grade, so he marched them off to school. He was responsible for teaching the basic information courses (more indoctrination) and his natural bent for conversation led him to engage the students in challenging discussions. He tested out his political theories and found willing listeners. For the first time, he was having fun. During his brief tenure as an instructor, his day room was awarded "Best Day Room in the Division." But his enjoyment was short-lived. When the former leader returned from leave, Marv was sent back to loading cannon.

"I was really pissed," he recalls. And he was not alone in his grumbling; the old leader was considered racist and the guys had really enjoyed Marv's discussions, so they set up *ad hoc* meetings with him outside of class to talk about their rights under the military code.

Relationships with his superiors again deteriorated, and Marv was denied regular leave. Gerty was ill again with colitis; Marv had accrued leave time and wanted to go and see her. In addition, a back injury kept him from training duties for a few days, so he argued to his sergeant that he wasn't needed around the unit; couldn't they spare him? The sergeant told him to apply again in several days. When he reapplied, he was again denied. Days later, because of Gerty's worsening condition, the Red Cross issued him emergency leave but the unit wouldn't honor it. "So I went to the orderly room and told the sergeant I would go home for one week. He warned me I would be in trouble if I did. I went anyway." His simple assertion reveals much about Marv – his pride, stubbornness, and integrity. When faced with a human need, or a belief that his position is the right one, he will not "adapt" to authority; he will negotiate, but not give in.

Gerty's health improved and Marv returned in a week, as he'd promised. He was court-martialed for being AWOL and convicted. Distraught, he threatened to hurt himself if he were put in the stockade, so he was sent to the post hospital's psychiatric ward. He is reticent about his state of mind leading up to this threat, but in the hospital he "met educated men and women" and thought he might happily finish up his army time there.

After three weeks, he was returned to his unit and given additional punishments of cleaning and KP. He did his jobs and took satisfaction in continued meetings with his cadre, "organizing" them and telling them their rights. The army officials could not have been happy about the situation, and more trouble was brewing. A few days into the punishment regime, just after Marv had finished cleaning, his sergeant called him into his office and ordered him to take care of the day room.

"I already cleaned it, Sergeant," he said, and turned to leave.

"Get over there, Davidov! It's a fucking mess!"

Knowing that could not be true and underestimating the nature of his predicament, he mildly repeated that he'd just cleaned it. The sergeant called over a couple of men to witness Marv refusing a direct order, then sneeringly told him to go over and see just how fucked he was.

Marv went to look. Someone had messed up the room in the fifteen minutes since he'd finished cleaning it. No one was around. Marv was court-martialed again, sentenced to 30 days in the stockade, and driven off under armed guard. By this time he was becoming inured to the injustice endemic to the system. Wasn't that what he and his students were discussing? This time, his anger seemed to sustain him as he reflected on the absurdity of armed men conducting him to jail for no reason at all.

As the cell door clanged shut behind him, Marv felt alone and frightened, but still angry. He took an assessment of his surroundings. His cell was lined up with six others, and there were seven more on the other side of the short hallway, each cell inhabited by one guy. Not alone, then. He soon learned that the hall was a temporary isolation unit, filled with men who had breached some stockade regulation and had extra punishment. They were fed a low-calorie diet: a boiled potato, onion, and carrot for lunch. Marv, however, was given a "full diet" and quickly determined that he could hide the food under his blankets and as soon as the guards left, share his meals with the others.

He was released into the compound in about a week and set about learning the stockade system and its inmates. He found stockade life not too different from ordinary army discipline, except that the men had to wear a "P" on their fatigues and salute by slapping their hats on their thighs. Physical training was more regular and work details more rigorous; as a consequence, work days began at 5:00 am with a heavy breakfast, and the full diet for the rest of the meals. Marv was on the "ash and trash" detail outside the stockade, breathing in fumes and dust from the post garbage dump. Once, he got to clean the stables of the General (Wayne C. Smith). He found it curious that the construction firm employed on the base was the Wayne C. Smith Construction Company.

The stories he heard from fellow inmates fascinated him. Many were army goof-offs— young, only interested in doing their time. A very few were rebels like himself; most were "poor unfortunates down on their luck and in jail for alcohol-related charges."

The time passed quickly as he worked, and listened. Release day finally arrived and Marv met with a division major who was to determine whether he would remain in the Army or be dismissed. After hearing his story, this good, sensitive man said, "I believe you. You were set up. With some discipline, you could finish your enlistment." Marv shook his head. He was beginning to see a path for himself that *could* not continue in the army. "I can be a better citizen outside." The major agreed, and told him "You'll be out in a week."

He was awarded a "For the Good of the Service" discharge, of which, as mentioned earlier, he is in complete and proud agreement. In a week he was sitting on a bus headed from Fort Campbell to Hopkinsville, Kentucky, where he would catch a train to St. Paul.

One final army experience left him convinced that he had made the right decision: a "civilian" climbed onto the bus as it was leaving the base and sat down beside Marv, though there were many empty seats. The man revealed himself as a CIC agent through a lengthy interview, as the agent described a character and set of circumstances (strangely like Marv's) that resulted in his "friend" being tossed from the service. "What do you think of my friend?" he queried.

Marv responded that there were good guys and bad guys in the service and the friend was "a bad ass." Apparently satisfied, the agent got off at the next stop. Marv reflects that those times, the McCarthy atmosphere and mainstream nervousness about spies were exacerbated by the army's protectiveness of its own privilege.

Although he did not hear about it until later that year, an FBI agent had interviewed his aunt (his father's sister) in Detroit about Marv's Army 'politics.' "She really knew nothing," he said, and must have been astonished at the questions. For now, as he watched the CIC agent walk away, Marv had never felt more liberated.

5

Oh, Freedom

When Marv returned to Macalester to register for his senior year in 1955, he found a note on his file: 'Hold to see the dean.' Macalester's dean of students was Dr. J. Huntley DuPre, a history professor and pacifist. Before his army stint, Marv had had a class with Dr. DuPre and remembered him as a fair though somewhat tedious educator. The professor set a rigorous schedule for his students, assigning a research paper biweekly that he would grade and comment on meticulously before returning the following week.

As he greeted Marv, the dean looked grim. He shut his office door and waved the prospective senior to a seat facing the large, unadorned desk. Marv, curious at this formality, studied the dean's expression. He seemed to be gazing everywhere but at his former student.

"We understand you had some trouble in the army," DuPre began. Marv looked around to see if there was anybody else in the room to make up the *we*. "I ain't part of the *we*..." he thought to himself. "The institution is the *we*."

DuPre might have thought Marv didn't want to talk about his army experience, but Marv had no qualms about sharing it. When he'd finished, DuPre gave him a brief, avuncular smile and said, "Now Marv, wouldn't you feel more comfortable if you transferred to St. Thomas, or the U?" There was that 'transfer' word again.

"I was a little crazy then," Marv admits. "And I thought, *I know why you want to ship me out.* The school song at the time was 'Dear Old Macalester, ever the same, always the same' If they let *me* back in, they'd have to change the lyrics. It wouldn't be ever the same, always the same... here's this crazy guy Marv."

"But Dean," Marv countered, "I don't need another school. It was here at Macalester that I was taught that if you see an injustice you have to do something about it."

"Marv, if you wish to return to Macalester, *we* suggest that you go out to the Veterans Hospital and see a psychiatrist.'"

The conversation continued, though the dean, despite his avowed pacifism, was unable to shake his impression of Marv as a young misfit in an otherwise functional system. Marv laid out what he believed were principled positions as clearly as he could, giving reasons for acting (and talking and organizing) as he did in the army.

"The only thing I could think of to ask was, 'They do that in the Soviet Union. You mean we do it here, too?'"

DuPre said, "Yes."

Marv did go out to the Vets Hospital and met with a psychiatrist. The man listened to his story, then wrote a beautiful letter to the dean that said, in part, "I hope that had I been subjected to the same set of circumstances, I would have had the courage to do what Marv did. Let him in."

Marv was readmitted and returned as a beginning senior for the summer term, taking two lecture courses.

As the summer months passed, Marv reacclimated to life in the Twin Cities and to his family, though he could not comfortably spend much time in the fourplex, where the atmosphere was far from tranquil. His studies and new friendships left him with little time at home, anyway. Marital arguments were still loud and often bitter; Louie, when he was not acting as silent buffer or backdrop, could be acerbic, and his oblique criticisms and sarcasm didn't sit well with his son. Gerty more than held her own in familial battles; she continued to have bouts of colitis but was otherwise as energetic and opinionated as ever.

The fourplex in St. Paul continued to house many of Gerty's relations, brothers and sisters-in-law, their children, and Marv's maternal grandfather. Evening mealtimes, especially on weekends and holidays, often involved a large, boisterous contingent of relatives and abundant food. In keeping with the family's Eastern European roots, the food remained traditional despite the growing popularity of processed and packaged foods. Gerty shopped at a kosher butcher whenever possible, and at the local markets almost daily, selecting the freshest if not the most tender cuts of beef, and whole chickens for roasts or stews.

After dinner, the tube still occupied a central place in the living room (no matter which flat hosted the meal). The men watched baseball games, wrestling matches, and emerging boxing stars like Rocky Marciano on *The Fight of the Week*. The whole family tuned in to the stampede of westerns and to the new quiz show, *The $64,000 Question* with host Hal March. Marv occasionally watched along with everyone else, though he often found the scene claustrophobic.

As Marv disengaged from the family scene, he spent more time on the campus of the University of Minnesota, where the beat culture offered lots of attractions, both social and political. He worked less often at the department store and, in the fall, not only transferred to the U but moved into an apartment in the Dinkytown neighborhood north of campus, where many students, artists, and activists hung out.

To Marv, the beats of Dinkytown, neither affluent nor down-trodden, had escaped the straightjacket of class by virtue of their avant-garde artistic and intellect gifts. They also formed the basis for a political elite that acted as a refreshing and much-needed corrective to the rigid and fearful norms and preconceptions of the McCarthy era.

Though the word "beat" had been in use since the mid-1940s, the term "beatnik" was unknown at the time. It was coined in 1957 by Herb Caen, a columnist for the *San Francisco Chronicle*, who, when the Russians sent the first satellite into space, remarked that Sputnik and the beatniks were "equally far out."

Marv was impressed by Jack Kerouac's understanding of 'beat' in its link with 'beatific,' or sacred. Kerouac described the beat generation as revealing "the secret holiness of the downtrodden." Beats admired communal ideals: brotherhood (less often sisterhood), justice, free artistic expression, and existential philosophy. "It was an interracial culture of talented, verbal, unique people," Marv later recalled. "Artists, poets, radicals, students, professors, met at the Ten O'Clock Scholar or the East Hennepin Bar." Some were drawn to the struggles of the union movement and stirrings for racial integration. Collaboration, rehearsed or spontaneous, was the order of the day. The revival of folk music, the Blues, and other art forms with black roots echoed the new consciousness.

Marv lived near the Ten O'Clock Scholar, and often met friends there for coffee. At night, there was the East Hennepin, with its long mahogany bar in the front room and the back room set up with booths large enough for ten people. "You could find anyone there from about 9 pm to 1 in the morning, talking about things of substance—art, culture, politics!" And relationships. Marv recalls sitting in a big booth at the Scholar with five other men, five women. "Joe Sweeny (an architectural student from New York) asked us, 'Has everyone slept with everyone else?' We looked at each other, saw all these nodding heads, and everyone broke into laughter."

Marv absorbed the culture and contributed to it as he studied and worked. He resonated to the ideals—and alienation from the mainstream—and probed its political underpinnings. With other beats, he adopted a new perspective on history and began to take "peoples' struggles" as his own.

In Marv's social psychology class the professor passed out a test purported to have been given to avowed socialists in the 1930s. Marv was the only student who scored close to 100%. "I didn't *know* I was a Socialist!" he declared. He was soon recruited into the Socialist Club at the university, where his political and ethical positions were honed and validated.

Marv and his friends were poor by most standards, managing to live "on the dregs of Capitalism" (as he quotes Meridel LeSueur) by doing odd jobs and sharing. He began to model for art students at the university and the Minneapolis Institute of Arts. He got to wear a jock strap, though the female models, he recalls, "worked in the buff." The going rate was $1.69 an hour—not much for sustenance even in the late 50s. Aware that some of the young women were single mothers, he suggested that they form a model's union and ask for a raise from the university. He agreed to be the negotiator.

"I went to the head of the Art Department, a Dr. Arnason, and explained how hard it was for some people to make it on that amount." Dr. Arnason claimed the department budget really had no money for a raise. Marv replied that the models were prepared to picket with signs in front of the art building, "and we are thinking of doing it nude." Dr. Arnason caved. "How about $2.50?" Marv was learning the value of creativity, not to mention audacity, in confronting institutions.

In his history of the 60s, *Freedom Riders*, Ray Arsenault described Marv as an "art dealer." Works of art, particularly films, were important to Marv, then as now, and during his Dinkytown years he also ran a business exhibiting and selling his friends' paintings.

In 1958 he became friends and lived for a year with Mel Geary, a painter who also worked as an exhibition designer and consultant to Edward Larrabee Barnes, the architect of the Walker Art Center. Before his death in 2007, Geary was considered among the best in the world in stained glass sculpting. He designed and installed stained glass windows and three-dimensional treatments in homes, churches, and public buildings throughout the eastern and Midwestern states.

Marv and Mel rented a spacious apartment across from the Walker and collaborated on art shows, holding them at venues in Dinkytown and in their apartment. On one hot summer day in 1958, they were to meet at home for dinner and plan a show. Usually quite punctual, Geary didn't show up at 6, or 6:30. At 7:00, as Marv was about to give up the evening's project, the phone rang: did Marv have $25 to bail him out? Mel wouldn't say anything more.

Marv rushed downtown—the first of many forays to a Minneapolis jail booking office. Mel, when released, was hot, perspiring, and disheveled; usually style conscious, he struggled to tuck his white shirt back into rumpled chinos as the two hurried out the door. He wouldn't speak until they were at home, seated at the table.

"What the hell happened, man?"

Mel was precise in speech, emphatic in his sarcasm. "I was standing in front of *our* building, *quietly* drinking a can of beer, waiting for you to get home, when this squad comes up the street, *creeping* along. So I duck around the bush, there beside the door, you know?"

Marv nodded, puzzled.

"The cops stop, get out of the car, both of them with their guns, and arrest me—on *suspicion.*"

"'Suspicion'? Of what? Mel, why did you duck?"

"Because, Marv, I'm black."

They talked for hours that night. Marv heard what it was like to be black in 1950s Minneapolis in a way that "political" discussion could not touch. Like many Northerners, Marv associated more virulent racist attitudes with the South, though he knew prejudice was endemic, even in his own family. He now saw that it was natural for his friend, this imposing, over 6-foot and heavy-set young man, to avoid contact with police. Despite his talents, he had to. Outside the university/art world he would keep his distance from compromising situations, or be invisible.

It was a shock though not a surprise. Marv had experienced racism in the army. Now it had invaded his adopted community, and it drove home the realization that even Dinkytown, which seemed a Nirvana in comparison with the wider world, was not immune from the nastiness of the wider world.

His crowd read the "new sociology" of C. Wright Mills and anarchist Paul Goodman's *Growing Up Absurd.* Mills moved sociology beyond the confines of academia, using it as a tool to analyze and confront the world's injustices. An admirer of Fidel Castro, Mills had visited Cuba to interview major political figures, and thought the country offered a third way between communism and capitalism. Goodman, a homosexual and iconoclast, became a guiding light for the counterculture in his efforts to challenge entrenched political and sexual mores.

Another individual who influenced Marv profoundly was the beloved and controversial social scientist Mulford Q. Sibley, his favorite professor at the university. Sibley held that for a pacifist, whether understandings came from religious or philosophical convictions, the commandment against violence was "as close to an absolute as one can discover... not only should one refrain from political or individual violence but one should also do everything possible to help create conditions and establish institutions which will discourage any form of violence."

"Mulford covered many sides of a political issue," Marv said, "but everyone who came in contact with him knew first what a gentle, compassionate man he was and second, his stance against all war and *for* structural changes in the system." Marv fondly remembered going to picket at the Federal Building during the American invasion of Cuba at the Bay of Pigs and finding Mulford, his sign held aloft, standing alone.

In a different way, Marv was also influenced by anarchist and bookseller Melvin McCosh, his sometime landlord, who had a shop at 1404 Fourth Street Southeast. McCosh owned a house one block away from the bookstore, and Marv, for eight months or so in 1958, lived there on the second floor with an ever-changing collection of "radicals, freethinkers and psychopaths," as McCosh referred to them. McCosh was a curmudgeon and an iconoclast in his own right, echoing the bohemian spirit of the surroundings. "He had a neatly printed sign visible on the shop's first floor, 'We give no discounts to University professors, clergy, and all other lower walks of life.'" At homecoming time, when the fraternity and sorority houses passed out balloons to the football fans, McCosh would put up a sign saying "Homecomers, go home!" Beside the sign was a blown-up condom attached to a straw.

But McCosh kept a kindlier eye on his radical roomers and community; he was an enthusiastic cook and would share his concoctions. He often made a large batch of beef etcetera stew and would bring it to gatherings or keep it warm in the shop.

That next year, Marv fell in love with Sally Oklund, a classics major at the University. "We slept together on a mattress on the floor, in a sleeping bag during the cold winter of 1959... we were vital, young, slightly absurd... there was so much to talk about, so much to do, moving in an exciting community of talented people."

Bob Dylan added his emerging talent to the community in Dinkytown. "Dylan and his friends were right after the Beats..., he'd be singing in coffeehouses, practicing, practicing on his guitar: not one of us could predict what would happen to him... For a time I lived right next to Dylan, above Gray's Drugstore." Gray's was at the intersection of 14th Avenue and Fourth Street—a mainstay of the community for more than 50 years—where today a glitzier strip of more generic shops and coffeehouses cater to students' needs. "Since my room was right next to Dylan's, I know how hard, *loud* and frequently he practiced." McCosh recalled Dylan less charitably, Marv remembers. "In general he wasn't very well liked," McCosh said. "He was sort of pompous. To be fair, I'd like to say something good about him, but I can't think of anything right now."

Born Robert Zimmerman on the Iron Range, in 1959 Dylan became involved in the Dinkytown folk music circuit before his move to New York. He enrolled at the University of Minnesota though he dropped out after a few months. The Dinkytown community, though, took him to its bosom, educating and inspiring him. He was a decade younger than Marv, who by the late 50s was no longer a student but was still actively engaged in campus culture and politics.

In 1960 Marv did DFL precinct work to elect John Kennedy— his last for the Democratic Party. The student arm of the Civil Rights movement became a gale force, sweeping conventional notions of politics aside. Marv and his companions were keenly aware of the Little Rock racial crises and the Montgomery Bus Boycott as Dr. Martin Luther King came into national prominence. In February of 1960, they saw on network television the four Greensboro College students walk into a segregated Woolworth's and ask for coffee.

"Boiling hot coffee was poured on them, lit cigarettes were put out on the backs of their necks. I was in a rage! Why couldn't the president do something," Marv fumed. "Send the FBI, the National Guard? Why couldn't they protect these courageous kids?"

He was part of a new group at the U, Students for Integration (SFI), who jumped at the chance when a national call came to picket local Woolworths, and organized a protest at the chain's downtown Minneapolis location. Buoyed by a sympathetic response from shoppers, SFI determined to do more. "A few of our SFI students drove to Nashville in March to support the burgeoning Students Nonviolent Coordinating Committee (SNCC), and came back talking about James Lawson, a ministerial student and the first black to be admitted at Vanderbilt Divinity Seminary."

Lawson was a mentor to many young men and women coming out of black colleges. He spent some years in India studying the Gandhian movement and was committed to Gandhi's philosophy and method. Nonviolent strategies would give young people the discipline and organization they needed, Lawson believed, and he conducted a rigorous series of nonviolence workshops, training students to withstand the racial slurs and physical violence.

In March of 1960, a boycott of Nashville department stores began. After protesters marched on city hall, the mayor called for desegregation and within three months of the first sit-ins, on May 10, lunch counters in Nashville began to serve African-Americans.

Members of the Minneapolis contingent took careful note of the months of planning involved and the response of Nashville's wider community. The boycott seemed to provide a textbook example of nonviolent theory: the purpose of a campaign is to build community rather than destroy it. The students in Nashville had shown that nonviolence is the opposite of passivity. It takes courage and discipline.

It wasn't long before Marv joined the nonviolent struggle for civil rights with the Freedom Rides. The strategy was daring but simple: black and white riders on interstate buses and trains would sit together, challenging racial segregation in interstate travel and upholding a Supreme Court ruling that such separation was unconstitutional.

The way had been prepared for them in 1944 by a young defense worker, Irene Morgan, trying to get home to her husband in Baltimore after a visit to her mother in Virginia. She found herself sitting in front of a white couple and offered to change places instead of stand when the bus driver ordered her from her seat. She'd suffered a miscarriage a few weeks earlier, but she was a determined, proud young woman, with a strong moral sense. She argued, the bus driver became enraged and summoned the police. A lengthy court case, aided by NAACP lawyers, finally made its way to the Supreme Court. The ruling in her favor, however, seemed to have little effect in diminishing the effects of Jim Crow in the South.

Leaders in the Congress of Racial Equality (CORE) and the Fellowship of Reconciliation (FOR) came together, impatient with the ineffectiveness of NAACP's legal approach to the problem of integration. Three of these leaders—Jim Peck, Bayard Rustin, and James Farmer—were to have pivotal roles in Civil Rights history: They formed a group of fifteen men, blacks and whites, called the Journey of Reconciliation, who, in 1947, traveled throughout the South in differing groupings, black men sitting in front and the whites in the back. This action and subsequent campaign were the inspiration for the Freedom Rides of 1961 in which Marv participated.

March 3, 2006. Marv arranged for my ticket to Ray Arsenault's lecture at the Minnesota History Center. Arsenault had spent several years gathering the stories of Riders and had recently published *Freedom Riders,* a 690-page history based on more than three hundred interviews with the living riders. Marv and others of the Minnesota Riders were guests and would take questions about their own experiences. I was excited to hear about these momentous events from the people who had actually been involved in them, but was disappointed to see that the audience was (as Marv himself fumed later) "99.5 percent white, and 85 percent elderly."

"What did you expect? These are historians, not activists. They bought tickets to a lecture series."

"I could have told [the Center] how to organize some invitations. I hope the audience learned something!"

Ray Arsenault began by quoting James Baldwin, "You have to take freedom, it's not given." He proposed that there were seminal times in history, "contingent moments" he called them, when an individual's acts of choice and commitment can transform lives and history itself. This was heady stuff: I thought of Marv and his groups stepping forward at the right times, and at many times.

In May 1961, the first group of Freedom Riders left Washington DC on regularly scheduled Trailways and Greyhound buses headed for New Orleans. They traveled in two groups. On the first bus, a Greyhound, seven riders were joined by a couple of journalists and two undercover plainclothes agents. Things were quiet until they headed into Anniston, in east central Alabama. There, rioters threw rocks, broke windows, slashed tires. The driver eventually left the bus, abandoning his passengers to make futile attempts to call a service station for replacement tires.

The mob, including churchgoers in their Sunday clothes [this was Sunday, Mother's Day], again surrounded the bus, pounding on it, cracking windows. A group of men and boys began rocking the bus, trying to turn it over. The mob broke several windows and threw Molotov cocktails inside. Ambulances finally arrived, and the smoke-injured, bruised passengers were treated at Anniston Memorial Hospital, albeit unwillingly, and were evacuated that evening by a rescue team.

The Trailways Riders were not so lucky. At the Birmingham terminal, a huge mob was preparing for an assault. Jim Peck, Wayne State Professor Walter Bergman, Charles Person, and the other Trailways Riders had no warning of what lay ahead. In Anniston their driver received word about the Greyhound and informed his passengers that the bus had been burned and riders hospitalized. Refusing to continue, he ordered the black Freedom Riders to "the back of the bus where they belong." Klansmen who had infiltrated the bus lunged toward two of the black riders, punching them. Both held to Gandhian discipline and refused to fight back but were repeatedly struck and kicked. Jim Peck and Walter Bergman rushed forward from the back to object, and the attackers turned their attention to the white "nigger lovers," beating them until they were unconscious.

By the time the bus pulled into Birmingham, the Klan and their law enforcement allies were all in place, armed with chains, metal pipes, and clubs. Bergman, caked with blood from the earlier beating, was smashed to the floor and kicked savagely. "Reporters asked Police Commissioner Eugene 'Bull' Connor why the police were absent," Marv said. "He smirked, 'It's Mothers' Day. I sent them home to be with their mothers.'"

At this point, Martin Luther King decided to halt the rides. The Klansmen had done what they set out to do: inflict deadly damage on the Freedom Riders and their project, and protect the Klan's "way of life" for the South.

Marv tells this story: "When Jim Peck was released from the hospital, he flew to Independence, Missouri, and with national media present, he confronted former president Harry Truman on his morning walk. Peck's head was still bandaged from the ferocious beating. 'Mr. President,' he said, 'This is what happened to me and the Freedom Riders in Birmingham. What is your position?'

"Truman, 'the buck stops here' decision-maker who made the

decision to drop bombs on civilians in Hiroshima and Nagasaki, answered, 'When I ran a haberdashery shop in Kansas City, if anyone entered my shop whom I did not want there, I would pick him up by the scruff of the neck and throw him out.' So much for that liberal president."

King's decision to end the rides frustrated students and other activists. SNCC worker Diane Nash argued in a phone conversation with James Farmer that "we can't let them stop us with violence. If we do, the movement is dead." Young SNCC people drove from Nashville to meet with Dr. King, declaring that now was not the time to stop the rides. They had the attention of the world; they must push on.

"Now the feds had to intervene," Marv remembered. King called a rally at Ralph Abernathy's church in Montgomery and gave a major speech denouncing the governor and the white supremacists. Once more, a mob formed outside the church. From the spot, King called Attorney General Kennedy, who assured him that the federal government would protect those inside the church. Kennedy immediately mobilized national guardsmen who used tear gas to disperse the mob.

Robert Kennedy's calling out the Guard propelled the Riders to national prominence. Activists around the country, like Marv's Students for Integration, were eager to join in. More press coverage came with more participation, especially from northern students. At the end of May, President Kennedy directed the Interstate Commerce Commission to ban segregation in all facilities under its jurisdiction, and when a Mississippi ride was planned, federalized the Mississippi National Guard to escort Freedom Ride buses to Jackson. These riders were then arrested, tried on the spot, and jailed in Jackson.

Marv and his coalition were ready to enter the fray: "Sponsoring organizations put out a national call for people to join the "jail-in" at Jackson. By June 5, about 100 people had answered the call and sat in jail... and my own life path changed on June 5."

6

The Road to Parchman Prison

June 3, 1961, began as a normal Wednesday of work and classes much like any other. Marv walked through campus to a temporary classroom building next to the new Social Sciences building, which was still under construction. There he ran into David Morton ("the first hippie in Minnesota" according to Marv) who was lounging on the steps. Like Marv, David had ties with the Art Department and with the local music and protest culture. His father Phil taught sculpture at the U and David himself was a talented guitarist who occasionally worked as a sideman for Bob Dylan. He and Marv had collaborated on an underground magazine and free-speech projects like a "hands off Lenny Bruce" campaign. In many ways their spirits jibed.

Standing stiffly opposite David was an armed campus cop, studiously ignoring him but carefully watching other students file past. Threats had been phoned in concerning the meeting about to take place. Raising his eyebrows at the policeman, Marv asked, "David, what are you doing here?" It was early in the morning for his friend and he obviously wasn't under arrest.

"I'm going to a meeting on the Freedom Rides, you know?"

Marv nodded. Everybody knew, though he had not been notified of this specific meeting. "Come on in with me," David said.

He did not think twice. He wanted to be updated on the current situation and was excited though apprehensive about linking up with CORE and SNCC organizers. If he was preparing to take a further step, it hadn't yet penetrated his consciousness.

Professor Dan Cooperman's stuffy office in "Temporary South of Mines" smelled of new plaster and disinfectant. About a dozen students and friends were gathered there to listen to Zev Aelony deliver an address. The meeting had been delayed because someone had thrown a stink-bomb into the room.

Zev was in his early twenties, a political science major who had spent time in Koinonia, an interracial intentional community in Georgia. Sickened by what he had seen of the poverty and racism of the deep South, he took direct action training with CORE in Miami. He told the group that the movement—a coalition now of the Southern Christian Leadership Conference, CORE, and SNCC along with activists from the Fellowship of Reconciliation and smaller groups like their own Students for Integration— had issued a nationwide call for people to join them on the Freedom Rides. SFI had raised enough money to send twelve people by bus to Jackson. The plan was for the Minnesota contingent to leave on Friday, June 9, and stop in Nashville for an orientation.

June 9? Marv worried. That was only two days away—less than that if they left early in the morning! Who could make those kinds of arrangements? And with the possibility of a longer time, incarceration…? Zev continued, somberly, "Chances are we will face at least a month in jail in Jackson, and the risk of violence is high."

Marv respected Zev, whom he took to be a thoughtful, experienced activist who would neither exaggerate the danger nor shrink from it. Marv looked around the room at the other young men and women, most of whom he had come to know and trust. They were mostly white (although the eventual Rider group, as Zev later remarked, "were all 'off white': four Jews, a Quaker, a Unitarian, an Irish Catholic."

When Zev asked that morning, "How many are thinking seriously of coming with us?" eight of the twelve who were present raised their hands. Marv didn't. A fairly good percentage, he thought, but of course these were serious people. Then Zev looked straight at him.

"Marv, you've been awfully quiet. What about it?"

Marv replied that he'd let him know by midnight. He went back to his room and called a friend, Bob Golding. "I have a chance to leave on Friday to join the Freedom Rides in Jackson. Tell me what you think."

"Go," Bob said. "You'll be making history." Marv asked him to meet at the East Hennepin Bar that evening to talk it over. That night, he went from table to table, asking what people thought, what they'd heard, what they would do. He encountered enthusiasm, trepidation, concern over young lives at risk in the South, and envy. "Marv, one of us should go," was the consensus, "and it should probably be you."

He called Zev at midnight and said, "Count me in."

The next morning, Thursday, though he knew he had much to do, he overslept. During the long night he was stricken several times by waves of fear as images of the recent violence that had been shown on TV replayed themselves inside his head. He chastised himself, asking, "What do I believe? Am I 'anti-racist'? Prove it."

The next day he packed lightly—it was the South, after all, what clothes did he need? And on Friday morning at 8:00 a.m. he stood outside the Greyhound bus station with six other prospective riders, various family members and friends, and reporters from the *Minneapolis Tribune* and the *St. Paul Pioneer Press*. Besides Marv (the oldest at 29), David Morton, and Zev, the riders were Bob Baum, Gene Uphoff, Harvey Abrams, and Claire O'Connor.

Bob was a self-described mystic and social critic who had studied existential philosophy and social movements; he looked as "clean as the Beatles' grandfather," Marv said (a reference to a character in the then-current film *A Hard Day's Night)*. Gene Uphoff was a Quaker whose family was active in peace circles; he played folk and rock guitar in local coffeehouses.

Claire O'Connor was working as a licensed practical nurse at the University of Minnesota hospital. Her family was active in political and social movements and her deceased father had been a union organizer; but as a white young woman of privilege she had little experience of poverty or racism and no knowledge of conditions in the South. She would later become active in antipoverty work, on health issues for women and teenagers.

Harvey, like Marv, was "a radical intellectual Jewish socialist," but unlike Marv, in the end he would not participate in the ride, to his great disappointment. When the bus reached Madison, he called home to let his family know what was happening, and his mother became so distraught he felt obliged to leave the group to attend to her.

Except for Marv (who had experienced institutional pressures and the racist culture of the army while stationed in Kansas) and Zev, none of the Minnesota riders had seen southern segregation and its effects.

The night before Marv left, Gerty advised him strongly not to go. She argued that the actions weren't necessary: After all, even the president opposed the rides. "What are you doing to me now?" she moaned. "You're killing me!"

"Gerty," Marv said, "If you can die from this I'll make sure you get in the Guinness Book of Records." Gerty turned to Louie for support, but this time Louie was on Marv's side.

"Look, Marv says he has to go, and we should believe him. I'm terribly worried, too, but we won't die."

Marv left hurriedly, a lump in his throat, his father's words echoing in his ears. He had failed to reassure his parents, and felt no satisfaction that he'd bested his mother with an awkward joke.

The six rode overnight to Nashville, and everyone talked excitedly for a while before quieting down. Marv had brought along a collection of "bus books" that friends had recommended: Louis Sullivan, *Autobiography of an Idea*, Gertrude Stein, *Lectures in America*, Martin Luther King, *Stride Toward Freedom: The Montgomery Story*, and Arthur Koestler, *Reflections on Hanging*. As darkness fell, he tried to read, then simply stared off into the night.

Marian and Nelson Fuson met the bus in Nashville and drove the group to their house. Marian warned them along the way, "Don't worry about the appearance of the place: we're going to have it fixed. The inside's undamaged." When they arrived, Marv was shocked to see that what used to be a wide, gracious front porch was a shambles. The front steps were splintered and the porch itself was severely damaged; planks and studs were blackened and a smell of burning wood still hung in the morning air. "What happened here?" Marv asked. "A bomb," Nelson answered bluntly. "You'll be briefed later. Let's get inside."

Nelson Fuson was chair of the physics department at Fisk University. He was the child of Presbyterian missionaries who had served in Guang-zhuo, China, and Nelson's experiences there led him to pacifism and he became a Quaker. At Quaker meetings held in the Fuson home plans had been developed to remove racial segregation in downtown Nashville businesses.

Fuson informed them that Diane Nash and John Lewis would be joining them in an hour. Should they wish to continue they'd be leaving from the Greyhound station for Memphis, then on to Jackson, Mississippi.

Diane, born in Chicago in 1939, had studied at Howard University and transferred to Fisk in 1959. She was a beautiful young woman—as a teenager she won several beauty contests—but she was humiliated by the prejudice she often experienced in public places. She sought ways to overcome her own anger and attended the non-violence workshops run by Reverend James Lawson. At 22 she became an unofficial leader of the 1960 Nashville sit-ins.

John Lewis (who later became a congressman) was already beginning a long career in the forefront of human rights movements. The son of sharecroppers in Alabama, he attended segregated public grade schools in Pike County. After hearing Martin Luther King on the radio, he decided to become a part of the Civil Rights Movement. Along with Nash, he helped form the Student Nonviolent Coordinating Committee (SNCC) and was chair from 1963 to 1966.

Diane and John had led several training sessions for groups of young people arrived from the North, but the situation was changing daily, almost hourly, as the Jackson jail filled up with protesters. A hundred men and women, black and white, had already been tried and convicted in the Jackson courts. They were now locked up in county and city jails, separated by race and gender, and more were arriving daily. There was talk of transferring Riders to the infamous Parchman Prison should the overcrowding become intolerable.

When Lewis and Nash arrived, they wasted little time before briefing the Minnesotans about the current situation. "The media are focusing on what's happening in Jackson now, so with the spotlight on the officials, the prisoners are being treated all right," John told them, "but we have no way of knowing what might happen at Parchman Farm." The new arrivals were given two hours to discuss among themselves, privately, if they wished to continue, or to return. There would be no Negro people available for this leg of the trip, so the six, if they chose to go on, would board a bus by themselves that very evening.

It took the Minesotans no longer than a half hour to agree, "We've come this far; we'll take the next step." Someone produced a guitar and the group sang a few Freedom songs together. The Minnesotans knew the songs from performances at the Scholar but the music had suddenly taken on a deeper resonance.

Diane briefed them on the jail strategy: a guilty verdict was a foregone conclusion, and Mississippi's disorderly conduct statute required jailed riders to post bond within forty days of conviction. The Coordinating Committee planned to post bonds on the thirty-ninth day, to maximize the effect of the Riders' legal challenge. If they missed the date, they lost their right of appeal and any alternative to serving their entire sentence. The Riders were to try and stick it out for thirty-nine days before being bailed out.

They would be taken to the bus terminal one at a time, in case any thugs were hanging around looking for Riders to beat up. *Wonderful,* Marv thought: *A bomb blows up the Fusons' porch, hostile white guys are lying in wait for us, and we're not even to Mississippi yet.* "I'm going to leave Koestler's *Reflections on Hanging* here," he quipped, "I don't want to give them any ideas!"

But everything went smoothly that evening. Volunteers got the travelers to the station without incident and they boarded for an overnight trip to Memphis, where a contact from SNCC would see that they got on the right bus to Jackson.

Marv slept very little on the bus. When they reached Memphis their man was on the spot, and within an hour they were on the last leg of their bus journey, drinking in the contrasts between the lush hills and the dilapidated dwellings in the "hollers" and flatlands. At the Tennessee/Mississippi border, they grinned at the large, colorful sign showing white people fishing, swimming, and water skiing: *Welcome to Mississippi, June is Hospitality Month.*

Once they were in Mississippi, a highway patrol car showed up regularly to escort the bus, siren blaring, whenever they passed through a town or city, announcing the presence of the Freedom Riders. A half hour stop was scheduled at Yazoo City.

Whenever he speaks about the Rides to a class, Marv pauses to ask his students about the significance of Yazoo City to civil rights. Usually, no one has an inkling. He tells the tragedy of fourteen-year-old Emmett Till, whose brutal murder there (less than six years before the rides) galvanized the Civil Rights Movement. The Riders had seen the photos, first published by *Jet* and the Chicago newspaper *The Chicago Defender*, of Till's mutilated corpse. His courageous mother allowed an open casket in their Chicago church, and his great-uncle had testified against the killers in Yazoo City.

The stop at Yazoo City seemed interminable. The young travelers waited in their seats, watching uneasily while white toughs circled the bus looking for Freedom Riders. Marv was too paralyzed by fear to get off the bus, though the others did, to visit the Whites Only rest room.

About three hours later, the bus pulled into Jackson. The terminal scene was ordinary, Marv thought, almost anticlimactic. The building was slightly dingy, with slate blue art-deco-style tiles on the exterior. The waiting rooms inside, both "white" and "colored," were nearly empty. The six white young people headed with their luggage for the colored waiting room and sat nervously at the lunch counter, waiting to order breakfast. Not one waitress approached them, because they were familiar with the scene; the only waitress remaining behind the counter busied herself, back turned, with arranging utensils.

Finally, Captain Ray of the Jackson Police Department entered the waiting room and drawled something the northerners did not quite catch. They turned on their stools and asked, "What?" "Pardon me?" Shaking his head, Ray told them to *move on*, and when they continued to stare at him in puzzlement, he said the magic words: "You all are under arrest." They breathed a sigh of relief; thank God, there would be no violence today.

They filed to a waiting police van and waited longer inside, passing the time by singing. At the police station in the Hinds County Courthouse, they were fingerprinted. Marv tried to relax his fingers, as he'd been taught, when the deputy grabbed and squeezed them. He yelped in pain at a vicious pinch and asked mildly, "I thought we were supposed to relax our hands to get a good print?" The deputy glared contemptuously but did not respond. The young people glanced at each other, smiling. If this was the worst, they could put up with it. They were immediately separated, however, and taken one by one into an interrogation room.

Marv's interviewer was a soft-spoken detective who asked questions as another man took notes. The second man certainly looked like a cop, Marv thought—grim-faced with chiseled features hardly softened by age (he turned out to be in his mid-sixties). This was Westbrook Pegler, a conservative syndicated columnist whose invective and biting sarcasm about civil rights workers were legendary.

Even by Southern standards, the diatribes Pegler wrote for the *Jackson Daily News* and other papers were often extreme. On June 16, his column for the *News* complained that "bands of insipid futilities of the type called bleeding hearts… invaded a really fine American city … [causing] a national uproar of indignation, disgust, pity and shame." He frequently ridiculed individuals he had met, labeling them as homosexuals or communists. Pegler said two of the Riders "wouldn't fight anybody for anything, but they didn't think it wrong of *them* to affront a local social system and kick up riots and civil war with painful, even fatal, results to men and women to them unknown."

Although Pegler was silent during Marv's interrogation, the detective's questions were acerbic: "What right do you all have to come here, disturbing the peace of our city?" When Marv tried to say something about supporting civil rights, he interrupted, saying, "Our negroes are happy the way they are."

What did that mean? Marv began, trying for some rational explanation that could reflect their Students for Integration discussions, "I don't think ethics should be determined by geography…" which on later reflection he thought was "kind of a wise-ass remark." The detective demanded to know where they got the money for the bus fares. Marv told him that professors and friends from the University of Minnesota and a couple of labor unions donated money.

"Which labor unions?" the captain asked sharply. Union organizers were considered dangerous agitators. For the time being, Marv thought he'd better not volunteer any more information.

The six were placed in individual cells in a small cellblock that faced the state capitol. Through a small window in the hallway outside the cells they could see a bit of sky and the capitol dome topped by the Confederate flag—flying *above* the U.S. flag, Marv remembered. Moments later, Jack Young, one of three black lawyers working with the Mississippi Riders, entered the cellblock and greeted them warmly. He briefed them on what was about to happen, expanding on what Diane and John had told them. They would be found guilty, convicted of a "breach of the peace."

"Even if we..." one of them began. Jack smiled and raised his hand, continuing the summary. "You will be quickly convicted and sentenced to four months and a $200 fine. As you know, the Movement is asking all of you to remain in jail at least thirty-nine days, after which we'll bail you out. The rumors persist that they'll send you to the state prison. Any questions?"

Well, yes, but they were mainly of a personal nature. They had to do with nerve and the fear that needed to be tamped down. For Marv, the central question was, could he live out his convictions?

Young's description was accurate. The jury comprised ten Baptists, a Presbyterian and a Methodist—all white men. Captain Ray testified that he was notified in advance of the Minnesotans' arrival; he had rushed to the terminal (with a prison van and a driver) where he found an angry mob outside that would compromise the safety of the northerners. "I arrested them for their own safety." This scenario was *not* the experience of Marv's Riders, but such things had happened. The jury deliberated less than half an hour; the verdict was Guilty, the sentence was four months and a $200 fine. All refused to pay and were escorted upstairs to a large room with a double row of bunk beds.

Several other Riders greeted them. One was Daniel Thompson, a lyric poet from Cleveland who read in the streets, junkyards, and other 'uncommon' gathering places of ordinary people. (He remained active in social justice movements until his death in 2004, and was celebrated for scratching out poetry on a Parchman Prison cell wall.)

They remained in the county jail for a week, in relative boredom but not much discomfort. Black trustees smuggled in newspapers and fresh fruit. One of the trustees told Marv and Dave Morton "the Jackson black community supported them wholeheartedly."

"Man," Dave said, "If jail is like this, we can do the time standing on our heads." Marv knew that a support network stretched across the country and that the nation was watching. Not all of the public was supportive, however, even in the North. In some quarters the Riders were seen as radicals, if not subversives. In a poll taken in the third week of June, of the 63 percent who said they knew about the Freedom Riders, 24 percent approved and 64 percent disapproved. The concept of nonviolence was little understood and even less honored; many thought the Riders were stirring up trouble and were not doing anyone any good.

Claire was separated from the group and housed with earlier arrested female Riders. (More than a quarter of the Riders were women).

At the end of the week, Captain Ray told the Northerners to gather their luggage for "a little trip." A black van was waiting to chauffer the eleven men—ten of them white—to the infamous Parchman Farm, the maximum security state penitentiary on 18,000 acres in Parchman, Mississippi. Inmates at Parchman worked under harsh conditions on the farm and in manufacturing workshops. Its reputation for abusing black men made it dreaded all over the South, and Blues songs from the region were littered with references to it.

An armed trustee in a prison-striped uniform opened the door to the van and motioned the new prisoners inside. Nervous, they began another round of freedom songs. Several miles and several songs later, the van lurched to a stop, sending them sprawling over the metal seats. The driver threw open the door and, hand on his gun, snarled, "If you bastards continue to sing, I'd just as soon shoot you as look at you!" They stopped.

Through the mesh-barred window, they could see ramshackle buildings and vast muddy fields where black workers were bent over, picking cotton in a light rain. The rain kept the van from being stifling, but they were all sweating, wondering what lay ahead.

The 140-mile trip to Parchman took about three hours. They entered the compound between high brick walls; Marv saw guards standing by with rifles, and prisoners laboring, some pushing hand plows behind mules. He noted that the stripes on the uniforms of black prisoners ran horizontally rather than vertically. A black trustee leaned against a three-pronged pole, watching the others; he had a shotgun slung on his back. Beyond him a white man sat astride a white horse wearing an amazing white cowboy outfit and a white sombrero. He paid no attention to them as the van rolled by, but seemed to be posing on a movie set.

"Wow," Marv said, "would you look at that! Could be 1861 out there—*Gone with the Wind*." In a few minutes, they pulled up outside a low brick building surrounded by an electrified fence topped with razor-wire. This building was the maximum security unit. It housed the most violent and incorrigible prisoners and also contained death row. For what seemed an eternity they sat in the late morning sun in front of the administration section. No one spoke. The driver seemed to have disappeared. The temperature in the closed van rose. In about a half hour they heard heavy steps and low voices; the words sounded like 'Guess they're cooked.' The van door opened and they breathed a sigh of relief. They were herded into the intake area, lined up beside a low bench in an otherwise barren hallway, and told to strip. Guards walked behind them, commenting raucously on the prisoners' nakedness: "This queer has pimples on his ass." "Lookit the little dick on that one."

The first thing taken away in jail after your freedom, Marv reminds activists today, is your dignity. That was no less true in the South during the sixties, but Parchman had a reputation for brutality that exceeded any norm for jails and prisons.

"Next step," Marv thought to himself, "the gas chamber."

For Bob Baum, another Minnesota Rider, the experience evoked the same associations. He spoke later of growing up "haunted" by the Holocaust, and saw obvious parallels between the anti-Semitism that had given rise to mass murder in Central and Eastern Europe and the racism so prevalent in the American South. For Bob, Marv, and perhaps for a majority of the white Riders, the association was natural. Nearly 70% of white Freedom Riders were Jewish—an amazing participation rate for a group that made up less than 2% of the U.S. population. But Jews in the United States had long been influential in movements for social justice, particularly in labor, and national organizations like the Anti-Defamation League of B'nai B'rith and the American Jewish Committee were in the forefront of civil rights advocacy. According to Charney Bromberg, a CORE member who spent 1965 to 1967 in Mississippi as a civil rights worker, "The civil rights movement [was] built in part through the black and Jewish workers' rights movements of the 1930s. It is absolutely world-shattering what transpired."

Once the prisoners had been stripped, searched, and humiliated in one way or another, the guards finally opened the electronically operated gate and the group trotted, still naked, into the cellblock where the male Riders were housed. Cells were arranged in a long row facing a single hallway with slit windows in the opposite wall about seven feet above the floor. What would have been the first cell was a shower room, where twice a week the inmates were allowed to bathe. They were given underwear, a tee shirt and shorts. Nothing fit; Marv's were at least three sizes too large, so that he had to roll and tuck the limp waistband to keep his pants up. Whites and blacks were segregated by cell but placed in the same cellblock for the first time in Mississippi penitentiary history. (Women Freedom Riders were housed in a block on another wing, separated from the men by the death row area.) As the new inmates passed, Negroes and whites in the cells put their hands outside the bars for high fives, shouting, "Where you guys from? What's going on outside?"

A guard escorted Marv to cell 14, the last one in the block. It was like all the others, six by nine feet with a toilet and sink on the back wall. The toilet was lidless, "so you couldn't commit suicide with a toilet lid." Two steel plates, the second three feet above the first and topped with thin, aged mattresses, jutted from the wall. Cell fronts were bars interrupted by a slot for meal trays, and faced a wall with one high window through which prisoners could see the sky but nothing else. Inside, Marv met his cellmate Heath Rush, a tall, thin Quaker from an Ohio college. Heath looked familiar but they couldn't figure out where Marv could have seen him until he remembered that the Ohio group had been shown on *CBS News* during an antipathetic Walter Cronkite report.

The guard on duty opened the cell door and growled at Marv to shower and shave his "damn Russian mustache." When Marv protested that he'd had it for ten years, the guard threatened, "If you don't, I will!" Deciding he didn't need a hostile guard messing with his upper lip, Marv complied.

By order of Governor Ross Barnett, the Riders were not allowed to exercise outside or work in the fields; they might contaminate the other inmates. "Besides, they wouldn't know cotton from weed," the governor quipped. And Marv concurred: "I plead guilty to that one."

The high point of the week was when the prisoners were allowed to shave, shower, and change their bed sheets. On their way to shower the inmates could see each other, and they used the opportunity for street theatre, adapting the sheets as props and costumes.

Despite the separation, their jailers soon learned that the Riders were united and not just in spirit. Marv and Heath "could reach out our hands and shake hands with Cordell Reagan, husband of singer Bernice Reagan, and Bill Mahoney. Bill was light-skinned and could pass for white; he had to tell the guard his color," so that the cells could be segregated by race. Black and white spoke—and sang—together.

"And what voices!" Marv remembers, "Henry Thomas and Cordell Reagan became part of the SNCC Freedom Singers who toured the country… Cordell later married Bernice, lead singer of Sweet Honey in the Rock."

The first night, after the evening meal, the men on Marv's cellblock held a devotional. It got to be a regular custom. Some of the riders were pastors, priests, or rabbis, and they often led these services. Marv recalled that on his first night, as the homily for the evening ended, a chorus began to sing Freedom songs, "Keep your Eyes on the Prize," and "Oh Freedom, O Freedom, before I be a slave/ I be buried in my grave/ go home to my Lord and be free."

"I lay on my bunk, tears rushing down my face—not because of Parchman punishment but because of the nobility of everyone in there. I had a moment of 'blessed human solidarity' like I'd never felt before and I said to myself, 'I know now what I will do the rest of my life. Search for this feeling again.'"

As the summer dragged on, the Quaker practice of sitting in silence was a frequent format, followed by ethically focused reflections. Marv's cell-block neighbor, Bill Mahoney, a Nonviolent Action Group activist from Washington, DC, once asked Marv to take a turn at leading a devotional. Marv said, "I'm an agnostic." Mahoney later wrote, "I asked the middle-aged art dealer next door to do an agnostic service."

"He was about eighteen, then" Marv laughs. "I was twenty-nine. I guess to him I was middle-aged." In his reminiscences Mahoney placed the Freedom Riders into three categories, based on their motivation—political, moral, or emotional—and described Marv as being "politically motivated."

The men used their ingenuity to devise ways to pass the free time during their confinement. Zev Aelony rolled up and dried white bread to manufacture chess pieces and played chess with his cellmate. There were the hallway promenades and theater. Some of the prisoners played Twenty Questions based on Bible texts (each prisoner was permitted that book, Marv declared sarcastically, "because the Power was religious"). But the richest, most unforgettable mode of communication was the singing, which infused the civil rights nonviolent resistance with the power of music. "I can barely carry a tune, but the movement's music traditions have been powerful for me. We've always had art and music as part of our programs."

One day at the beginning of the fourth week of incarceration, the jailers brought in two SNCC field organizers, one black and one white. They were put temporarily in the same cell. Sheriff Tyson ordered the black man, "Negro, I want you to clean up your filthy cell."

The man replied, "Sheriff Tyson, you know me by my name. Refer to me by my name and I'd be happy to scrub this cell, which as you can see is already clean."

Purple-faced and furious, the sheriff called for "wrist-breakers" (metal handcuffs tightened with a crank) and had both men thrown into solitary confinement—the Hole. This was a 6' x 6' metal box beneath the cellblock with little light, no furniture, and a small drain in the floor for a toilet. The first prisoners to see the men dragged away began singing, mocking the jailers when they threatened to remove the mattress from anyone who wouldn't shut up: "Come and take my mattress, oh yes, come and take my bedding, oh yes." The singing swelled and spread into a deafening chorus as, one by one, the mattresses, toothbrushes, sheets, and stray personal effects were seized.

Removing the thin mattresses was not a paltry punishment; the bunk beds were quarter-inch steel plates, perforated with one-inch holes, extremely uncomfortable for sleeping, since the prisoners wore only briefs and t-shirts. But the men kept singing as their comforts disappeared.

The jailers weren't satisfied. At nightfall, workers came by and removed window screens. Clouds of mosquitoes, attracted by the 24-hour lights and fresh meat, "were a kind of biological torture which none of us had foreseen." Still they sang. At 2:00 a.m., a large diesel truck pulled up and a large hose snaked in through a window. A powerful spray of DDT drenched prisoners. Early the next morning, guards told the inmates to wash down the bars and walls to get rid of the now lifeless bugs.

For three days, the guards ramped up the discomforts and miseries. The small, high windows were closed in the heat of the day and the air circulation turned off. At night, the air would again be turned up to maximum, Marv said, "which made the steel sheets that were our bunks rather cold and left us shivering."

On the fourth day, suddenly and without explanation, all of the Minnesota men were put into the first two cells and given new striped uniforms to wear. "They told us visitors were coming but not who they were. I thought maybe my mother was going to come."

Marv was pleased with his new garb. He thought of Cagney and Bogart films and it felt natural. Simultaneously, everyone's mattresses and prison comforts were returned, and the two men in the Hole were let out. A sense of suppressed excitement filled the cellblock, but it seemed the Minnesotans were the only inmates to be visited.

"In came two reporters, Sheriff Tyson, and a man and a woman I didn't know." The Minnesota Riders' families had been calling Governor Elmer Andersen to intervene on their behalf and to investigate. The two officials he sent were Assistant Attorney General John Wright and Human Rights Commissioner Gladys Brooks. The access was to be considerably less than the officials wanted, but to increase the likelihood of a favorable report from the media, the delegation was treated to a lavish dinner at the warden's home, and it was also taken on a tour of local black schools and more presentable black neighborhoods, to impress the northerners with the "happy Negro communities."

But Marv and the other Minnesotans were granted five minutes each under the scrutiny of the sheriff. "I met Sheriff Tyson's eyes over the head of the Assistant Attorney General... I *did* tell [Wright] about the SNCC workers dragged to solitary, about the DDT and our protest and the removal of mattresses. The only result I saw was that I stopped getting mail."

Minnesota woman Rider Claire O'Connor had posted bail just before the visitors arrived and was not interviewed. When she returned to Minnesota, she presented a dark vision of her prison treatment. The experience of women Riders was physically similar to that of the men, but emotionally it was qualitatively different, particularly for the younger ones. Whereas the men were scorned and treated with contempt as agitators or dupes, southern officials' attitudes toward the female activists verged on the pathological. The authorities' assumption was that the women riders had crossed some line of racial and sexual decency. In reporters' conversations with southern officials, the southerner often brought in, unasked, the topic of miscegenation. The young women were thought of and referred to as "civil rights whores." Claire reported that inappropriate sexual questions were only a small part of the special harassment women experienced. Among other things, it also included repeated vaginal searches with a Lysol-dipped glove—the same glove for all the women.

Though her distressing jail memories did not fade with time, Claire also later recalled the positive experiences of learning and communal time with the other women Riders. The daughter of a union activist, she maintained that she was never *not* socially conscious. In Hinds County Jail she shared space with forty white women Riders and about sixty African American women. "The jail was crowded, with little room to sit down, let alone sleep. We pretty much just talked all day, there was nothing else to do," O'Connor said. "It's a surprise to me now, there was no tension, I cannot recall hearing a single raised voice." In Parchman, the women were more isolated, in a tight cluster of cells on the other side of death row; but like the men they kept their spirits alive by singing and underwent the same deprivations as a result.

Once Claire had been released, two FBI agents whom she describes as "absolutely brutal" shoved her around, then drove her to the airport in a prison van and dumped her off, alone. She made herself as inconspicuous as possible during the boarding and on the flight until the plane landed in Minneapolis.

Meanwhile at Parchman, the male Riders were transported from Maximum Security to a new brick facility, the First Offenders' Unit. Marv's cellblock residents were now housed in a large dormitory room with fifty cots in the middle. "Like a herd of antelopes, we began to run around the room about twenty-five times, the first exercise our legs had in a month!" Marv said.

When the running stopped, the men formed a large circle to meet. They decided as a group to ask for a meeting with the Warden, Fred Jones. Jones had already brought about some reforms at Parchman by setting up a system of leave time accrual, eliminating chain gangs and beatings, and establishing cohabitation shacks for married prisoners, black and white. Guards were not armed—only trustees, black and white.

The group requested that they be returned to maximum security to avoid any special privileges. The warden denied the request, stating, "More Freedom Riders are arriving, including thirty Jackson High School students, and you all are overcrowding that facility. Anyone who wishes to make a symbolic statement, line up in front of that door where we have some solitary confinement cells to accommodate you."

Twelve men chose that option. Marv did not. He wanted to find out who his new companions were and why they had come. "I knew the time would pass faster that way."

They were still forbidden outdoor exercise, though they could move about freely in the large barracks and eating area. Now the Mississippi Freedom Riders, including the recent arrivals in Jackson, were all assembled face to face for the first time, so those who had been in maximum security could catch up on the news. The guards and cooks in this area were trustees, and in the evening after the dishes were cleaned, the cooks brought steel guitars and sang the prison songs for which Parchman was famous. The prisoners in return shared their repertoire of protest and freedom songs.

One afternoon, Marv heard melodious deep voices singing Gospel and folk. "We all went to the windows." The singers were ten Negro men chopping weeds. Catching sight of the faces, the singers approached the building. One of them called out, "Are you them Freedom Riders we've been hearing about?" When they responded, "Yes, that's us," the singers applauded: "All of us are behind you!" It brought tears to Marv's eyes. He asked one of the men when he'd be released.

"I get out in 1981!"

Marv groaned. Twenty more years in this place. He could barely imagine it.

And then one day, nearly two months after the arrest, it was over. "The warden's assistant read off our names, and we said goodbye to our comrades. We would miss them—maybe even some of the trustees—but not Parchman."

Marv's first taste of freedom was the stale pack of cigarettes he found in his street clothes upon his release. The four-hour trip in the Black Maria to Jackson was the Freedom Riders' last experience of confinement, and Marv smoked as the group chattered excitedly all the way back. (He ought to have kicked the habit back then, he now admits ruefully.)

An AME church in a poor Negro neighborhood gave them a welcoming banquet. Then the Minnesota men were driven to a black businessman's home where, again, they had a lavish meal, a barber trimmed their hair, and they cleaned up for a late night flight home.

"They were so enormously kind and generous," Marv said, "no doubt involving risk to their families." They sat watching a gorgeous Southern sunset as Dave Morton strummed a guitar. They knew they'd be home in the morning, returning to relative safety, while the struggle for freedom would only intensify for their hosts.

In Minneapolis, hundreds of friends and supporters greeted the party at the terminal. After a short rally, the crowd formed a caravan to Mayor Arthur Naftalin's office for a press conference. The tired travelers met up with Claire O'Connor and each of the six spoke of their experiences—the SNCC men being dragged off to solitary, the way the women were treated, the "mattress rebellion," and the good people they had met in and out of Parchman. They spoke of the inspiring spirit of the movement and thanked whatever gods had motivated them to make the journey. An old friend of Marv's, Sinker Jones, thanked him personally for doing it for him and "his people." Marv felt honored, answering, "I'm so glad I could—but I did it first for me, *then* for you and the people I don't know."

Brother Jerry, his family's emissary, drove Marv straight to Lake Carnelian where their uncles had a lakeshore cabin. "The whole family was there, everyone excited to see me home and safe. But no one seemed particularly eager to hear my story and that rather shocked me."

On his first night back, Marv slept in the refreshing air of north-woods Minnesota, and he swam in the lake the next day. That night the family gathered to watch the 10:00 p.m. news. There was Marv, speaking of Parchman and the South. They eyed him uneasily and said little.

Yet for Marv himself, the experience at Parchman was central. And the Freedom Rides themselves had a profound affect on the nation's history. Five months after the first Freedom Riders left on their historic trip, the Interstate Commerce Commission (ICC) in conjunction with U.S. Attorney General Robert Kennedy issued a federal order banning segregation based on "race, color or creed" at all interstate public facilities. The law became effective on November 1, 1961.

Speaking engagements began to come in, and Marv was launched on a new and deeper phase of activism. He spoke at Rotary and Sertoma Clubs, high schools and colleges, at women's clubs and at one or two black churches. In St. Paul, Rabbi Bernie Raskus invited him to speak at Temple of Aaron.

They were not done with Mississippi. Although five cases would be selected for a representative appeal in Hinds County, the Riders learned in September that *everyone* would be called back for arraignment. Only eight failed to return.

In late October Marv took the train back to Jackson for his appeal. "We met Bill Kunstler, who worked on the federal appeal and held a mass meeting in the Negro Masonic Auditorium, where 3,000 local negro citizens joined us." At the arraignment Captain Ray of the Jackson Police testified again that he had arrested the group to protect the Riders from an angry mob waiting outside. The defense attorney assigned to the Riders' cases, Carson Hall, told Marv that he could help question prospective jurors and the captain, but that "I could not win this case if I were Clarence Darrow." Again, the all-white jury affirmed the conviction and, pending appeal, Marv returned to more extensive speaking in Minnesota.

The Freedom Riders' cases finally reached the federal courts in 1965 and the convictions were overthrown. Bail money was turned over to the Movement for voter registration. "After that," Marv says, "much of the nation caught the spirit of a radical active nonviolence: we changed its social reality forever."

In November 2001, as much of the nation reacted to the trauma of the Twin Towers attacks with new forms of racial discrimination and prejudice, the Riders gathered in Jackson for the Fortieth Anniversary of their historic journey. Zev, Marv, Bob and his wife Heather Baum, David, and Claire joined around seventy-five participants. The sixth of the original group, Gene Uphoff, a doctor at a clinic in a depressed neighborhood in Portland, Oregon, couldn't attend. All except David and Zev flew to Jackson, where Claire had reserved rooms in a down-town hotel. David and Zev decided, for memory's sake, to bus.

Marv's first surprise at the hotel was seeing a proclamation from the sitting governor (Ronnie Musgrove), declaring it "Freedom Ride Day." The welcome was a stark contrast to Governor Ross Barnett's hostile stance. He was also thrilled to see so many of the original Rid-ers in attendance. Even Jim Forman was there; Jim was battling colon cancer and was a shell of his former self, but he retained the electric presence that had brought him respect as an activist and organizer. "For me," Marv later said, "one of the high points was listening to Jim talk about the early development of SNCC."

The next morning the group toured the Hinds County city and county buildings, including the Jackson jail. The police chief and chief's assistant were black; they opened a cellblock on the fourth floor, where women riders were housed before Parchman. Several women walked in, slowly, holding hands. In a moment, the entire group were clasping hands, singing, while tears poured down their faces.

"Every black official we met said, 'We would not be sitting here except for what you did in 1961.' Of course, we knew they were be-ing generous, that thousands during Freedom summer, the Mississippi

Freedom Democratic Party activity of 1964, and all the local and regional struggles played major roles. But it was thrilling to see a manifestation of our collective effort."

On a tour of Jackson, city officials, police and deputy sheriffs welcomed everyone with hugs and thanks. Jackson appeared prosperous and growing, but the economic inequities were still obvious. In the shadow of the state capitol, grinding poverty was evident, and a young student from a Southern college told Zev Aelony that day that though the group may have done something important a long time before he was born, this was no time to just retire.

For Marv there were flies in the ointment. "The only people I had trouble with were two of the three *rabbis* who returned." Much of the tense discussion was centered on the long-standing animosity between Israel and Palestine, though one rabbi argued with Marv about the means used by Danish citizens to protect Jews from the Nazis during World War II. Marv argued his case strenuously, drawing upon events he had become deeply familiar with while teaching nonviolent activism at St. Thomas. The rabbi listened politely but persisted in his denials of the effectiveness of nonviolent resistance, and in the end Marv was reduced to saying, "Rabbi, you do not know what you are talking about!" The rabbi turned away.

That incident profoundly frustrated Marv, but the excitement of seeing so many people who wanted to meet them far outweighed the negatives. There were black city council members, white history students from Ole Miss who eagerly took oral histories from each Rider, a young black judge just appointed to the Mississippi Supreme Court, and the first black mayor of Jackson, who dedicated a plaque to them.

The group returned to the Twin Cities glorying in the experience. At his next St. Thomas class, Marv recounted the day-by-day reunion, emphasizing the changes he witnessed, telling the students, "I want you to know that every effort we make to seriously change social reality counts, especially when people work together in the right ways, sustain the activity, and take risks!" He added, reflecting on the human foibles of his heroes, "We who went on the Rides were not unusual people; but we sometimes became unusual by virtue of what we did. And if we could do it, you too can do it."

In the weeks following the Freedom Riders' return to Minneapolis in 1961, Marv shared his experiences with others and eventually helped arrange a speaking tour for Clancy Sigal, author of the classic tour of working-class America, *Going Away*. Marv and Herschel Kaminsky, a Dinkytown radical, picked up the writer at the Minneapolis Greyhound station. As they crossed the Mississippi on the Third Avenue bridge they noticed a mother slowly wheeling a baby in a carriage with a toddler straggling along clutching her hand. The mother appeared to be poorly dressed and her shoulders were slumped. Clancy asked them where this woman would go to get the help to survive. They admitted they had no idea what systems might be in place. Clancy erupted, "You're supposed to be radicals! Why don't you know?"

Then Sigal said something Marv never forgot: "One of your main tasks in life is to locate your world view, your political morality, and to live this out in a commensurate way *in public* with a minimum of compromise. Make your private and your public life one, so that you are not schizophrenic." With these comments, Sigal gave Marv the words for his life mission.

Today, Marv delights in challenging idealistic students who want to "make a difference" by changing themselves, or maybe *one* person in their lives. "That's bullshit! How ineffective. You want the masses involved!"

7

Canada to Cuba

The Cuban Missile Crisis gave Marv another opportunity to link the causes of peace and antiracism. Once again, his journey would take him into the heart of the segregated South, as part of the Quebec to Guantanamo Walk for Peace.

When Fidel Castro's revolutionary government nationalized Cuba's banks and industries in the early 1960s, U.S. policies hardened to outright hostility. The Eisenhower and Kennedy governments initiated an embargo, followed in April of 1961 by an invasion at the Bay of Pigs. The CIA assumed that Castro's regime was unpopular and were confident that once the counter-revolutionaries had established a beachhead on the Cuban mainland, the people would rise up to demolish the Castro regime. The country would return to a paternalistic, Batista-type government catering to the interests of the multi-national corporations that wanted to do business there—not to mention the middle-class Cubans who were now fleeing in droves.

But the CIA was wrong. The Cuban government quickly defeated the U.S.- backed force of Cuban exiles. It was an embarrassing defeat, and the Kennedy administration decided to tighten the economic and military screws.

What had been a regional embarrassment for the United States became an international crisis when it was discovered that the Soviet government had placed short-range nuclear missiles on Cuban soil. A game of brinkmanship followed, though it was hardly a game. The entire world teetered on the brink of destruction for twelve days before Nikita Khrushchev announced on October 28 that the installations would be dismantled.

Because of the "imminent danger to humankind" the Committee for Nonviolent Action (CNVA) in New York put out a call for activists to join a Canada to Cuba Peace Walk. In 1960 CNVA had sponsored a San Francisco to Moscow Walk for Peace, urging unilateral nuclear disarmament in the United States, England, France, and the Soviet Union. Jerry Lehman, one of the marchers, came to the University of Minnesota to speak, and he made a deep impression on Marv.

The Quebec to Cuba walk seemed like a natural course of action for Marv. He called Neil Haworth, CNVA executive secretary in New York, and described his own background; Neil heartily accepted Marv as a marcher, and Marv drove to New York to meet him.

In mid-June 1963 the two joined the walk at Griffiss Air Force Base in Rome, New York, where walkers from different cities had agreed to join forces. The plan was to demonstrate for five days against nuclear arms, including the bombs going into B-52s. A hundred marchers, joined by townspeople from Rome and the surrounding area, gathered at the base's main entrance base. At first the vigil was quiet and low-key; the time passed with music, street theater, and talks by activists from around the country. On the fourth day about twenty young people, including Marv, climbed the fence, with the idea of walking slowly to a runway and presumably blocking planes.

They were no more than a few steps into the base when special Department of Defense police vehicles arrived to scoop up the protestors, carry them to the gate and deposit them outside. Those who were able repeated the action again and again for the next six hours, until it began to get dark and everyone returned to camp.

That night the Canada to Cuba walkers held a public meeting in a Rome-Utica hotel, where CNVA facilitator A. J. Muste outlined the purpose of the walk and their position of unilateral disarmament. The marchers and supporters in the hall greatly outnumbered members of the general public, though the atmosphere was charged with tension. When a young man rose belligerently to challenge the stance on disarmament, Muste praised him. Guessing correctly that he was in the Air Force, Muste said, "It takes a great deal of courage for you to be here alone and voice your view. We have a deep respect for you."

Marv never forgot Muste's gentle demeanor and response as an example of nonviolent practice. Muste's thinking about weapons and pacifism had a profound influence on Marv, as did his emphases on nonviolence, respect for human life, and social justice.

Muste had become a pacifist when World War I broke out in Europe. He worked with the American Civil Liberties Union in Boston and as a religious leader assisting Massachusetts textile workers. From 1940 to 1953 he was executive secretary of the religious pacifist organization Fellowship of Reconciliation, which stimulated the formation of CORE. After "retirement" at 68, he stepped up his activism and was unstinting in his opposition to war and especially to nuclear arms. Even *preparation* for a war that contemplates using radioactive weapons, Muste believed, was a degradation of mankind, indicative of "extreme mental sickness." Marv's anti-weapons work came later, but the Peace Walk strengthened his passionate opposition to any corporate systems that exploited human fear for profit.

On the same day that the community meeting took place, a companion pointed out to Marv a man who was to be another major influence and long-time friend and mentor, Dave Dellinger. Dave was standing on the picket line, smiling and chatting with soldiers on the other side of the gate. He looked like he was enjoying both the day and the company enormously. No point in being shy, Marv thought, and he walked up to introduce himself, initiating over 40 years of precious friendship.

Marv suggested to the marchers a game of touch football; sixteen men and women volunteered. Dave was on Marv's team. Marv watched, astounded, as the 49-year-old outran the younger people, moving fast and gracefully without hurting anyone. After the game (their team won handily), Marv walked behind Dave and his young son Ray, observing their affectionate banter as Dave had his arm around the boy. "I made up my mind then, I wanted to know this man and his family."

David Dellinger was well known in the pacifist and anti-nuclear communities, as well as among those who worked to bring racism to an end. He worked closely with A. J. Muste and was one of the most influential pacifists of the late twentieth century. He was the founding editor and publisher of *Liberation Magazine,* a monthly that from 1956 to 1975 offered thoughtful editorial and investigative pieces that fed the pacifist and radical left.

On the morning of June 18, 1963, the Walk prepared to move out, beginning from the front gate of Fort Griffiss. There was a significant delay as a young mother of three, Joanne Collier, sat in a solitary vigil in the middle of the road blocking traffic. For some reason the military police moved slowly and cars were backed up for about a mile before they arrested her. The marchers had time to bid her goodbye and wish her well before they took up their packs and gear and filed off. Marv was moved by her dignity and solitary calm and later obtained part of her testimony at trial. Her words about nuclear danger seem timeless:

Dave Dellinger

Three years of writing letters, carrying petitions, and visiting Congress ... have convinced me that it is not sufficient to present our desires and good ideas for peace to the government—that it is the people who must make peace. We can do it by ... nonviolently obstructing its operation, placing our own bodies as a barrier between men and the weapons they build, service, and stand ready to use.

The group walked fifteen to eighteen miles a day, taking back roads and walking on the shoulder facing oncoming traffic. Their signs carried a variety of messages such as "Quebec to Guantanamo Walk for Peace," "Nuclear Disarmament," "Freedom to Visit Cuba," "Practice Nonviolence" and dozens more. They were crafted of thin plywood sheets with black and red lettering, and were designed to withstand weather while being highly visible and lightweight.

The organizers saw to it that a van with supplies, medical needs, and changes of clothing met the walkers at scheduled stops. Brad Lyttle, a member of the executive committee of CNVA, had already driven the entire route from Quebec to Miami, making contacts with peace groups and seeking home hospitality wherever possible.

An early leg of the trip was through rural areas of the beautiful Pocono Mountains, where hospitality was the rule. Farmers or their wives would spontaneously meet the walkers, curious about the mission, offering refreshments and rest.

In Binghamton, New York, a Methodist Church had opened its fellowship hall for overnight, and supporters brought groups of the marchers home for dinner. That evening, a rally with speakers was planned in front of City Hall. Binghamton reporters had interviewed marchers on the road, so a crowd of about 600 people filled the city square by the time they arrived. A group of counter-demonstrators picketed the rally, holding signs that read "Captive Nations Week."

Brad Lyttle chaired the rally. Then in his early thirties, Brad was a tall, fair-skinned man with straight dark hair and an imposing but gentle presence. He was a precise speaker, carefully measuring his words. He gathered the attention of the crowd easily, but there were murmurs among the counter-picketers that swelled as younger speakers were introduced. The arrangement was to share the speakers' duty in alphabetical order, and Marv was scheduled to take the podium following a seventeen-year-old, who presented a short statement explaining the mission.

Never having spoken to so large a crowd, the teenager was nervous and the right-wingers began to heckle him. Marv had done some homework that day on a hint from Dave. He went to the local newspaper files and discovered that a civil rights martyr, William Moore, grew up in Binghamton. Moore was a postman and a Marine veteran of the Iwo Jima campaign who later became a committed pacifist. He had been a frequent picketer at City Hall, often by himself, on antipoverty and antinuclear campaigns. The year before, he had undertaken a solitary march to the South, with letters in his postal bag for the Governors of Alabama and Mississippi. He wheeled a supermarket cart with his belongings and displayed two signs: "Wanted – Dangerous Criminal at Large – Consorter with Pimps and Prostitutes, Jesus Christ" and "Eat at Joe's, Black and White." One April evening, on a lonely stretch of rural highway near the town of Attalla, Alabama, he was shot in the head and killed.

Marv began his talk by declaring, "I am honored to be standing in the shadow of a building where William Moore expressed his thoughts to your community about the issues that deeply concerned him." The heckling ceased.

He went on to speak about the Cuban Missile Crisis and his fears for humanity if governments and ordinary people could not learn to live together. He emphasized that the *integrated* Walk would bring black and white marchers every day deeper into the South where Bill Moore was brutally murdered, and gave a brief account of his own experience as a Freedom Rider. When he turned around after "respectful applause," he was stunned to find Bill's wife Mary Moore on the stairs, waiting to shake his hand.

Mary stayed for several hours talking with the group, and the next day she brought Marv to Bill's gravesite on a hill overlooking the city. "Why did he make that strange journey alone? Why was he killed?" she asked him. He had no answers, but knew that the Quebec to Guantanamo Walkers would carry Moore's memory and commitment throughout their own journey.

As the march approached New Jersey, Marv was sent to arrange a stop and stay at the cooperative community known as St. Francis Acres. There, Dave Dellinger and the community of pacifists operated a radical publishing house, a farm, and a school. Marv became acquainted with Dave's wife, Elizabeth, and the children, Patch, Ray, Danny, Natasha, and Michelle, "one of the most extraordinary families I have ever known."

David Dellinger had been moved by the possibilities of communal living since his years as a graduate student before the second world war. Traveling in Spain on his way to Oxford in 1936, Dave came to admire the non-hierarchical communal settlements established by the Popular Front. Francisco Franco had just launched a military attack on the Front, which had only recently come to power, and Dave was tempted to remain and join in the defense of it, but he understood that all factions were taking lives, and felt that he could never pick up a gun. The following year he undertook a journey of three years across the United States, learning to live as a poor person, dependent on others. He remained steadfast in his vision through the 1940s and 50s—not an easy time for people with pacifist ideals—and eventually found both a partner, Elizabeth Peterson, and a place to nurture his ideas.

Author and activist Barbara Deming was also on the walk and has chronicled her experience in *Prison Notes*. At the time of the walk she had already long been involved in nonviolent activism, and was known for her application of nonviolent theory to the women's movement. But her roots were in Quaker schooling and her vision of the promise of nonviolence extended beyond its feminist applications. In 1961 she walked with the San Francisco to Moscow Walk for Peace, where she met Brad

Barbara Deming

Lyttle, protested atomic bomb testing at the Atomic Energy Commission building in New York City, and later joined the Nashville to DC integrated walk for peace. A brilliant journalist and poet, she taught dramatic literature and published fiction and nonfiction works. She spent much of her life teaching and advocating for personal empowerment.

Marv's admiration for Barbara is boundless: "I had never met anyone like her. There are people in this world with whom you become more mature just standing next to them. It seemed like every bit of Barbara's attention was directed like a laser beam right on you, every pore of her being concentrated on the needs of others. She radiated a sense of power and peace. Just by being in her presence you grew!"

Marv occasionally demonstrates to his students at St. Thomas some of the body language Barbara employed. "If a confrontational situation arises, or if you have to call a halt, or if someone is threatening—and there is space to do this!—raise your left hand, a 'stop' signal, while you extend your right, indicating 'I'm open to listening.'"

Excitement grew as the walk approached New York City, where the group was met and joined by James Baldwin, Norman Thomas, Dorothy Day, and others. Near Columbia University, a small mob of Cuban exiles attacked the support van, shouting "Communist! Communist!" They grabbed signs from marchers and attempted to break into the van's doors to get at those inside. They were unsuccessful in starting a fight, and drifted away, but were a portent of the days to come.

Marv was discovering that he could articulate the purposes of the walk well, and began to speak more often in the rotation and work with the march leaders as they met with government officials. In Washington, D.C., he joined Brad Lyttle to meet with Robert Follestad, the State Department's Cuba Desk Officer.

Brad described the walk to Follestad, telling him that the group intended to walk from Havana to Guantanamo to urge nonviolent solutions to a crisis that had nearly destroyed humanity. Follestad nodded, agreeing that the Missile Crisis had been profoundly dangerous.

"Given the nature of the conflict, don't you think that U.S. policy was one of darkness and stupidity that was counterproductive?" Brad persisted. The response that followed was a non sequitur: "Cubana Airlines uses planes that are old, but safe. They leave from Mexico frequently." Marv couldn't figure it out. On his own initiative, he telephoned David Brinkley to report on the meeting; Brinkley, Marv said, was flabbergasted but did no follow-up reporting.

The Walk arrived in Washington, DC, just in time to join the momentous People's March on Washington; this march had been organized by a variety of civil rights and activist groups to highlight the severe frustration at racial inequity and to counter the violence of the early sixties. The participants, along with sponsoring organizations including NAACP, CORE, Southern Christian Leadership Conference, Urban League, SNCC, and various labor unions, were demanding the passage of meaningful civil rights legislation; elimination of racial segregation in public schools; a major public-works program; the passage of a law prohibiting racial discrimination in public and private hiring; and a $2 an hour minimum wage.

On August 28, 1963—a horribly hot, sticky day—more than a quarter of a million people, four fifths of them black, marched to the Lincoln Memorial. There were pleas for basic human rights from nearly every segment of American society, including members of Congress, labor leaders; SNCC leader John Lewis; civil rights figures Gordon Parks and Roy Wilkins; clergy; James Baldwin; film stars Sidney

Poitier, James Garner, and Marlon Brando; and popular singers such as Mahalia Jackson, Marian Anderson, Joan Baez, Peter, Paul and Mary, and Bob Dylan. Martin Luther King, the young, charismatic leader of the Southern Christian Leadership Conference, capped the day with a historic speech.

The way Marv tells it, Dave and radical journalist I. C. Stone very nearly missed the speech. Dave and 'Izzy' were at the back of the speakers' platform. After the first part of King's prepared remarks, Stone whispered, "This is boring, let's go down and walk among the people!"

The scuttlebutt among organizers was that many of the talks, notably John Lewis's, had been vetted and toned down. March organizer Bayard Rustin had asked that all speakers hand in the text of their speeches the night before; Robert Kennedy and Bishop O'Doyle insisted that Lewis temper his rhetoric where he denounced the President's bill as inadequate. At a hasty conference, A. Phillip Randolph and Bayard Rustin convinced Lewis to get rid of the controversial passages.

The March on Washington was intended to build nationwide support for the passage of the 1964 Civil Rights act, but many in the nonviolence movement thought the event heralded a return to "coalition politics," an antithesis of the nonviolent confrontation at the core of the black protest movement. King was about to change that view.

As Dave and Izzy prepared to creep off the platform, King visibly put aside his prepared speech, paused, and began again, "I have a dream!" The speech, celebrated and lauded for its unifying message, was more than a utopian vision. Marv, Dave, and those already spurred to political action heard the challenge in King's words: "There will be neither rest nor tranquility in America until the Negro is granted his citizenship rights. The whirlwinds of revolt will continue to shake the foundations of our nation until the bright day of justice emerges."

They heard his call to the people, "some of you have come fresh from jail cells…" and understood. They heard, "go back to Mississippi…go back to Alabama…" and knew they were on their way. They resonated to a message that was largely incomprehensible to the general (white) population.

In the evening, the CNVA contingent was invited to a hotel party hosted by SNCC field secretaries. Marv was thrilled to be among the courageous young people again, and to be entertained by the likes of Joan Baez and Bob Dylan.

Over the next week, SNCC and CORE representatives came to help train the walkers for the next leg of their trip. The group was to select only thirteen of the thirty-nine willing walkers to continue the journey into the South. It was critical, the committee believed, to leave slots open for southern black people to join in. In secret ballot, after each of the thirty-nine had presented his or her credentials and commitment, they ranked the contenders 1 to 39. None of the walkers was satisfied with the low numbers proposed; they decided to send representatives to New York to persuade CNVA to expand the Walk. Marv was elected to be one of the persuaders.

The committee met for fourteen hours on Saturday and nine on Sunday, discussing each name. A strong homosexual candidate was rejected because of fears that young, attractive males could be subject to rape in southern jails. Marv struggled to include all of the thirty-nine: "They've come so far! How can we say we're inclusive if one of our first acts is to keep out our comrades!"

The unbending aspect of Marv's nature was showing itself, and he felt his face flush with anger. The elders, experienced nonviolent practitioners, kept patience, knowing Marv would learn. Calmly, they explained that the group should be diverse, but capable of withstanding harsh physical conditions and extreme mental stress. Marv had proved himself in Parchman, but what lay ahead was uncharted territory.

Bayard Rustin argued for inclusion of a young black amateur boxer, Ray Robinson, who was tough and resourceful. In the end, his name and three others were added to the thirteen, an expansion to seventeen walkers. Ray was to play a significant role in the hardships to come.

8

"We mean you no harm"

November 1963. The integrated group that left Washington, D.C. had little trouble in Virginia, with only occasional epithets thrown at the marchers and their signs. To defuse potential violence, group representatives would meet with the state governor's office in each state they entered, and with sheriffs and police departments all along the way. The CNVA's practice was to persuade the authorities that it would be in everybody's interest to let the group pass through. They had not come to stay in any community. "All we wanted," Marv says, "was have people see us, to speak if the opportunity presented itself, and walk into the white downtown, offering leaflets to anyone who would take them. In most cases, the Power would initially say, we don't want you to do this here. So we'd stop talking, and say 'We'll be back in the morning.'" The marchers spoke in front of the Post Office in Chapel Hill, North Carolina, where a few people threw eggs at them, at Duke University, and at North Carolina State.

The first major trouble came in Gaffney, South Carolina, a small agricultural town in the middle of cotton fields and peach groves with a downtown district that in the 1960s spanned five blocks. On a Saturday the district was bustling with shoppers.

The group chose white women to pass out leaflets before the rest of the marchers entered the downtown area, on the theory that locals would be less likely to harass them. The women met with no opposition though few were interested in their leaflets. At the end of the fifth block the entire group met up with a gauntlet of fourteen white men who stood, arms folded, on either side of the sidewalk. They had been advised in Washington not to show fear in such a situation, and not to touch anyone, either—it might set off a donnybrook.

Ray Robinson, the black boxer who had joined the group in Washington, was in the lead. He had made it a habit to carry the lead sign, saying he had to see how much people hated him. He stepped forward confidently with, "Good morning, gentlemen," and the other marchers repeated the same greeting as they passed through the long line of glaring faces.

An hour later, the marchers arrived at the black neighborhood on the outskirts of town. At the far end was a large clearing where fifty-odd cars and pickups were parked helter-skelter, white men having driven ahead to stand beside their vehicles or sit on the hoods, waiting. Marv was close enough to take in the looks of hatred on many white faces. The marchers hesitated. Suddenly, in plain view of the hostiles, a young black man stepped down from his porch and shook hands with Ray. He handed him a five-dollar bill, then shook hands with each marcher, saying, "God bless you."

At that point the crowd drifted away, gunning their motors but abstaining from further confrontation. Marv remembers with awe the young man's quiet bravery, the touch of a hand, and the eyes of "every angry person in the crowd witnessing that incredible act...I still weep when I tell the story."

The rest of the long walk through South Carolina was uneventful. The authorities had assigned two troopers to accompany the group and these policemen became friendly, learning their names, at times accepting cheese sandwiches and other simple road fare. Days passed when the marchers encountered no opposition at all. It was almost as though they were invisible. At one point, walker Yvonne Klein made a bet with Marv that the group would make it through the South unscathed.

In Georgia, the marchers slept on the floor in African Methodist Episcopal churches, making suppers and breakfasts in the church kitchens. The first main base was near the University of Georgia, where Charlayne Hunter, one of the school's first black students, had just graduated with a degree in journalism. The walkers were impressed with the neat red-brick buildings and tree-lined streets of the old campus in Athens, but they knew they might have difficulty finding space to meet there. A prosperous university town, Athens retained handsome antebellum mansions and a lively, though segregated, community. Searching for a meeting location, Marv met with a priest at the campus Newman Center. "Dorothy Day's a sponsor of our walk," Marv told him proudly. The priest responded coolly, "She is not one of my favorite people."

At the Methodist Center a young pastor enthusiastically agreed to set up a meeting at a black church; fifty students and faculty attended, and the university newspaper interviewed the walkers.

Leaving Athens the next day, the group walked thirty-five miles to Dacula, a ramshackle village on the Winder Highway and the CSX railroad line between Athens and Atlanta. A patrol car sat at the head of the town's main drag; two local cops stared at them. Marv walked over and stuck out his hand, through the open window: "Good morning, officers," he said, "Would you like a press kit about our walk?" They left his hand dangling: "We don't want none of that shit."

Around noon all seventeen walkers sat eating lunch alongside Highway 29 when a car sped by, swerving close enough that they could see a man, a woman, and a child inside. The man screamed, "God damned nigra lovers!" Barbara Deming waved and smiled. A few minutes later, the same car backed fast into the clearing, narrowly missing a group on the ground, and a powerful young guy jumped out, waving his fists. Marv noticed that the Dacula cops, who had shadowed the walkers through town, were gone. The man headed for the nearby pile of signs and began to smash the plywood and plastic to pieces.

Walker Peter Gregonis, a short, wiry man and World War II veteran, came up to him and said in a quiet voice, "Please stop that." The man punched him in the face, knocking him down. Peter immediately got up, holding his hands open before him in a non-threatening way. The man slugged him again.

Marv found his legs walking under him right up to the guy, in a sort of out-of-body sensation.

"We mean you no harm," he pleaded, but the man drew back his big fist and swung. Marv ducked, catching the blow in his back, which toppled him. The entire group then slowly drew near, saying, "Please don't hit them. Can't we talk?"

Breathing hard and shaking his head, the man climbed into his car and drove away. Ray picked up the lead sign, one of only two that remained intact, and Marv said, "Let's go, walk some more. We'll probably see him and his friends later." The marchers repaired a few signs and moved off, keeping between their escort van and car, which played leap-frog on the opposite shoulder of the highway, driving ahead but not so far ahead that they couldn't keep watch.

A half-hour later the marchers passed a closed restaurant, and their assailant was waiting in the darkened parking lot with a dozen of his friends. As the group slowed, two of the women walked right into the crowd, offering leaflets. The men (they were all men) seized handfuls of leaflets and ripped them, yelling "F--ing nigra lovers. We know you're doing them, go back to your lovers!" The women rejoined the group and the mob allowed the marchers to pass.

State Route 29 is a major trunk highway from New York to Miami with a fair amount of truck and tourist traffic. Some passers-by gave them friendly waves or greetings, others tried to spray them with gravel. Suddenly the CNVA van came up fast behind the marchers, its passengers shouting, "There's two carloads coming! Get ready!" As marshal of the walk, Marv ran up and down the line, repeating the warning.

Minutes later, two cars pulled up across the highway. The same man who had attacked them earlier ran across the road and then slowly approached the oncoming marchers.

High Noon, Marv thought, and images of Gary Cooper standing alone on a dusty street came crazily to mind. The tough ignored Ray, who carried the wooden sign, but tore up the other signs one after the other. He then punched two of the male marchers, who did not retaliate but merely replied with, "We won't fight you. We mean you no harm." His friends stood beside their cars chuckling. Once again, this seemed to confuse the attacker, who departed hastily with his friends, tires screeching.

Marv had had enough. He shouted at the walkers to get in the vehicles. "A few people demanded that we walk further. I screamed, 'Get in the damn cars. You elected me marshal. We'll debate in Atlanta!'" People scrambled inside.

Decisions were made all along the route by consensus, with a voice vote if agreement could not be reached. Experienced leaders helped the group forge a decision-making process for themselves, but conversation was difficult at night when everyone was exhausted, or on the long road when they had to remain alert. Sometimes decisions had to be made on the spot.

Marv drove the lead van, Yvonne Klein the car. Five miles down the road, a car sped past them on the left. A lumpy bag sailed toward the van's windshield; Marv tried to swerve away, but it smashed through the glass on the passenger side in a hail of rocks and eggs, the glass cutting him and two others. Edie Snyder, former secretary to A. J. Muste, was riding shotgun. She was petrified but stuck her hand out to clear away some of the mess so that Marv could see.

Edie later recalled: "I was sitting next to Marv, wiping blood off his face. How could I have forgotten that! I do remember Marv cracking a joke and both of us laughing while trying to get out of that scene a.s.a.p." Although most of the windshield was crazed and splattered with egg, Marv said he could see well enough through the "hole" to keep driving, holding a steady pace as the car chased them to the Georgia border before racing away.

In Atlanta, the party made repairs, rested, and spoke in different venues around the city to gather support. Returning to the area of the attack, they resumed walking, moving for two days without incident. The third day, they entered Griffin, 35 miles south of Atlanta, and began to pass out leaflets near the southernmost limits in the black area of town. As they passed a long, low building—the black high school—students hung out the windows and stuck their hands out to grab leaflets. A policeman following them stopped one of the women and told the group to quit, that he would not allow them to continue. The walkers responded that they would respect his wishes and stop for the day. However, they said they had a constitutional right to distribute information and that they would return in the morning.

That evening they were given hospitality in a small Negro church in Macon. The minister did ask them to leave within a day, because of the danger to his congregation. It may be hard to understand, Marv says, the fear that small black communities felt at the mere presence of their visitors. The walkers were welcomed with dignity and hospitality; their commitment was honored; but the level of violence was so high in the South that they also felt undercurrents of hostility to their presence.

In the morning, Marv volunteered to remain behind when the group returned to Griffin. He would seek another host church after he had cleaned up the dishes and mopped the floor.

Talking about that day from his dialysis couch in November 2005, Marv is acutely uncomfortable. He impatiently shifts the tubes that are cleansing his blood, as though he'd like to thrust them aside to return to November 1963 and do things differently.

"I must have smelled something coming on, because I volunteered to stay behind and wash the dishes! I don't know if I suspected some violence would happen, because the cops in Griffin had said, 'You're not going to leaflet this black high school,' and we had said, 'We'll be back.' And they looked really serious! Anyway, I offered to stay, somebody had to do that, find us a new place and so on. I don't know if I thought, wow, they're going to get the shit kicked out of them, I better stay out of this, or I thought somebody's got to do this and it's important, and I'll do it. I don't like violence, I've been in the wrong trade."

He laughs, an abrupt bark of glee at his own ambivalence. He insists people can't know until it happens what their reaction will be: whether they'll freeze and try to become invisible, run away, or walk right into it. "I've done all three in my life."

He was nervous all day. The physical tasks helped; he did the cleaning, repacked and stored everyone's luggage, and lined up a new host church a few blocks away. He was alone, working quietly for a change; he didn't hear what was going on until late afternoon, when the phone rang, and the caller (he can't remember who it was) gasped that there had been injuries and arrests. Pearl Ewald was on her way to the hospital. Soon several of the walkers returned and the story spilled out.

Dozens of police had met the walkers at the high school and a smaller number of black citizens gathered as witnesses. When the first walker offered a leaflet to a black child, police arrested the leafleter. The walkers lined up silently to continue and were arrested one by one. Their practice was to say gently, "I refuse to cooperate with an unjust arrest," and sit down; or they would simply stand and quietly accompany a policeman. But now a Georgia Bureau of Investigation cop walked among them with an electric cattle prod; he began using it, thrusting it toward the women's and men's genitals to make them move.

The Griffin sheriff ran over to him, pleading, "You don't have to do that! My guys will carry them!" The sheriff then picked up a sobbing woman and carried her to the bus. The action was over within minutes. The local police ticketed and released the demonstrators from the bus.

Pearl Ewald, who had been watching, horrified, suddenly clutched her chest and collapsed.

Pearl was the usual CNVA van driver, a 70-year-old Quaker and a veteran of nonviolent campaigns. The year before, she'd led a small group of elders who kept vigil in front of the White House wearing black armbands on which were printed in white letters the words, "Bomb Tests Kill People." Their vigil went on for several days until an exasperated judge sentenced them to twenty days in jail. According to a *Nation* writer, the judge reproved the offenders "in a voice such as one would use for a frightened puppy," speaking to "four people whose unabashed gentleness was awesome."

Now Pearl was on her way, half-conscious, to a southern hospital. Because the Griffin hospital didn't have a cardiac facility, the group found an ambulance driver who would take her to Macon. Ray Robinson and Kit Havice rode with her; Brad followed the ambulance in the van. Within a few minutes, the ambulance driver was stopped for speeding and the multiracial passengers questioned. The driver and ambulance passengers were waved on, but Brad was arrested and jailed.

Marv and the group didn't find out about Brad until the next day. In the meantime, Ray called Marv from the hospital, at his wit's end because Pearl demanded to be taken to a black ward. The hospital was segregated and refused to admit her. Ray asked if Marv would call to see if he could find her a doctor to deal with the hospital. Marv called about ten doctors, telling the medical men what their group was doing and what had happened. They all said, "Sorry, can't help you." The eleventh one said, 'I don't care who y'all are, she's sick, I'll do what I can. I'll be right over.'

The doctor persuaded Pearl to let him examine her in the hospital, which then admitted her under his care. To everyone's relief, Pearl recovered quickly, although the angina attack had been severe enough to fell her.

The next day, the group learned that Brad had been booked into a small county jail in Macon which the locals informed them was "very inhospitable to any enlightened people." Marv knew they had to go and get him out.

They walked into the sheriff's office, an anteroom off the lockup, just large enough to house a few beat-up wooden desks and some file cabinets. There were pictures on the wall of grinning men in uniform standing beside politicians, and of deer carcasses fresh from the hunt. The sheriff, a jowly, hefty man, sat placidly, smoking a cigar. They told him who they were and that they'd come for Brad Lyttle.

"You can have him for 100 dollars cash," the man said. Then he glowered and said, sneering, "If you bastards come through here with Nigras I'd just as soon hit you on the side of the head with baseball bats and throw you in the creek dead. You're not walking into our county."

They had no doubt he meant it.

They gathered up Brad and his backpack and returned to their new host church for another night, then delayed the walk for a week, returning to Atlanta. The time spent on gathering support and enlisting national pressure was critical. The father of one of the younger walkers, Tom Rodd, worked in the Kennedy administration's Arms and Disarmament Agency, and the senior Rodd was anxiously watching his son's progress.

The sixth day they drove to Griffin to continue, noting a large police (and media) presence and several unmarked cars that held FBI agents. As the group later learned, the FBI had visited the sheriff. A mile or so into the walk, a deputy crossed the road, hand on his holstered gun, and stood blocking Ray's way. He reached out and yanked off the black man's SNCC button. Ray lowered his head and walked around the lawman, smiling; the marchers quietly followed, holding their signs high. Marv believes they made it through that county because of the national pressure put on the governor and directly on the local sheriff. If they hadn't been a "mostly white group," they might not have had help.

On November 18, the group entered Macon, Georgia. They had negotiated with the police chief there, promising to be in and out of the city in a few hours. "Sorry," the chief said, "in and out is fine, but you all can't leaflet here. We got an ordinance. Not even our own citizens can leaflet." Marv invoked the Supreme Court decision that struck down an ordinance against passing out leaflets: *Lovell vs. Griffin, Georgia,* which he had learned about during his training.

The cop eyed him glumly, and said, "This ain't Supreme Court country! We'll arrest you if you try."

The first person to offer a leaflet was duly arrested, and most of the others followed, except for two who stayed back to communicate with CNVA and other groups. That very morning, they were tried by a judge and sentenced to from three to fifteen days, depending on whether people walked to the paddy wagon when arrested, and whether they stood for the judge in the courtroom. A number refused on principle to stand, saying "Your honor, we only stand for the highest authority, you're not it." A number of faith-based activists, including Quakers, felt honor-bound to resist unjust authority and its trappings.

Inside the Macon jail, the group began to hold intentional, friendly conversations with the other prisoners; everybody had heard that under circumstances like theirs in the South, authorities would sometimes pay racist inmates to beat up civil rights activists. The CNVA planning committee had discussed the possibility of resistance during incarceration. The new prisoners had told their captors they would not work during short-term sentences like this one, because they were arrested unjustly. "What do you think will happen?" they asked.

The long-termers answered, "They'll take you behind the Green Door."

The cons didn't say what that door was.

The next morning, when the prisoners lined up for work detail, the walkers refused. Fifteen of them, men and women, were marched downstairs, and the warden himself ushered them into a solitary cell behind a thick, green (and windowless) door. The cell had room enough for ten people to sit down. The only light was that coming in under the door.

"So we took turns sitting and lying down. People began to fast, drinking water. It was a tough circumstance, but this group was becoming very, very tough, dedicated. Three of us, including me, who *had* stood up for the judge and walked when arrested were released the third day."

Spirits were high for the two days Marv was inside that stuffy room. They talked quietly, solicitous of one another, caring for each other's physical needs, especially for rest, to the extent possible. Food was brought in three times a day and was shared, or refused except for liquids. But when the guard came to remove the three who had short sentences, they feared for the others, some of whom were going to be in there for up to twelve more days. The three released were CNVA coordinator Brad Lyttle, chemist Erica Enzer, an immigrant from Czechoslovakia in her late 30s, and Marv. All they could say to the others was, "Hang on, we'll see what we can do for you!"

That night, Brad Lyttle spoke before a mostly black crowd at a rally in a Macon AME church. "Don't rely on Washington to lift Jim Crow!" he exhorted the quiet but tense rally. "We have to have faith in our own resources. Dr. King's Southern Christian Leadership Conference and SNCC have taken Gandhi's nonviolence farther than it's ever gone!" Then he described the conditions for the walkers in jail, behind the Green Door, telling them that the next morning people would picket Macon City Hall and inviting the crowd to participate. There were worried rumblings and nods of assent, but the three walkers knew not to expect a large turnout.

The morning of November 22, 1963, was uncharacteristically cool for South Georgia, frost crisping the grass, and the early sun was giving way to dark clouds and a damper chill. It was to be a bitter and threatening day for the peace walkers in and out of jail, for the movements for peace and freedom, and for the nation as well. Marv pauses when he tells the story to classes and asks them the significance of the date. A few remember.

The three carried with them Barbara Deming's single-page flyer, "Peace Walkers or Freedom Walkers?" In her leaflet, Barbara had tried to summarize the important links between the peace and freedom movements. She began:

We have been asked: "Are you Peace Walkers or Freedom Walkers?" We are both. The same belief makes us walk with signs calling for disarmament and with signs calling for Freedom Now. We believe that all men, everywhere, are brothers. We believe that we have not been born to destroy one another, or to exploit one another, or to humiliate one another, but to try to live together in peace, as one human family.

Such beliefs are not consistent, she wrote, with a denial of full citizenship to "the Negro people...the country cannot withhold what they ask for any longer without doing itself great damage." The pamphlet went on to describe how the same values shaped the Peace movement: "The nuclear weapons men possess now are so unspeakably destructive that unless we learn the difficult new way of struggling nonviolently for what we believe, we may help the human race to commit suicide."

On that morning of November 22, Marv and others from CNVA, joined by about a dozen black members of the AME church, began their picket of Macon City Hall. They carried signs saying "Fifteen Peace Walkers in the Hole of Macon Jail" as well as "End Racial Segregation," "Walk to Cuba for Peace," and "Demand Fair Trade with Cuba."

A crowd of counter-demonstrators began to form just across the street, and their numbers grew. About 11:00 a.m., Brad left to do a television interview. At the same time, Marv met with the police chief.

"What would it take," Marv asked him, "to persuade the sheriff to let our people out of the Hole?"

"Listen," the chief said, "If we get an agreement that you'd walk through Macon without leafleting, they'd be out of jail today!"

That didn't seem too onerous. Marv asked if they could confer with their people in jail. The chief assented and added, "You'd have to work fast. The mayor can call the judge and make arrangements, but the mayor goes home at 3:00 on Fridays."

Brad returned from his interview and they began to talk about the chief's idea. Just then, one of the counter-demonstrators ran up to them, shouting. "*Your* president has been shot in Dallas!"

The emphasis was significant, Marv thought later; at the time he was simply stunned. He couldn't explain that their protest was *against*

Kennedy's Cuba policy. Then everyone was gathered around a radio on the street—marchers, police, and the groups of demonstrators, hushed. Kennedy was dead.

In the confusion that followed, the five CNVA walkers quickly put their heads together and decided to follow the chief back to city hall. He led them into the jail where they were permitted to meet with the entire group.

News of the shooting had already reached the prisoners. Radios were tuned in and guards stalked back and forth through the cellblocks, quieting prisoners, locking some down. Their group was released from the Hole and given an all-too-brief time to clean up.

Marv had learned enough details in the last hours to tell his friends, "Kennedy is dead. They have a man named Oswald who is in some way connected to the Fair Play for Cuba committee." He didn't stop for the confused questions from those who could find speech. He went on, "There may have been a coup attempt. Now, what we think," he looked around to Brad and the others for confirmation, "we urge you to join in making an agreement that we won't leaflet in Macon. We can still walk, if we want. The city will drop the charges against everybody, and release us."

A coup attempt? The marchers were attuned to the national mood that gave rise to this bizarre suggestion. Animosity to the Kennedy administration was plain to see in the South in 1963. In the marchers' view, it came from a racist, 'anti-liberal' right wing. Even before the assassination, the atmosphere in Macon was charged. Young white men had been racing cars back and forth in front of their host church; black elders stood guard outside with loaded shotguns. The reporter who had interviewed Brad kept his motor running, he said, out of fear of the Ku Klux Klan, and told him, "I have information that a group of local men are plotting to attack you."

Reports of violence had haunted them throughout the march, and Marv was not the only one suffering with fears that sometimes approached obsession. The jailings and communal spirit had strengthened the group in many ways, but the mounting hostility they saw in the eyes of many townspeople sapped that strength. Was there something brewing?

"Rumors were rampant," Marv later recalled, "that a right wing coup was in motion to launch another invasion of Cuba. Some people even thought we should send a team to Florida to confront right wing Cuban exiles planning another invasion!"

They could not stay longer at the Macon church; that much was clear. The group could not reach consensus about where to go, how to rest and recoup themselves. Several had begun to fast in jail and, despite the sudden release, were unprepared for quick decision and action. The best options seemed to be to stay in Atlanta, maybe for several weeks, or to go to Koinonia, an integrated Christian community near Americus. The walk would be suspended for a time. They decided to meet again at 1:00 a.m., taking turns trying to sleep in shifts and walking the church grounds with flashlights, guarding the community. At 1:00, they decided to leave Macon for Atlanta at 6:00 am.

That night Marv contacted Staughton Lynd and Howard Zinn at Spelman College. Both taught history to black women students and were setting up Freedom Schools for the civil rights movement. The purpose of the call was to explain the group's predicament and the need for housing and safety. Both men agreed to help; they would stay at Staughton's overnight and he would arrange accommodations at Mennonite House in an Atlanta Negro district.

The new day was overcast, and at 6:00 a.m., as they lined up to leave Macon, a thin rain began to darken the soil. They packed hurriedly and set a plan to caravan closely, with a system of signal lights if one car was attacked. The police chief drove up before they left, in civilian clothes, and shook hands with each one of them. "You're making the right decision to leave now," he told them somberly. A humane person, Marv thought, but the chief's friendliness did not allay his fears.

The drive over the wet, almost-deserted highways that day was tense but uneventful and they arrived at Staughton's house before noon. Over the next few days, Marv and the Walkers watched television with the rest of the country in fascinated horror, as Jack Ruby shot Lee Harvey Oswald, reporters speculated about assassination plots, and evidence mounted that the nation and, in fact, the world was in some sort of terrible danger.

Marv was feeling an immense personal strain. He began to argue with other walkers over policy and even meaningless trivia, and he knew he had to get away to regain his balance. Thanks to Bayard Rustin's suggestion that the walk should proceed immediately to Florida, Marv hit on the idea of contacting a friend who taught Humanities at the University of Florida, Ed Richer, and asking if he could visit Ed for a "rest cure." Richer was welcoming: "Come on down."

Marv admitted his stress to the group; everyone understood the need for time off. Those who could afford it headed for home. The rest would be staying in Atlanta for several weeks. While in Florida Marv met a new group of activists and enjoyed his time with the Richers. In his absence, the walkers planned the first demonstration since Kennedy's death, an integrated walk into Atlanta's downtown where they would stand with signs opposing violence. A. J. Muste flew into town and the walkers held conferences with progressive groups in Atlanta. Most planned to join the vigil, although a few black leaders demurred, thinking such an action so soon after the president's death might be counterproductive.

On Friday, December 6, Atlanta police, without a warrant, poured into the Mennonite house and roughly lined people up along a wall. They threatened them with arrest or expulsion from the city, by force, should the demonstration go forward. Muste's response was a call to Dr. King, who arranged to have a walk begin from the church where he would be preaching on Sunday. He would have each walker introduced to the congregation, and urge his listeners to join in. This was a brilliant stroke, Marv said: the plan succeeded, police did not interfere, and the vigil was honored as a memorial.

In the next two weeks, the marchers repaired their equipment and made new signs for the next phase of the walk. Brad took an advance team into southwest Georgia, seeking housing along the route to the Florida border. Marv was still nervous and irritable, suspicious of the new administration and the temper of the country. His own temper was often at the raw and he found himself at odds with several others in the group. He felt that some of them, in their desire to emphasize civil rights activities, had lost sight of the world peace/Cuban phase of the project.

This would not be the last time that Marv insisted that a movement retain an appropriate and clearly defined focus for action. Such concern remained present throughout his career as an activist, and it brought him time and again into confrontation with men and women he honored but whose vision or strategies conflicted with his own.

Barbara Deming also worked to sustain a vision that included freedom, disarmament, and the walk to Cuba as aspects of a single struggle. Unlike Marv, she wasn't disturbed by the varying emphases of the walkers.

Tom Rodd left for home. His father felt that his job might be terminated if Tom did not leave the project. Tom's loyalty to his father took precedence and, Marv felt, rightly so. He was wondering himself whether he should go now for a time, before more violence burst out.

The meetings became intolerable for Marv; he was fearful for both himself and his friends if they remained in the South at this critical time. One night as he was tossing and turning in his sleeping bag, he could not stop thinking about his conversation with Mary Moore, the widow of William Moore. Like Moore, Marv had been the "postman" (marshal, often in lead position) of the walk. He began to sense a presence, Moore's presence, in the room, and he became obsessed with the idea that were he to continue, he would be shot. The next evening, as he and Yvonne Klein were sipping tea, his fears and frustrations erupted in a bitter argument. He told her of his doubts, particularly about his own behavior in this crisis. He knew that the presence of others on the firing line kept his courage up but he said now he couldn't predict his behavior, or anyone else's. He had to go. They parted and "kissed goodnight as friends" and he knew he would leave the next day for Minnesota. His resolution brought him peace. That night he slept well for the first time in many weeks. He was able to explain his decision to his friends, who seemed sad to see him go. But at that critical juncture, Marv could see no other way.

9

Brief Respite

He was pleased to be back with family in St. Paul, and relates glee-fully nights of pleasure with his friends, "eating *full* meals, drink-ing, making love, and telling the story." Very soon, Marv found himself fund-raising for the project. He spoke at the Newman Foundation, the Student Peace Union, and the University of Minnesota radio sta-tion. He began a lifelong habit of phone conversations with Movement contacts, including the walkers in Atlanta. From those calls and sparse news reports, he learned that the walkers resumed their walk in Macon two weeks after he left, honoring their pledge not to hand out leaflets. Barbara Deming initiated an appeal of their Macon conviction, chal-lenging the anti-leafleting ordinance, and word came that the Georgia authorities would appeal the ordinance themselves—a victory, of sorts.

Brad Lyttle began negotiations with Albany, Georgia, police chief Laurie Pritchett, who had devised an ingenious strategy for containing the efforts of the Albany Movement, a civil rights coalition that in 1961 began a campaign against segregation. That coalition had expected the police to respond with the violence typical of other small southern towns, and thus bring national publicity to their cause. But Pritchett, who con-sidered himself a strong, politically astute leader, had done his research. "I found his [King's] method was nonviolence, that his method was to fill the jails, same as Gandhi in India. And once they filled the jails, we'd have no capacity to arrest and then we'd have to give in."

The chief figured out how many jails were within a 60 mile radius and got permission to use those facilities. When the mass arrests start-ed, the protesters were sent hither and yon to be locked up—anywhere but to the Albany jail.

Pritchett's approach to the Albany demonstrations, including arrests of Martin Luther King in 1962, worked to end the campaign before the Movement could secure any concrete gains. The Movement ran out of willing marchers before Pritchett ran out of jail space. By August of 1962 it was clear that King's coalition was ineffective in bringing about change in Albany, but he had learned the important lessons that he and the SCLC would carry to Birmingham.

By the time the CNVA's Peace and Freedom Walkers arrived in Albany, the Albany Movement was leery of endorsing their strategies, particularly as regarded Pritchett. An advance team that included Barbara Deming, 18-year-old Ronnie Moose, and Ken Meister went to visit with the Albany Movement leaders to outline their hopes and ask for support. Civil rights strategists had hoped the public demonstrations would resume at some point, but the Albany leadership was not optimistic. The advance team was more successful with SNCC, who arranged for them to stay in the Albany SNCC hospitality house.

Many activists had received support and training during the previous year at the Albany House, where the accommodations were simple and "rules of the house" encouraged self-government. For the trail- and jail-hardened peace walkers, the environment offered respite rather than restriction, and the very presence of Movement workers and strategists buoyed them.

Marv remained in contact as his friends negotiated with Chief Pritchett, and passed on the information to supporters in the Twin Cities. The chief had offered them only one route—Oglethorpe Street, which formed a sort of racial divide on the edge of Albany's black neighborhood that local whites and blacks seldom crossed. "Oglethorpe or nothing," Pritchett said. "And if any local Negroes join you as you walk, *on Oglethorpe*, I'll pick them out of your line and arrest them."

Brad calmly told the chief that the walkers routinely entered towns by the alternate business route so that shoppers in the downtown areas would have "exposure to our message." Brad favored formal speech, with a cool politeness that seemed to ignore disagreement. The chief objected that at Christmas, he didn't want to congest the already crowded streets, and Brad replied that the fourteen walkers would walk single file, at least five feet apart, and obey every red light and traffic direction. Brad gave Pritchett copies of the walk literature, including biographies of the walkers, but the meeting ended without agreement.

Marv searched the national news the next day, December 23. Nothing. He kept calling Albany House until he reached a SNCC worker who gave him the word: fourteen walkers—nine men and five women—had walked down Oglethorpe to Jackson and were arrested as they crossed to the forbidden side. The arrests were peaceful, each of the walkers declaring their belief that they were within constitutional rights. Pritchett's report said they were "detained for deviating from an agreed-on route and resisting arrest."

Later several members of the group stepped up nonviolent resistance by refusing to walk to the courtroom—they'd have to be carried from their cells. The chief said No, they could rot in jail; they would not be tried until *all* appeared. Eleven began a water-only fast.

C. B. King, lead attorney for the Albany demonstrators, represented two of the walkers; others represented themselves. CNVA activists Dave Dellinger, Ross Anderson, Bob Barber, Candy Kricke, Johnathan Stephens, and Al Uhrie drove from New York to support the team, and in a driving rain on January 9, they demonstrated in front of the court building. They were also arrested, bringing the total to twenty.

The trials were farcical. C. B. King, a tall, dignified and experienced trial lawyer, represented them. Marv said, "He impressed everyone who heard or saw him in action, except for his opponents in the white power structure." C. B. addressed the court calmly, eliciting from witnesses and even from the chief that there *had* been no disorderly conduct. He laid the basis for a constitutional appeal.

In her journal, Barbara Deming wrote that the police chief, the officers and Judge Durden himself seemed scarcely to listen. Pritchett and the officers interrupted the defense often—when they weren't talking and joking among themselves. Eventually all the prisoners were found guilty and sentenced to thirty-one days, with time already served deducted from the sentence. One of the prisoners looked at the papers and saw their names and the dates already filled out. He asked, astonished, "Were these prepared before trial?"

"Yes," answered Judge Durden, who was the sole decider of guilt in this bench trial, "but if you'd been found not guilty, of course, they wouldn't have been used."

Back in Minneapolis, Marv began to get snatches of news about those fasting in prison, including Yvonne, who on January 11 was taken to the hospital suffering with extreme weakness. Two others were hospitalized, and the last couple of days before release, all the fasters were given vitamin shots. On January 10, out of the blue, CNVA representative Marge Swann called Marv: "Would you consider coming back? The walk desperately needs help."

Marv's spirits soared. He'd been fund-raising to get back, for he now understood that he was bound to the walkers so viscerally that his very being felt torn by the separation. He talked about them wherever he went, despite the depression that had dragged him down, and searched the papers for news daily. He told Marge that he'd been raising money; he'd step it up and be back in Albany in a week.

Within days Marv was on the train to Chicago, with Albany as the final destination. He loved riding alone on the train, settling in with a pile of books and cigarettes. But he didn't read much that day; he peered out the windows at the wintry stubble fields and thought and smoked. As the train rumbled into Birmingham, where it stopped at a station built before the Civil War, he couldn't help thinking about wars, especially that between the North and South. "I imagined all those broken bodies, southern and northern soldiers lying in anguish and pain, and I kept thinking about how useless it all was, that war, the wounds in society's flesh still far from healed a hundred years later."

Wakeful and apprehensive, he watched children walking along the tracks to school and thought about how many children had faced fire hoses and dogs. They were only children, yet so brave, so hopeful. They daily faced worse than he had. Why was he so nervous? What could he do? Winter scoured the passing Georgia landscape with a cold, driving rain, the rusty red earth split by streams that reminded him of blood. He would be in Albany within hours.

He made it in time to welcome the imprisoned fasters home. They had been released after 24 days of incarceration. He called the SNCC house; Peter Gregonis answered and welcomed him back with a gleeful,

"Marv! Where the hell you been?" and said two guys would be down to pick him up immediately. After half an hour he spotted two young black men eyeing him, but they did not approach and Marv looked down, then walked away, worried. He called the house again and two of the people he knew, Ken and Ronnie Moose, came to fetch him.

They embraced and everyone began talking at once. The young black men nodded, now smiling. They'd been at the station but had to be careful. "Oh, how good it was to be back," he remembers, "despite that tiny crack of fear in the back of my skull that never really left me." Ronnie warned him not to be shocked at the appearance of some of the "kids, very thin from fasting."

At the house, the group had just finished a meeting and everyone was sitting around sipping tea. Barbara Deming saw him first and approached him gently, giving him a warm kiss. Then Edie Snyder shrieked and ran over to throw her bird-like, fragile arms around him. Yvonne Klein gave him a kiss and asked what he had been doing while they were starving, "but with a mischievous glint in her eyes" Marv recalls.

He replied, "Yvonne, as damned corrupt as I am, I was eating, drinking, and making love—getting ready to come back!'"

Everyone laughed, and Ray Robinson picked him up in the air with his huge, strong hands. "How relieved I was to be back with my friends. But how right Ronnie was. My God, I could see the blue veins in each girl's arms, clearly defined."

They talked for hours, filling Marv in on the last miles, the court struggles, and what it had meant to see their brothers and sisters suffer in jail. Could it possibly make any difference to the Albany Movement, who still had questions about them? They told him about the wiles and weaknesses of Police Chief Pritchett, and Barbara's futile attempts to reason with him. They regaled him with stories about C. B. King and the Albany Movement lawyers. He shared their high spirits, but he also felt guilty that he hadn't been with them from Macon to Albany and all during this Albany jailing, the ordeal of the fast. "I had lost my nerve. I had to learn the art of pacing my energies, creating a consistent flow of resistance." He was beginning to get an idea that the ordeal was by no means over, not for this group nor for himself.

10

Launching *The Spirit*

In the morning, the reassembled group embarked on a new phase of the peace walk. Young people from Albany's "Harlem," the student wing of the Albany Movement, came to meet them, convinced that these northerners were serious and their project was meaningful. With at least part of the local black community in support, the walkers would make another attempt to penetrate the white downtown.

Marv was determined to redeem himself. His new mantra was "create a consistent flow of resistance." He'd be part of the walk's negotiating team that would offer local authorities not one, but eight alternate routes, each traversing a part of downtown.

On January 15, the team entered the large anteroom of the city jail that served as office for Pritchett and his staff. Brad introduced Marv: "Chief Pritchett, I'd like you to meet my good friend Marv Davidov, who's been in Minnesota getting ready to rejoin us for this leg of our walk." He made the point that their venture was enduring, and had nationwide support, at least as far north as Minnesota. Marv and the chief shook hands. Marv felt his hand squeezed in a warm, meaty grasp. Pritchett was a large man, 6' 2" or so, Marv thought, and weighed about 220 pounds. He had close-cropped blonde hair and steely blue eyes that stared at you without a hint of laughter. None of the surface affability that characterizes his amused drawl on sixties television clips was apparent at that moment.

Turning to Lyttle, Pritchett asked pleasantly, "Well, Brad, what do you have for me?" His manner acknowledged that negotiations go forward but that acceptance of the walkers' plan was doubtful, and *his* was the authority. Brad and Marv presented the eight alternate routes, pointing out that now (after Christmas) their little group could not possibly add to congested city sidewalks.

The chief nodded, but said that the city council was no longer predisposed to negotiate and would accept a route along Oglethorpe or nothing. He had some information, moreover, that was bound to alienate the council. Perhaps the walkers had not operated in good faith in their time away from the streets of Albany.

"What do you mean, Chief?" Marv asked bluntly. The chief produced a news clipping from a Denver paper. Kit Havice, one of the marchers home after the jailing, had expressed hope in an interview that the walkers could "defeat" Pritchett. It was an unfortunate choice of words. Brad urged the chief to understand that their goal was only to walk as an integrated group. They had no desire to personalize their resistance. They would not and could not "defeat" anybody. Pritchett thanked them, unsmiling, and said not to get their hopes up. Marv thought, "We are really up against a formidable force in Laurie Pritchett." Although he was disgusted by the man's incredible misuse of power, he later admitted, "I had a peculiar respect for him."

Back at the SNCC house, young people cranked out leaflets by the thousands on an erratic mimeograph machine, explaining the nature of their resistance from many viewpoints: civil liberties, the history of Albany's freedom movement, human rights, and the challenge to nonviolence that segregation represented. These expressions of nonviolent protest and witness echoed sentiments articulated a few months earlier by Dr. King in his "Letter from a Birmingham Jail" and "I Have a Dream" speeches—the interrelatedness of all communities, the moral necessity of confronting injustice wherever it appears, and the importance of sacrificing for freedom.

In the hiatus before the next phase of the march, Brad asked Marv to pick up a donated Plymouth in Miami. During the three-day trip, Marv met with SANE and civil rights leaders and stayed with Phil and Thalia Stern, who, unbeknownst to him, had arranged interviews with the *Miami Herald* and the Larry King radio show.

Marv was nervous. His recent retreat and return had left him with mixed emotions. But he had wonderful mentors in Dave, A.J.,

Barbara, and his hosts from SANE; they seemed to see a clear path for the nation—one that was not being followed. Marv cherished thsee same ideals and convictions, and knew he had a gift for expressing them. Within hours, he had become a television media person in Miami.

Meanwhile, in Albany, Chief Pritchett called to tell Brad that he was sorry, but the city council remained firm—Oglethorpe or jail. Brad paid the chief another visit and reiterated the original offer of eight alternate routes each including a tiny portion of the (white) downtown.

"I have cells ready," the chief replied, "with clean mattress covers."

Marv returned to Albany with the beat-up Plymouth and attended Jewish services Friday evening with Joe Tuchinsky, a recent recruit from Chicago who'd served five days during the first jail-in. Joe was to coordinate activities at the SNCC house during the next phase of the project. Albany had a small Jewish population, like many mid-sized Southern cities, but Marv found little support at temple for the walkers' position. Marv and Joe spoke with the rabbi for a few minutes, but he seemed remote, almost hostile, particularly regarding any suggestion of anti-military views.

On Sunday the group ate a farewell meal that Marv remembers vividly: meat loaf, underdone peppers, and potatoes "hard as major-league baseballs." Everyone ate voraciously just the same, in anticipation of the likely fast.

The march began at 10:00 a.m. the next morning near the point of the December arrests and proceeded for one block. The group crossed Oglethorpe and was allowed to move forward a few feet into the "forbidden" downtown before Pritchett and a line of Albany police and state troopers moved in. Pritchett, through a crackling megaphone, ordered the walkers to return to the highway. The seventeen marchers murmured their refusal to comply, Brad simply saying that the order was a violation of a Constitutional right.

Most of the walkers had put on two sets of clothing for protection against rough handling, and also to provide for a change if, as they assumed was likely, they were arrested. At the moment of arrest, fifteen sat down, having determined that they would not cooperate. Many of these had been in the first jail-in. Marv and Erica Enzer remained standing and walked to the Black Maria. Marv had never "gone limp," believing this noncooperation would provoke the cops. Sometimes, he admits, "I was afraid for my ass and tenderly protected it whenever possible." But he also felt the need to acknowledge the humanity of the policemen, in the hope that such small gestures of consideration might move the officers to deeper reflection about the situation.

Pritchett ordered his men to remove the seated walkers by stretcher into the paddy wagon, which they did "gently, for the most part, laughing at us." But Ray Robinson told Marv and others later that, during the unloading in the alley behind the jail, the black walkers were more roughly treated: "A cop stepped on my stomach, he walked on me." The blacks were dragged off to a separate cellblock and the women were carried into another wing.

Marv was ushered into a cell with five other white walkers. Cells were metal cages eight by ten feet wide and twelve feet high, with a bare bulb burning constantly in the middle of the room. Bunks were the usual metal sheets extending from the walls. They did indeed have mattresses, but there were only four of them. After a while the jailers brought in two more mattresses and Marv made his temporary home on one of them pulled beneath a bunk. After talking excitedly about what had happened—it all seemed to happen so quickly!—the walkers grew quiet, wondering what the days ahead would bring.

Marv could not forget that some of these men and women would resume fasting after only an eight-day respite. What would happen? Was he strong enough, was he in shape to fast? Yvonne had already begun: She'd been arrested earlier in the week for picketing and leafleting at a segregated fall-out shelter downtown and had been re-fasting after only four days outside jail. He worried about Ray, too, who brought his corrosive anger at racism to his intention to fast. Ray's determination to succeed, coupled with his fury against the system, made for an odd vulnerability. He schooled himself to refrain from retaliation and let himself be dragged to and from his cell. But on one occasion, to keep himself steady, he grasped a toilet so tightly he wrested it from its foundation (and had additional charges filed against him).

For Ray Robinson the civil rights movement had become a calling. Brad Lyttle characterized him as a born leader, open and forthcoming, who put himself "out in front of the project, though the nonviolence angle puzzled him. We urged people not to get angry or hate the people we were struggling against. … He was the main target because he was so big and outspoken."

Marv lay into the evening hours, gathering his own determination as the others dozed or talked quietly around him, and listened to the din of the jail hallways. He thought of Minnesota, covered in heavy January snow, and of his friends who were no doubt gathered at the Scholar, eating and drinking. He yearned for a drink. If he closed his eyes he could project an ice-cold stein on his eyelids. He chased his mind from that thought! Instead, he got up and drank a tumbler of water from the tap.

During the next few days, the men in his cell drank great rivers of water every day, but no one touched the food. "… the hunger pangs were torturous the first day, and the next and the next."

Barbara, older than many of the women, began to accept a bit of food each day after an episode during which she lost consciousness and then descended into hallucinatory fears. The men and women made games of their condition, passing notes from cage to cage; they concocted imaginary meals and encouraged one another with their wild, funny creations. At other times, however, they remained silent, intent on guarding one another's privacy as new inmates were brought in daily for drunkenness, domestic violence, and street crimes, filling the cell block with roars of outrage or aimless clamor.

Marv was unable to tune such disturbances out. He felt a certain attachment to this degraded part of humanity that moaned, swore, hurled insults and put the moves on others. Many times he felt tears spring to his eyes, not with the sense of the human nobility he had felt in Parchman, but with an understanding that he shared a bond with *these* outcasts. The system would just as soon consider him and his friends "throwaways," too. The thought stirred his familiar fury at injustice and quickened his resolve. Damned if he was going to let the Power get away with it.

Outside the jail, CNVA representatives and the Albany Movement's

C. B. King were working to gain their release. News of the fast was spreading, mainly in nonviolent circles but also, little by little, in the mainstream media. A. J. Muste and Dave Dellinger continued negotiations with Albany authorities; Dave and C. B. visited jail when they were permitted, whether or not they had good reports for the inmates.

But words of encouragement were hard to come by and time dragged. Marv had never worked so hard to maintain patience. He felt physically strong, despite the hunger pangs. He and his cell-mates leaned on one another lightly, mixing teasing with support and mutual confidence. The guards' treatment of other prisoners, especially the black men, sickened them. They feared for Ray, whose past record of violence they knew, and prayed he wouldn't break.

On February 14, Valentine's Day, Marv decided to end his fast, in order to preserve his physical and mental ability for the longer project. (It was his nineteenth day.) He was determined that the walk for freedom must continue on to Cuba, its original destination. He sent an explanatory and unapologetic note around to the other cells that he was breaking his fast "for love," he quipped, "of my stomach."

About the twentieth day of the second jail-in, Pritchett let the walkers meet together to set strategy. Some wanted to finish the thirty-day sentence and try again. Others were worried that the Albany Movement did not fully support them; they wanted to "get out and address the Cuba phase of the project." After two hours, Pritchett ended the meeting.

Dave, A. J. Muste, and C. B. King were let in to consult and asked if the walkers could hold on. "SNCC saw real possibility in our struggle and the Albany City Council would look at a compromise. The compromise at first failed, then on the 26th day won, and we were released."

The *Student Voice*, a publication of the Albany Student movement, described their release as a "victory." The paper went on to compare the walkers' fate to their own very similar civil rights story, which had been one of repeated obstruction and intimidation.

The day of release, SNCC field secretaries from all over the South walked across the forbidden line in small groups, leafleting about voter registration, and for the first time were not arrested. "A large crowd of negro Albany citizens turned out to support the walk group and we walked the 13 miles out of town," Dave Dellinger later wrote in *Liberation*. "Walkers used ferocious tactics coupled with a gentleness of spirit to make the breakthrough.'"

Several walkers, including Barbara Deming, soon went home to heal and prepare for the next antinuclear campaign. Ray Robinson also left, though he remained committed to nonviolent strategies and civil rights. He was later killed at Pine Ridge Reservation during the stand-off with the FBI in 1973.

But for Marv, the walk wasn't over in Georgia. After some weeks of retraining and recovery at the SNCC house, the march resumed with several young men and women, black and white, bolstering the ranks. In early summer the group reached Miami, where supporter Scott Herrick had donated a small but bay-hardened 24-foot motor launch named *The Spirit of Freedom*.

CNVA had been negotiating with the Johnson administration during the summer of 1964 about the travel ban to Cuba. The *Spirit* made twelve trial runs in the Miami harbor that summer, and each time the Coast Guard stopped and inspected it. The boat was to set sail again in late October at the tail end of the hurricane season—not a propitious time for sea voyages—and the group planned to dock in Havana. Five walkers practiced their sea legs with a short course on the bay. On October 27, under overcast skies, they embarked, motoring down the mooring channel to open water. They were not on the sea half an hour before the Coast Guard halted them again.

Marv, Brad, and three other crew members watched helplessly as the Coast Guard cutter secured their launch to a tow hitch, and pulled it alongside. Minutes later, two guardsmen boarded their boat and ordered them to stop their engine.

"Are we under arrest?" Marv demanded. "You can't arrest us on the sea!" He wasn't sure about that, but at that moment Brad was in the cabin, radioing newsman Ed Arnow that the Coast Guard had illegally stopped them on the high seas. Before the guardsmen returned to the cutter, they had switched off the engine, seized the boat keys and locked the cabin door, effectively keeping the crew of the *Spirit* from food, water, and "the head." Then the Guard towed them a few hundred yards down the dock, away from the main gate, and welded the launch to the dock, stationing an armed guard nearby.

Brad fumed. "This is the way the U.S. Government conducts its foreign policy!" The commander, through a bullhorn, pleaded with the crew to leave the ship, saying that their mission was a life-saving one, not a foreign policy decision. However, he went on, "We are just following orders from the secretary of state."

Scratching his head over the discrepancy, Brad shouted, "Just untie us! We're not doing anything wrong." Marv added, "We'll leave for Cuba now and be out of your hair." He gestured with his boatman's cap to illustrate, sweeping it from his bald crown in a mock salute. The commander turned on his heel and moved away without responding. No one else approached the launch until a couple of sailors appeared with stanchions and rope. They proceeded to rope off an area of the dock so that the men could clamber up and take some exercise; Marv could smoke there, rather than risk igniting the boat laden with gas tanks for the voyage. The *Spirit* crew settled in for the wait, figuring that with their experience, "they could fast for days."

In the morning, media people were allowed access to the area to interview the crew. Supporters demonstrating at the main gate, however, were refused entrance. Marv happened to be up early, waiting for the reporters and watching the demonstrators through binoculars. He spied a man carrying a sizeable canvas bag approach the closed gate; as Marv watched, the young man was turned away. Suddenly, he leapt onto a low wall between the public walk and the channel, jumped into the water, and began to swim, towing his bag behind him.

This strange incident was somehow captured on film; Marv gleefully shows the 10-minute video to his St. Thomas classes, pointing out the small head splashing in the water and himself, ducking or retrieving unidentifiable projectiles.

The brave swimmer turned out to be Phil Stearns, a team member of the CNVA San Francisco to Moscow Peace Walk who happened to be in South Florida visiting his grandparents. When he heard a radio report that the Coast Guard was holding the *Spirit* crew captive and they could not get at their food, he sprang into action.

Waking his companions, Marv cried, "Some guy is swimming to us!" The cutter partially blocked their view but they could see splashing. Soon, Phil was within fifty feet— so close! But Marv could hear the shouts as a nearby Guard cutter started up and eased toward the swimmer, trying to bring him aboard. Dozens of sailors then appeared at the dock, watching as the interloper, treading water, began to lob apples and lettuce over the small cutter toward Marv. Marv jumped to catch them. He caught three. Then the swimmer threw a head of lettuce. Raising an oar, a guardsman intercepted it and the sailors cheered.

Skirting the cutter, Phil finally reached the *Spirit of Freedom,* with his sack still in tow. Three pairs of arms stretched out to lift him on board. Marv ceremoniously handed him an apple.

Later that morning, the commander came to parlay: "If you come onto the dock, we will release you." They refused and made themselves as comfortable as possible on the deck, munching on Phil's provisions. Within an hour, guardsmen boarded and carried each protestor off the boat and onto the back of a pickup truck. The truck slowly drove to the main gate and guardsmen unloaded its unwilling passengers, depositing them on the pavement outside. Then, as the would-be sailors watched, guardsmen lifted their motor launch by crane onto the dock: they could no longer swim to it.

On October 28 the crew visited the Miami attorney who had authorized the capture of the *Spirit,* accompanied by a few reporters. The attorney tried to explain that the McCarran Act justified the action. One of the reporters gasped and grabbed his pad, asking the attorney to repeat his words. Marv groaned. He knew red-baiting was still a lively worm in the American psyche, but he hated to see its legal ramifications invoked by a government representative.

The McCarran Act (or Internal Security Act of 1950) was an outgrowth of the anticommunist fervor that had gripped the nation in the fifties. The Act required communist organizations to register with the attorney general and established the Subversive Activities Control Board to investigate persons thought to be engaged in "un-American" activities. A key institution during the Cold War, the act allowed for the detention of dangerous, disloyal, or subversive persons in times of war or "internal security emergency." Although much of the act has been repealed, the ghosts of chauvinism that gave rise to it remain, and the debate over internal security and civil liberties is one of the central issues of our time.

The crew were devastated.

"Naturally, we demanded he rescind the order. He said no. We sat in his office. Within half an hour federal marshals carried us outside the building. We stood in a circle on the sidewalk for a while and the reporters interviewed each of us. We made our exit plans. We ended seventeen months of action that day."

Edie Snyder (Maris Arnold) reports that after the walk reached Miami and "its boat, the *Spirit of Freedom,* was confiscated by the Feds, another walker and I returned to Albany to see if we could facilitate dialogue between the totally polarized black and white populations." They were thrilled to meet again with the lawyer C. B. King, lunching with him at the Albany Holiday Inn "the day after the [Civil Rights] Act was passed. It was very ordinary. No one even looked at us. It took extraordinary deeds to make an ordinary act possible."

What were the accomplishments of the walk? Marv names the Quebec to Guantanamo project as the one that first integrated peace and freedom issues on a broad scale: "My own decision to join the CNVA walk was driven by the plan to walk through the *south* to Florida. My experiences with the Freedom Rides shaped my knowledge of what racism did to people. And so I could see the possibilities of confronting racism and showing people around the world that people in the U.S. knew that justice and peace *had* to go together."

He remembers a meeting he had a year later with Chief Pritchett: "You didn't get what you wanted, did you?" Pritchett asked. Then, surprisingly, he said, "Barbara is an extraordinary person. She sent me the manuscript of her book, *Prison Notes.* " Almost as an afterthought, he started talking about gains in employment for the Negroes in town. He mentioned bus drivers, and said, "I even have Negro cops."

11

"He's got himself in a terrible jam"

What does Marv mean by "revolutionary nonviolence"? He caught the phrase, as he caught so much inspiration, from David Dellinger. Through the 1960s Marv pored over *Liberation Magazine* for both its ideas and its calls to action. "And I began to study a far-off place called Vietnam. Not many peace activists yet looked that way. By the winter of 1965, all kinds of speakers were coming to the Twin Cities speaking out against the U.S. engagement in the war. And, of course, *Liberation Magazine* was on top of it!"

As mentioned earlier, Dave Dellinger founded, published, and edited *Liberation Magazine* from 1956 to 1975. The periodical was a mouthpiece and source of inspiration for the worldview of the pacifist left, advocating resistance through nonviolent direct action. Some conscientious objectors who considered their anti-war stance as a matter of individual conscience were uncomfortable with this new emphasis on direct action. They considered it too confrontational.

Marv's experiences in the South had strengthened his belief that confrontation of some sort was inevitable. He had come to see that even the most seemingly futile confrontation could play an important role in addressing social ills by *engaging* the agents and institutions of social injustice.

Back in Minneapolis, he was close to family again, which had both advantages and disadvantages. One afternoon early in 1965, he announced to the press that he had decided not to pay federal income taxes to protest the government's savagely inhumane policies in Indochina. The local media decided to do a story, and they came to interview not Marv, but his 64-year-old Jewish mother.

Gerty called him: "They're coming."

Marv: "Who's coming, Gerty?"

Gerty: "Press people are coming to interview me. I'm so nervous I took a pheno. What should I say to them?"

"Gerty, just tell the truth, as you taught us."

She admitted the reporters to the apartment, offered them something to eat, "no doubt," Marv said, "because she thought they looked emaciated." She then sat with them in the living room (the very *clean* living room) to answer their questions—a slim, trim woman who had retained her athletic grace.

The initial question was the most obvious. It came from a local newspaper reporter. "Mrs. Davidov," he said, "your son Marv has been a Freedom Rider and Peace Walker. Now he says he will not pay federal income taxes because of the Vietnam War. What do you think of that?"

Gerty paused for a moment, thinking. She asked, "What do you mean, pay taxes? He hasn't earned a cent in years." Marv says the cameras were shaking, the reporters were laughing so hard.

"Mrs. Davidov," another asked, "you have two sons. What do you think of your two sons?"

At that time Marv's brother Jerry was working with the Street Department in St. Paul. Gerty said, "Yes, I have two sons. One son sits in the streets, the other cleans them." At this point the media people were howling at what became her most famous statement.

Marv began to throw in his lot with the emerging Minnesota New Left, including Students for a Democratic Society (SDS). The SDS political mission, as outlined in the 1962 Port Huron Statement, harshly criticized the materialism and discrimination in American society, and advocated "participatory democracy," immediate withdrawal of U.S. troops from Vietnam, and an end to corrupt government and U.S. economic imperialism. The new SDS leadership was organizing a demonstration in Washington in April of 1965. "They wanted removal of all troops," Marv said, "while *liberals* called for 'immediate negotiations.' That was when I joined the radicals."

As SDS expanded through campuses in the Midwest and West, the character of the movement changed. Although suits and ties were prevalent among serious activists in the early sixties, more casual dress became widespread: western-style clothing, denims, flannel shirts and boots for both sexes, and loose "granny dresses" for some women, suggesting an active, outdoor lifestyle. At the same time, protests became more militant and demonstrators more focused on a single message: out of Vietnam.

For Marv the message was more complicated: the issues of peace, freedom, human and civil rights, and fairness for labor were linked. Moreover, he thought groups working on local justice issues could coalesce, bolster their causes with numbers and, above all, *organize.* CNVA worked on coalition-style organizing, hammering out agreements on a range of issues. Civil rights organizing among black youth had gained new strength and numbers despite the jailings and beatings.

In August 1965, riots broke out in Watts, a predominantly black neighborhood in Los Angeles. President Johnson's programs to build a "Great Society" were unable to mask the realities that racial injustice and poverty at home and war abroad were ruining the hopes of youth and minorities. The Watts riots destroyed buildings and stores, millions of dollars worth of property. The response of civil rights leaders Robert Moses, David Dellinger, and Staughton Lynd was swift: they organized the Assembly of Unrepresented People in an effort to fuse the civil rights and peace movements. Marv returned to D.C. for the Assembly of Unrepresented People: "We were 7,000 strong—union people, SDS, civil rights workers—all calling for radical reform in labor relations and human rights, and an end to the war."

On the twentieth anniversary of the Hiroshima and Nagasaki nuclear bombings the assembly gathered in Washington for workshops and direct action. "Police arrested 325 of us as we marched toward Congress. That time I spent three days in the D.C. House of Corrections. They did not correct me." When Marv was released, he went immediately to New York to meet with Muste, Dellinger, and Lyttle, asking them to appoint him field secretary for CNVA. "What that meant was I got a national mailing list and a few hundred bucks. I organized a speaking tour from New York to Berkeley, at first traveling by bus from city to city, campus to campus."

At State University of New York at Buffalo, a professor gave a small house party for Marv where he met Catholic Worker David Miller.

Miller also had been at the August action, and Marv made an instantaneous connection with a kindred spirit. After the party they went out for a beer. Marv was ready to hit the road for the Midwest and beyond, and he was eager to bring David's perspectives along with him. Maybe he could entice David to speak or organize locally.

"David, what are you doing about the damn war?"

"Marv, I'm thinking about burning my draft card in public."

Marv was shocked. A new law was in the works under which it would become a federal offense to knowingly destroy or mutilate a draft card. After brief debate, the House voted one August afternoon 393 to 1 for the bill, which was aimed at what its proponents described as "beatniks and so-called 'campus cults.'" The penalty was five years' imprisonment or a $10,000 fine or both.

Although not the first card burner, David became the first to put the new law to the test. He had contacted his draft board in June of 1965 to let them know where he was, but that he was opposed to killing and would not cooperate with the draft call. He told Marv, "So I've got the card, the new one, with me."

"I think that's great, David. I think that kind of courage could really spark a national movement. I'd do it myself if I hadn't already been kicked out."

David didn't have to wait long for an opportunity. That October peace groups and sympathetic labor unions called for "International Days of Protest" in response to the continuing troop buildup. David was asked to give a speech as a representative of the draft "non-cooperator" position. He agreed.

"So on October 15," Miller later recalled, "I dressed in a dark pinstripe suit that my mother bought me as a graduation present several months earlier, a white button-down shirt, a narrow dark tie, and short hair." He said the first thing that came to his mind: "I am going to let this action speak for itself. I know that you people across the street really know what is happening in Vietnam. I am opposed to the draft and the war in Vietnam."

In the afternoon breeze, the matches he lit nervously (he was not a smoker) went out one after another. Someone held up a cigarette lighter, which worked like a charm. He was not arrested at the rally, amid the crowd of cheering supporters; three days later the FBI swooped down on him in Manchester, New Hampshire, where he had gone with several Catholic Worker comrades to set up a literature table at St. Anselm's College.

In the weeks following his appointment as a field secretary for CNVA, Marv had meetings in Detroit, Cleveland, and Chicago, riding cramped and bone-jarring buses across the Midwest. In Chicago, he bought an ancient Chevrolet and drove to Minneapolis. "Here were my old friends, now hanging out in the Mixers bar on the West Bank. We had some great talks—everyone wanted to do *something* about the war. It was early days yet in Minnesota for resistance, though some of our friends were being called up."

He visited family members and saw Mulford and Marjorie Sibley who gave him some encouraging words. Then he hit the road again, enjoying every moment, especially when the landscape began to rise beyond the Missouri River. His destination was Berkeley, California, a center of antiwar action, where in May, groups of students had burned draft cards, marched coffins to the local draft board office, and burned President Lyndon Johnson in effigy. Thirty thousand people attended a teach-in on Vietnam between May 21 and 23 on the Berkeley campus. The Vietnam Day Committee (VDC), a group partly founded by former Berkeley graduate student Jerry Rubin, organized the event.

Marv arrived just as the huge October International Days of Protest were taking place all over the world. At UC Berkeley, a mass rally with speakers, music, and comedy was to be held on campus before a march to the Oakland army terminal.

It was early afternoon when Marv arrived at the VDC house, a two-story Victorian near campus. He felt instantly at home—a large central area on the ground floor was sparsely furnished with card tables stacked with papers, placards and supplies, and a mimeograph machine stood in the corner. Volunteers gathered around the tables or sat on the floor, hand-lettering signs. The SDS, the Communist Party, and a variety of small Bay Area activist committees were all organizing for the march from Berkeley to the Oakland army terminal where U.S. troops and supplies embarked for Vietnam.

"I walked into the house and met Jerry Rubin, Bettina Aptheker, Steve Weissman and others on the staff. I explained who I was and volunteered to help them for a few weeks. I think I was the only person fully committed to nonviolence on staff, but that day I was still a volunteer. They later named me one of twelve staff members and paid me $50 a week."

The evening rally went late, despite the number of young students and children with their parents. Everyone wanted to march. The crowd was serious and disciplined—fifteen to twenty thousand people marching eight abreast down Telegraph Avenue toward Oakland. There were children, grandmothers, college and high school students, and a busload of Ken Kesey's Merry Pranksters.

At the Berkeley-Oakland border, hundreds of police wearing riot helmets and wielding truncheons blocked the way. The march stopped less than a dozen yards from the police line. As spectators and a group of right-wing counter-demonstrators milled around between the march and the police, a subcommittee held an *ad hoc* conclave.

"Wisely," Marv said, "leadership turned the march around because of darkness and marched them to Berkeley Civic Center Park. On a flatbed truck, Country Joe and the Fish took the stage." (Country Joe later promoted itself as "the band that stopped the Vietnam war.")

The marchers were anxious after seeing the riot police and needed some bolstering. The group played the anti-Vietnam song "I-Feel-Like-I'm-Fixin'-To-Die Rag." One of the song's many verses went

> *Yeah, come on all of you, big strong men,*
> *Uncle Sam needs your help again.*
> *He's got himself in a terrible jam*
> *Way down yonder in Vietnam...*

(© Tradition Music, BMI, 1965 renewed 1993)

As they sang, the marchers regained confidence. People were clapping. "The mood was better, still electric but not angry," Marv recalled.

Then Robert Scheer, who'd written a concise and powerful history of U.S. involvement in Vietnam, spoke to the crowd. Heads were nodding in agreement as he laid out the background to America's ill-advised involvement in the conflict. Country Joe came on again… and suddenly there was a bang! A tear gas rocket hit the stage, sending clouds of gas up and inflaming the musicians' eyes. They jumped off, pulling off their t-shirts and fanning the air with them. As soon as the gas cleared a little, they climbed back onto the flatbed to thunderous applause.

The next day the crowds returned to the park, rejoining about a hundred who had remained there overnight. Hundreds of police were

also on hand, and when the marchers reached the Oakland City line the parade was halted again. A small gang of Hell's Angels appeared and one of them ripped a banner reading "Get out of Vietnam" from the VDC lead marchers. They yelled, "Go back to Russia you f-ing communists!" Marv insists that the Angels first rode through the police lines, the police watching but not interfering: "We

Jerry Rubin

stopped and people stood quietly talking or sat in the street. Abruptly, Oakland cops separated and Sonny Barger led his Hells Angels charging toward us, stealing a banner and scaring the shit out of people, bikes backfiring and rearing up like prehistoric beasts."

In a matter of minutes, Berkeley police surged forward to move the Angels back; Oakland police pushed through the crowd from the other direction. An Angel wound up on the ground bleeding, clubbed by an Oakland policeman. The Berkeley police captain ordered his men to disperse the crowd. Berkeley's International Days of Protest ended at the Oakland City Limit.

VDC leadership regrouped and began planning for the next march. They would take their time, meeting and putting pressure over the next few weeks on the Oakland political establishment. "This time," Marv remembered, "we did three or four weeks of preparing. All kinds of rumors were flying, that we revolutionaries would get Harry Bridges' longshoremen to come with their tools to protect us." (Under Bridges' leadership, the International Longshoremans' and Warehouse Union (ILWU) had supported peace and human rights campaigns. Bridges condemned U.S policy in Indochina and in 1965, the ILWU called for an end to the war in Vietnam, the first American union to do so.)

But hiring bodyguards, at least to protect marchers from the Angels, turned out to be unnecessary. Ardent VDC supporters Alan Ginsberg and Ken Kesey sponsored a party for the Angels: "The reports were that they all dropped acid and were doing spiritual chanting together by daybreak. Whatever the reason, the Angels backed off. Sonny Barger, their leader, even came to talk to VDCers about the gang and what they represented."

In mid-November, VDC called a strategic meeting of the groups who wanted to be part of a November 20 demonstration and march. In a large auditorium on campus, representatives of antiwar groups took the stage, debating how the march was to be defended and what the tactics should be.

Marv gave an impassioned talk for nonviolence, talking about Dellinger and what civil rights activists did in Mississippi and Georgia. A lot of heads were nodding, but others argued for some form of "self-defense." At the end of the session, Ginsberg rose and gave his opinion: "One hundred women dressed in Sunday best and carrying flowers will lead. Peter and I will be on a flatbed chanting *Om, Om, Om* to calm any attackers. If attackers come through, marshals will give the signal and 25,000 people will drop down and do pushups. Or people will approach the attackers with crosses, as if to face Dracula. For the next line of defense small children with water pistols will squirt them in the groin, make it look like they wet their pants. If all else fails a trained group of queers could yank down those pants and … !"

The last words became part of the lore of Berkeley. Marv shouted again and again, "Listen to the poet! Listen to the poet!"

Ginsberg's joking pleas were expanded with creative embellishments and serious suggestions for maintaining the spirit of nonviolent resistance. Finally, after the auditorium quieted down, the vote on a proposal for a nonviolent march was taken. It lost, three to one.

Marv was appalled. He came to the conclusion that the vote

had been stacked, and that many who called themselves leftists had never attended VDC meetings and had entirely different ideas about protest.

By that time Marv was on the payroll. He had become familiar with the influential speakers and the volatile character of the Berkeley culture, but he had been in California for only a few weeks. He hadn't had time to nurture the level of trust required to influence the vote significantly. At the time, he didn't have enough perspective to see it that way. "*The fools*, I thought. *Allen gave the most creative plan for non-violence I had ever heard. In their sectarian zeal they couldn't see reality.* I told Jerry Rubin and the staff, 'I quit. The vote was stacked and it's going to lead to disaster.'"

He called A. J. and Dave in New York, seeking advice. They both counseled him to hang in there, suggesting that with time his approach would begin to make more sense to the Berkeley activist community.

But it was too late. Marv had quit. He was resolved to leave, but not before seeking validation from a different quarter. He traveled to the Joan Baez Institute for the Study of Nonviolence in Carmel Valley to speak to her and also to Ira Sandperl, Joan's mentor in nonviolence. Marv had seen Joan at the 1965 Assembly of Unrepresented People and was eager to see her again. The Institute, founded that fall, was intended as a refuge and study center for organizers. It had been open a month when area residents complained that an influx of hippies and subversives might threaten their property values. The Institute had then closed temporarily but was to reopen without incident in December.

A retreat to the Institute was an inspired choice. Marv knew that for Baez and Sandperl nonviolence was a way of life. The Institute's founders wanted to teach ways to create a new world of nonviolence, by studying and experimenting with alternatives to violence on every level. They spoke of enabling "a new kind of person" and envisioned a growth of the Gandhian point of view. Joan's music was central to her expression of nonviolence. She believed that the nonviolent person incorporated honesty and integrity in all of his or her activities and re-lations in life. She and Ira wrestled with the notion of "satyagraha" and how to present Gandhi's philosophy as a political reality.

When still in Quaker high school in 1956, Joan Baez had attended a three-day conference of the American Friends Service Committee where she was inspired by the main speaker, a twenty-seven-year-old Martin Luther King. Before long she was speaking on civil rights issues herself and being regarded as a leader as well as an entertainer. She and King remained friends until his death. It was also through the Quakers that she met Sandperl, who was a student of Gandhi's work.

Ira was a tall, thin, monkish-looking man with a hawk-like nose and deep-set eyes. His ascetic appearance was softened by a wide smile that invited and honored others' opinions. When Marv appeared at their door, Sandperl had just been re-reading Gandhi's autobiography *The Story of My Experiments with Truth*. During dinner, he quoted Gandhi to Marv: "When I despair, I remember that all through history the way of truth and love has *always* won. There have been tyrants and murderers and for a time they seem invincible, but in the end they always fall—think of it, *always*."

Marv needed advice on how to relate to leftists who didn't really get it. There had to be a way. He told them his story and both were happy that he had quit the VDC. Marv also shared the sadness he felt at leaving Berkeley. He had come to appreciate and even love his colleagues in VDC.

Ira said, "Truth and love *can* operate in the workaday world."

Joan chimed in. "Gandhi sounds lofty, but you look at the world now. What's the truth about Vietnam, about killing? What's the truth about racism? Love means you don't accept these things, you have to reject that kind of violence—all violence."

"Yeah," Marv said, with a touch of bitterness, "but some of these guys ask what's the point of making yourself a victim—of making freedom movements fail, putting the leaders in jail. The authorities don't *mind* if we're nonviolent, some people say; it makes the cops' job easier."

Joan shook her head. "You have to do it anyway. There has to be discipline, self-discipline for nonviolence to work. You keep your mind on what you're striving for, not just for yourself."

Ira had been in jail. "Everyone is reaching for something beyond themselves. First time I was in jail, one thing I was struck by was that phrase, 'I have to get my kicks.' It wasn't from another activist. It was the regular cons, and I heard it a lot."

"What's that mean, 'Get your kicks'?" Marv asked.

"I think it was a form of reaching out, getting free of the oppressiveness of the system, of whatever obstacle stood in the way of—I don't know—freedom, authenticity."

Marv nodded. He could see that "kick" in Ginsberg's humor, and in the free speech movement that Jerry Rubin and others had instigated at Berkeley, in the creativity of the young men and women there. He just wasn't sure what it had to do with Gandhi, or with sacrifice or love. He felt like he was being a devil's advocate. He took a different tack:

"People accuse us of being nay-sayers. Gandhi struggled with the concept of *non*violence, didn't he? How come you call your center the Institute for the Study of Nonviolence?"

Ira laughed. "We didn't have the nerve to call it the Institute for Truth and Love."

Joan said, "The exciting thing is that Gandhi gave us ideas about how you put all this into an organized movement. Before him, people were engaged in their personal *witness* but it wasn't an organized movement."

Marv agreed. He, Dave, and others on the CNVA staff talked about doing "witness" actions, where a person or a small group offered to be arrested and maybe got a little publicity but didn't really contribute much to the movement.

Ira frowned, seeming to wonder if he had answered Marv's concern. "In my experience, there is a real quest for *truth* in the anti-war movement, but not love. The young people can say 'No' to the nation-state, 'No' to the draft, 'No' to killing, and organize around it, but genuine love sticks in people's craws."

Joan turned to Marv. "You're right, Gandhi worried about the word. But he understood that people first have to turn away from violence. In this country there are infinite guises of violence that we have to reject. Nonviolence *incorporates* truth and love. It's not one above the other," she repeated.

"So, what's positive in nonviolence?" Marv persisted.

Ira said, "Generosity, warmth. You know, absence of hostility and pettiness. It doesn't mean I'm uncritical. Gandhi said the seeker had to be tender as a lotus and hard as granite."

Heady stuff, Marv thought. He remembered Dave's advice and repeated it: "Be where the action is, Dellinger keeps telling me. In prison he found out some people who were committed pacifists did not behave that way when conflicts heated up. And some who rejected nonviolence did finally select nonviolent solutions. 'You never know until the mob comes at you.'"

A few days later, Marv was back with the VDC. "Joan and Ira were a little upset that I went back," he remembers. But when he returned from Carmel, he kept talking to people quietly, including Jerry Rubin. Jerry called him up and said they had been rethinking strategy and were going to have another vote. "If the vote is fair and reasonable, will you return to the staff?" Jerry asked. Marv said yes. They met again and this time the vote was two to one in favor of a nonviolent defense of the march. Marv was among those selected to do the nonviolence training and lead the marshals.

"Joan and Ira had been of tremendous help, at least to my thinking in those days."

The day before the march the Hells Angels called a press conference and announced they would stay away. Despite this promise, VDC negotiations with Oakland officials reached an impasse. Officials did not want the marchers to pass the city border. Finally, they offered a compromise. Marchers would be permitted to move beyond the Oakland-Berkeley boundary but only as far as DeFremery Park in Oakland, not to the Oakland army base. In a vote, the VDC cadre agreed. Marv thought the alternative location pointless but went along with the majority. On November 20, from 6,000 to 10,000 protestors walked to the park and demonstrated peacefully.

As Marv recalls: "Awhile later, the Vietnam Day Committee fell apart, for many reasons, sectarian infighting being one. Jerry Rubin and others joined Bob Scheer's bid for elective office in the 1966 Democratic Primary. He was one of the first anti-Vietnam War candidates."

Rubin asked Marv to work on the campaign. Because the candidate was Scheer, whose antiwar analysis Marv respected, he did go to the first meeting, where the discussion focused on the best way to announce the candidacy. Everyone agreed that Scheer should choose a venue and a visual backdrop that would show the full spectrum of support for a peace candidate. "Why not at the Oakland Army Base?" someone suggested. Marv thought it was time to jump in: "I hadn't spoken yet. I said, 'All of these suggestions are fine, but why not announce from over the fences and *on* the base—show them where serious peace people stand?'"

Bob stared at Marv, seeming not to recognize him. He replied, "I'm interested in serious politics, not fantasy." Fantasy! Marv flushed angrily. He *had* been serious, and considered Bob's dismissive reply disrespectful. There was no debate: "I thought at the time that politics and I were through," Marv said. "I left Berkeley for Los Angeles."

Scheer lost but won 40 percent of the primary vote and carried Berkeley, a showing against an incumbent that in some minds demonstrated the strength of the New Left. But Marv remained disenchanted with what he saw as the "corporate liberalism" of Democratic politics.

In Los Angeles, he hooked up with a coalition of groups who were building an Artist's Tower of Protest on a lot on the Sunset Strip between Hollywood and Los Angeles. The idea for the Tower came from the Los Angeles Artists Protest Committee, an organization of a hundred or so local artists who wanted to make a visible statement against the Vietnam War. The construction was a 58-foot steel tetrahedron with a large yellow sign reading, "Artists Protest Vietnam War." The tower framed 418 two-foot by two-foot paintings by local artists.

Marv helped develop a nonviolent defense of the tower as it was being constructed. "I talked to the artists and local antiwar people, and we had teams watching the site and engaging in dialogue with some would-be vandals."

He was there for the dedication day: Susan Sontag spoke and also Donald Duncan, a Green Beret vet who said, "We are not protesting our boys in Vietnam, we are protesting our boys *being* in Vietnam."

The tower was dismantled after a few months of continuous controversy and occasional physical attacks, but its power as prophetic symbol was memorialized in 2006 when a new Peace Tower, initiated by some of the same artists, highlighted the Whitney Museum of American Art Biennial.

A. J. Muste sent Marv a few hundred dollars for continued field organizing in Los Angeles. Although the coalition of artists was an inspiring and friendly group, Marv knew the defense of a single site was unlikely to lead to a broader antiwar effort. He needed a base of operations. He did what he often did when at an impasse: he called Dellinger. Did Dave know of someone in L.A. who could back him? Dave named acting coach Paton Price, one of his conscientious objector prison-mates during World War II.

"Paton invited me to his home shortly after I called," Marv later recalled. "He was a short, bald man with a sharp nose and a slight Texas accent. He had trained at the American Academy of Drama, and caught on at Warner Brothers as a coach. He trained people like Don Murray, Kent McCord, the Smothers and the Everly Brothers, and a young, very handsome cowboy-like kid with an exuberant singing voice, Dean Reed."

That first night Price invited some people over to listen to Marv—Don and Kent, Hope Lange, and some other actors. Marv spoke about the Freedom Rides, the Walk, and Vietnam. "They were blown away! Hope and Don bought me drapes for my apartment and the others raised about a thousand dollars to help get me started."

Marv was star-struck by these listeners and today drops surprising names from the California/Hollywood mid-1960s. He was gratified to see antiwar sentiment carried into the arts, into film and music, and made the most of his opportunities. He spoke around the city, at universities and rallies, gaining wider recognition for antiwar organizing. "I looked hard in L.A. for how to be useful against the damned war. One day early in 1966 I spoke in the free speech area at UCLA. I could always draw a crowd in those days and perhaps 200 people gathered. At the end, I said, 'Anyone who wants to work seriously, come up and talk.'" A few people did. Among them was a handsome blonde named Vicki Esken, a graduate student working on her doctorate in sociology.

It was almost instantaneous, the pull Marv felt toward this beautiful young activist. Within weeks he would be deeply and passionately engaged in a relationship, then a marriage that was as tempestuous as it was short.

12

Summers of Love and War

Marv and Vicky's first social evening was not a resounding success. He had invited her to come over with two of her friends for a chat, but his brother Jerry was due to arrive the same day for an extended visit. He returned from the airport with Jerry in tow to find Vicky and two of her friends, Marty and Gary Hinman, waiting outside his apartment door. Marv invited them all in for a glass of wine and conversation. The evening ended early and apparently wasn't what Vicky had expected. He thought she seemed cool, perhaps embarrassed to be the focus of his attention, but he couldn't help it: she was so beautiful.

The next day, Marv and Jerry took off for a touring trip.

"You know, I've been thinking a lot about that woman," Marv told his brother, "I think I'll call Vicky when we get back."

He did call, soon after he put Jerry on the plane to Minneapolis.

"Who *is* this?" was the querulous greeting at midnight.

"Marv. I have to tell you I've been thinking a lot about you."

"Why do you have to tell me in the middle of the night? Don't you remember, I work two jobs and I'm sweating blood on my thesis. Anyway, Marty and Mady are inviting me to dinner day after tomorrow. You come." She hung up.

Marv beamed at the phone, oblivious to her annoyance. Dinner!

The excitement Marv felt as this new chapter opened in his personal life only compounded the emotions already seething in his work with some of Hollywood's glamorous activists and actors. His gifts as a speaker and organizer were growing, and he felt driven to put them to the service of the movement in any way he could. For example, he had scheduled himself to hop a bus in three days for Miami Beach to see friends and do some speaking. And he was under consideration to join an important, possibly dangerous delegation to Saigon under the auspices of CNVA. The 88-year-old A. J. Muste, Barbara Deming, and Brad Lyttle were also among those being considered. The mission's objective would be to learn firsthand about the Vietnamese situation and initiate dialogue with U.S. personnel stationed there. The group were also planning to stage an act of protest at the American Consulate, so the Vietnamese would know that Americans didn't universally support the war. "No one knew what the U.S. and South Vietnamese authorities would do. And thirty crazy people had volunteered to go. CNVA would select seven. I very badly wanted to go."

Marv's head was spinning. He wanted to go to Saigon, but he wanted to stay in California and pursue Vicky.

Conversation at the dinner with Vicky and her friends the following evening was intense. After dinner Marv took Vicky's hands in his. He told her about his hopes to travel to Saigon and his dilemma. "You may think I am absolutely insane, but I would marry you tomorrow."

Her face turned bright red. Martin and Mady gasped. It ended the party. Marv walked Vicky to her car and stood next to the rolled-down window, staring, not knowing what to say.

"After what you just said upstairs," Vicky growled, "why the hell are you just standing there? Get in the car, I want to talk to you!"

Marv climbed in, and they talked in the parked car for an hour or more. She told him that, yes, she did think he was nuts. She was dating a couple of men and had been involved with one of them on and off for five years. But Marv was persuasive.

"She drove to her rental cottage in the Silver Lake district, where we made love, falling asleep exhausted. I don't remember much about the cottage. In the next two days we walked, went to the beach, held hands through a film, and spoke about our dreams for the future, growing up, our families and friends, study." On the third day, Vicky drove Marv to the bus station, saying, "Write and call me when you get to New York, and when they make the selection." They kissed, and Marv boarded a bus for the four-day ride to Miami Beach.

Marv spent the time sleeping intermittently and writing page after page to Vicky. By the second day, he was exhausted; the fluorescent lights in the bus and the endless stops at small town stations were starting to sicken him. When an older man boarded and sat next to him, he mentally shrank from the man's smile, thinking, "My God, I hope he's a deaf-mute, I can't talk to anyone." The man took out a pad and pen and wrote, "I am a deaf-mute, would you care to converse by writing to me?" Startled into laughter, Marv began to recover his equanimity. The universe was surreal but it seemed to be on his side. The two men had a friendly, brief conversation before Marv drifted off to sleep.

His presentation in Miami Beach went well. Fifty or so people attended a house party, where he made a hundred dollars. He called Vicky, who reminded him that he was to tell her immediately when the delegation to Saigon was picked. Two days later he was in the CNVA office in New York, joyfully reuniting with Dave, Barbara, Brad and A. J.

He asked for a few minutes alone with A. J., who was looking more stooped and frail than Marv remembered. Still, his movements were brisk and he was obviously on fire with the mission before them. Muste was the acknowledged pacifist leader, a man of great political and spiritual stature. Marv believed that here was a person who could advise him in his personal turmoil. Elements of their personalities harmonized; A. J. had a sharp, but "almost perversely prophetic mind." He seemed always ready to take action beyond the point where most people, even on the left, began to pull back. In one-on-one communication, he was enormously effective, offering counsel that was both tender and incisive. He stared at Marv, his eyes glittering with emotion.

"OK, Marv, what's going on with you?"

"I think I'm falling in love. I met this wonderful woman in L.A." He waved aside Muste's troubled and questioning look, and continued, "If I were chosen, I'd be honored to go with you to Saigon, but my insides are telling me I should return to L.A."

Muste had to ask him how long he'd known the woman, and how well they were aquainted. "Not long," Marv told him honestly, adding that the instinct to be with her was more real than anything he'd ever felt.

"And how does *she* feel?"

"We talk incessantly when we're together. But really, I never have asked her. She said I'm supposed to tell her what your decision is."

There was a long silence as they studied each other. Then Muste sighed.

"Marv, it's true you were chosen. All seven of us on the committee picked you—everyone admired your work and your honesty on the Canada to Cuba walk. However, I don't have to tell you that this mission has the potential to be dangerous. If, and it's a big if, Vicky wants you in Los Angeles, perhaps this is the time in your life to go back there."

They shook hands, and Marv was moved by the light, dry sensation of his friend's hand, like a bundle of twigs in tissue. Then A. J. squeezed, exerting a powerful, even painful grip. Marv grinned, "I'll let you know in the morning."

Vicky called that night and came right to it: "What's the decision?"

Marv countered, "Do *you* want me in Los Angeles?"

"Yes, darling."

"That clinched it for me," Marv later recalled. "I hopped a bus for St. Paul and told my family and friends. Then I flew to Los Angeles, where she picked me up at the airport. I had never in the short time I knew her seen her so radiant. We went back to her apartment where we made love until we passed out."

For the next couple of months they were together constantly, delighting in each other and learning their personal histories and idiosyncrasies. Vicky was fascinated with Marv's antiwar work. She considered herself a radical, at least intellectually, and was learning what it meant to be part of the movement. She did not always agree with the notion of self-sacrifice to further a cause, wondering if Marv and his CNVA friends were pursuing a viable course of action. She did not share his guilt and sorrow, which he had not entirely concealed, about pulling out of the Saigon trip.

But Vicky understood in her bones that these were dangerous times for political resisters. Marv's class analysis, reflected in class distinctions between those who went to war and those who got to stay home, struck a chord. The system favored the elite, who could get exemptions and deferments from the draft, over working class and minority young men. The couple watched television coverage avidly. Antiwar sentiment was spreading beyond their own revolutionary enclave as ordinary people gained greater access to uncensored information.

Marv kept in touch with the CNVA team. The seven activists arrived in Saigon on April 15 and spent the next week meeting with media, USAID workers, religious groups and students. The team found little support for the South Vietnamese government among the people and no support at all for the U.S. presence. Even if people did not support the National Liberation Front, they believed the Vietnamese themselves should resolve issues. At a news conference, young people later discovered to be security agents who were "told to break things up" began throwing eggs at the CNVA group. "A front page of the *New York Times* showed A. J. standing, his hand raised in the air, demanding that the South Vietnamese agents cease throwing eggs and screaming 'Communists!' at them. For some reason they stopped."

On April 21, the group decided they would try one last time to demonstrate at the U.S. Embassy. As they walked from their hotel to the embassy, they were stopped several times by security police before finally being loaded into police vans and driven to the airport, where, a few hours later, they were put on a plane out of the country. Marv talked to Barbara in early May. She said that in the back of the van to Tan Son Hut airport, the frail A. J. cradled his head in his hands, looking very tired.

"Are you sick, A. J.?" she asked.

"No. I'm just thinking how we can do it better next time."

A. J. did return to Vietnam in early 1967—to North Vietnam, where he and a delegation of clergy met with Communist leader Ho Chi Minh, shortly before A. J.'s death.

In June 1966, Vicky and Marv decided to be married. Their prenuptial period was as stormy as their beginnings: When Vicky brought Marv to meet her parents, Vicky's father Nate at one point aimed a toy pistol at Marv and asked if he was going to marry her. "Who knows?" Marv joked. This was a month before the couple formally announced their engagement to her mother Ann at a luncheon.

Nate and Ann fought a delaying battle that the young couple allowed for about a month, but Marv and Vicky persevered. "We visited the family rabbi, who knew what a fine upstanding young woman Vicky was. As for me... I got into a heated debate with him about whether the Jews were nonviolent when they marched into the gas chambers."

Vicky asked him later why he had gotten into that quarrel. "He started it, baby, and who do you think you are marrying, anyway?"

They had a house wedding, inviting family members and Movement friends. Marv wore a dark blue suit borrowed from his uncle Sam and Vicky a white wedding gown that had been her sister's.

"She was as beautiful as any bride. I walked up to take her from her father's arm and he would not let go! I had to figure out how to take her from him without exerting physical force. I managed it somehow." Then they were under the Hupa, in front of the rabbi. Everyone expected Marv to make a political speech. Marv really wanted to say something, "especially because every time [the rabbi] mentioned God, he looked up. I was thinking, why do you only look up? It's sideways and down—it's in the people's eyes and the champagne!"

The next days rushed by. The couple drove to Chicago, then Miami Beach, then New York to stay with Dave Dellinger and Elizabeth and, in late July, over to the CNVA farm in Voluntown, Connecticut.

The Voluntown farm was the center from which CNVA embarked on nearly all of its demonstrations. The farm was forty acres of dense woods and open fields around buildings housing a dozen or so activists. Dave and others chose the site because it was close to Groton, home of the Electric Boat Company's nuclear submarines, where CNVA held regular vigils.

Voluntown's communal living style, shared decision-making, and resistance to violence attracted Marv, though Vicky considered such an idea a distant dream; this trip was supposed to be a honeymoon and she had studies to continue.

About a week before the couple arrived, a group of pseudo-patriots called the Minutemen had staged an invasion of the farm. According to Bob Swann, two Minutemen armed with shotguns walked in the back door of the farmhouse and ordered people in the room to sit down. To everyone's good fortune, local police had been monitoring the group. An officer followed the men, saw the open door and rushed inside, yelling, "Put down your guns!" Unfortunately, one of the weapons accidentally discharged: "The tiny shells of the shotgun sprayed a two-inch hole in the leg of one of our members, who was sitting only five feet away. The police officer rushed her to the hospital, where she stayed for a couple of weeks; the Minutemen spent longer than that in jail."

When Marv and Vicky arrived, Voluntown residents were still shaken but unstinting in their hospitality. They welcomed the young couple, talking late into the evening about movement events in California and the regular vigil at the entrance of the Electric Boat Company. Marv and Vicky would be taking part the next day. The employees were sometimes belligerent, the residents said, but workers were more afraid of losing their jobs than they were of "the Russians."

The following day, Muriel Humphrey was scheduled to christen a submarine, and a larger crowd than usual gathered, including workers and townspeople, to watch as dignitaries arrived. "The two of us and a priest in a clerical collar were standing at the back of the crowd when five angry workers came up to us and started to yell at the priest." One of them, who had been staring at Marv for some time, walked up to him.

"Don't I know you from someplace? I'm sure I've seen you."

The man finally remembered he'd seen Marv on the Joe Pyne show. "I was famous. He said I was talking about communism or something!" Joe Pyne was a pioneer of confrontational talk show, gaining wide popularity in the sixties for targeting hippies, homosexuals, and feminists. By the time Pyne interviewed Marv in Los Angeles, the show had been nationally syndicated. Pyne supported the Vietnam War, and many guests found his style offensive and vitriolic. The Anti-Defamation League accused him of catering to bigots. "But he also supported labor unions, and he had a soft spot for guys that would stand up to him," Marv remembered. "So this worker was impressed with me. So we shook hands, then he called his friends over. 'This guy was on the Pyne show.' Ah, the awesome power of TV."

After a long road trip, the newlyweds were more than ready to settle down to a "normal" activist lifestyle—at least Vicky was. After driving to Minnesota to spend a little time with Marv's family, the couple returned to California, where Vicky resumed her studies. Marv hooked up with a project called The Crafts of Freedom, a worker-owned cooperative based in Mississippi that made dolls, leather handbags, puppets, and other crafts and shipped them to centers of antiwar activity around the country. Marv marketed the items through house parties, spreading them on the floor, selling, and gathering donations for SNCC, who was sponsoring the co-op. He accepted the work as part of his vocation to build a movement, though it wasn't much of a living.

As the war dragged on the draft resistance movement burgeoned. As many as forty thousand men were being called up each month, and the unfairness of the selection process was becoming crystal clear. Resisting the war consumed the couple's time: "Our lives were study, demonstrations, meetings, house parties, and warm, close friendships with people who were resisting."

Marv himself continued to be haunted by recurring depression, under the gloom of which it seemed that society was crumbling, that the dreams of young people were doomed.

"Since 1949 I have had a bipolar condition. Extreme depression, followed by rockets under my ass, and then depression again. It was not really diagnosed until about 1989. I suffered a great deal, deprived of spontaneity, humor, and my extraverted nature. And it destroyed my marriage. I told Vicky about this condition before we were married. We thought we could handle it. Turned out we could not."

In February 1967 Marv roused himself to organize an antiwar speaking tour in Miami Beach and Chicago. While on the road he learned that A. J. Muste had had a stroke and died. It was a great loss, both to Marv and to the movement. Then Marv learned from Vicky that she had gone back to her old lover. He threatened to fast until she promised to stay with him six more months, and she agreed to his proposal. (She left him for good six months later to the day.)

In the spring of 1967, during their last few months together, the couple worked together on draft resistance and antiwar demonstrations. California was becoming a mecca for young people that year, as media reports proliferated about the antiwar demonstrations taking place there. The state's reputation as a locus of counterculture activity and sexual freedom also contributed to the allure. Early in the year, the first Human Be-In was held in San Francisco's Golden Gate Park—a preface to the Summer of Love that followed. Counter-culture icons such as Timothy Leary, Allen Ginsberg, Gary Snyder, Ram Dass, Dick Gregory, and Jerry Rubin were on the coast, and the musical scene was similarly rich in talent and innovation, with The Grateful Dead perhaps leading the way. A series of "be-ins" culminated in the Los Angeles be-in preceding an address by the president and a huge demonstration that Marv (who helped plan the event) calls the "Century Plaza massacre."

It was to begin in Rancho Park, a baseball field off Wilshire Boulevard, and march past the Century Plaza Hotel, where President Johnson was to speak at a $1,000-a-plate fundraiser. The hotel has a grand nineteen-story edifice fronting the Avenue of the Stars. It was still under construction in 1967 on a former backlot of 20th Century Fox Studios, but it already held the glamour and prestige of a five-star hotel.

On the afternoon of the march, movers and shakers of the Democratic Party gathered at the hotel in tuxes and gowns, while a mile away, on the baseball diamond, thousands of young people cheered folk singer Phil Ochs and boxer Muhammad Ali, who had become a folk hero because of his antiwar stance. Ali had been convicted earlier that month by an all-white jury for draft evasion, which carried a five-year sentence, and the World Boxing Association had stripped him of his heavyweight title. That afternoon, according to Marv, Ali stood at home plate and said, 'They stripped me of my championship because I would not fight in their war. No Viet Cong ever called me nigger. Am I not the people's champ?" Marv cheered wildly, deeply moved, as many in the crowd were, by Ali's remarks. Ali then climbed onto a flatbed truck where he autographed draft cards for half an hour.

Marv's admiration for Ali has been reflected at recent peace events in his light-hearted *schtick*: he emerges from backstage wearing sparring gloves and a boxer's dressing-gown embroidered on the back (Barb Mishler's handiwork). He spins around and sheds the robe to assume a fighting pose, then sings out,

> "Don't mess with me, I'm the Jewish Muhammad Ali.
> I float like a butterfly and sting like a … Gefilte fish."

At around 6:00 pm, June 23, 1967, the march toward the hotel began, with local leaders of the antiwar movement walking eight abreast, joined by such luminaries as Dr. Benjamin Spock and H. Rap Brown of SNCC. The president flew over in a helicopter and could not miss seeing the twenty thousand marchers. Other helicopters with machine guns poking out their doors also circled overhead. "We were to the far right of the boulevard," Marv recalls, "potted plants on an island in the middle, on the other side an outdoor restaurant and the hotel's circular driveway. Cops and firemen with drawn water hoses guarded the entrance."

The crowd kept their distance from the spectators lining the streets, and spontaneously stopped in front of the hotel far away from the entrance. The hotel guests, many of them California Democrats in gowns, ties, and tails, stood on the balconies of their rooms as the scene developed. Several thousand people began the infamous chants, "One, two, three, four, Johnson stop your bloody war!" or "Hey, hey, LBJ, how many kids have you killed today?"

Los Angeles Police Chief Reddin announced through a bullhorn: "You only have a permit to march on by. So do it. In the name of the people of L.A., I order you to move on."

Energized, the crowd yelled, "We *are* the people of L.A!"

A roar of motorcycles drowned out any further dialogue as the police whizzed by, moving the line of people onto the sidewalks. At the same time, about 300 police in riot gear began to beat back the demonstrators with long batons. Joining hands in front of the police attackers, the demonstration marshals urged the crowd to run ahead to safety.

A policeman hit Marv in the back and knocked him down. "They came swinging at the mass of demonstrators *and* those just watching. They hit men, women and children. One mother's polio-ridden son got his brace caught in his mother's dress somehow. They were both knocked to the ground. People ran in panic, chased by cops rabid with rage."

Drivers stopped and shouted out their windows at the police, "Don't hit them!" The drivers were dragged from their cars and beaten. Even the hotel guests standing on the balconies began screaming at the police chief, "Call off your cops!"

During the attack, Marv lost track of Vicky. He was worried sick. In the chaos that was the aftermath of the police riot he ran from group to group, questioning people and trying to help organize transportation for the injured. No one had seen Vicky. Finally, still anxious, he was dropped off at their house toward 9:00 pm. Vicky arrived a few minutes later with eight friends who had been invited to a dinner party that night. She wasn't hurt, but everyone had stories to tell of police brutality.

The rest of the summer passed more quietly. Los Angeles, like San Francisco's Haight-Ashbury district, Berkeley and other San Francisco Bay Area cities, drew thousands of young people from around the world to join in the antiwar experience. But Marv found that the "love" ideals were difficult to sustain as overcrowding, drug problems, and crime drained the "golden" neighborhoods and government oppression sapped the movement. Marv himself was worn out; his marriage was barely intact, held in place by a promise and the shared commitment to war resistance. The couple were rarely together, both busy with study and meetings, Marv spending more time with a chapter of the War Resisters' League and arranging services for draft resisters.

Vicky came to the conclusion that she should leave, and she moved out in November. Marv, mourning but determined to use his energy to save young men from Vietnam, threw himself into work with the War Resisters League. He also worked with Sherna Gluck's draft resistance group, which may have been the only such group at that time led by a woman. He was convinced that the acts of mass civil disobedience such as the draft card burnings at universities would put strong pressure on the Johnson administration. The president was bound to see that many of those resisting the draft were young, middle-class, and from educated backgrounds.

And it did seem as though inroads into public opinion were being made. In February 1968, the Gallup poll showed that 35% approved of Johnson's handling of the war; 50% disapproved. In March, antiwar candidate Eugene McCarthy had a decent showing in the New Hampshire primary. The war had never been popular, but now the mainstream was waking up. Still, the tide was not turning fast enough to save a generation of young men. Marv wanted to do more.

He was handed an opportunity in early spring of 1968, when a War Resistance League friend leaving his apartment tripped over a sleeping body. "The kid turned out to be a deserter scheduled to go to Vietnam. He didn't want to kill or be killed so he split from camp and somehow picked up a flyer put out by WRL. We developed a small committee to get him out. I volunteered to escort him to Canada."

The safest way to escort someone wishing to emigrate and go underground was by car. Marv and the young man flew to Seattle but were unable to rent a car. Marv had cash but no credit card. They bussed to Tacoma and got a hotel room to think it through. Bussing was considered the worst way to make it past border security. The Canadian group advised him to wait a couple of days and go by ferry on the weekend. "Meanwhile, the kid had fallen asleep. I woke him and gave him the options. He desperately wanted to go that night by bus, so we did. Within half an hour into the bus ride, again he fell asleep. At the last U.S. stop the driver announced, "Have your ID ready for Canadian Customs." I woke the kid up telling him, "Get your ID ready.""

"I destroyed everything," he said.

Marv had to think fast. Why they hadn't discussed this possibility was beyond him. He grabbed the kid's shoulders. "Okay. I'm your uncle, all right? You get off first and tell customs that I'm your uncle, your dad's brother. I'll talk for both of us."

Mopping his forehead, hoping his balding head would make him look old enough to be the uncle, Marv told the border guard, yes, they'd be visiting friends for a couple of days.

"What is your occupation?"

Deciding to put some truth into the situation, he gave them the name of the Mississippi Cooperatives and explained a little about the organization. After what seemed like a long time, the border guard said, "Go on through."

Back on the bus, the kid was jumping up and down in his seat with delight shouting, "We made it!"

There has never been a definitive accounting of the number of draft "evaders" who made it through to live in Canada during the 1966-72 period. The number is probably in the tens of thousands.

Marv gladly claims responsibility for saving—if only for a time— one of them.

13

Beginnings of the Project

In late summer of 1968, his marriage over, Marv returned to Minnesota. "I sadly said goodbye to the friends and comrades I had made in two years. However, as soon as I started driving east, layers of anxiety peeled off. I always delighted in the long drive through mountains and deserts." But the soothing effect of the Mojave desert and Rocky Mountains vanished when his car radio picked up news from the Chicago Democratic Convention. Every small town he passed through seemed to have the convention's televised display of police brutality.

By 1968, the U.S. had 500,000 troops in Vietnam. Yet on January 30 and 31 of that year North Vietnamese and NLF soldiers occupied many provincial capitals and held the grounds of the US Embassy in Saigon for half a day. This offensive shifted the war from its rural base to South Vietnam's urban areas, a turning point of both the war and public opinion. The assassinations of Martin Luther King in April and Bobby Kennedy in June added further to the growing sense that the nation was on the wrong track.

People from the Movement planned to gather in Chicago during the Democratic Convention to express their concern and dismay in the strongest possible terms. In the event, fewer people came than the movement had anticipated, owing, in part, to Mayor Daley's well-publicized threats. As Marv puts it, "Mayor Daley had ordered before the convention that his cops 'shoot to kill looters.' This was a direct warning to the many thousands who might have come to protest, so only about ten thousand people came."

Daley's comments exacerbated nervousness within the Democratic party about holding the convention in a city that had already endured riots after King's assassination. A great deal of pressure was exerted to change the venue to Miami, where press crews had already set up for the Republican convention. But Daley promised to enforce the peace in Chicago and reportedly threatened to withdraw his support for Humphrey if the venue was changed at the last minute.

As he drove the endless prairie miles back to Minnesota, Marv listened anxiously for news of his friends. He knew Dave Dellinger would be there; he was a coordinator for the Chicago demonstrations. At the time writer Terry Southern characterized Dellinger, whom he had not yet met, as an "old-fool-person, a kind of leftover leftist from another era who didn't know where it was at right now, just a compulsive organizer." Southern changed his mind once the two had met.

"We are not seeking a confrontation," Dave had said. But confrontation is too mild a word for what took place outside the convention hall. Chicago streets were an armed camp; over the five days 11,900 Chicago police, 7,500 Army troops, 7,500 Illinois National Guardsmen and 1,000 Secret Service agents came down in force on demonstrators. The television coverage, with young protestors singing out, "The whole world is watching!" showed the swinging batons, the blood, the faces twisted with hatred or horror. Dellinger and seven other male leaders of the Chicago protests were later indicted for conspiracy and crossing state lines to incite a riot. Dave later told Marv that he considered it a sexist indictment. "There were many *women* who also deserved the honor."

Marv followed the trial of the Chicago Eight closely. "A number of left sectarians were ready to bury nonviolence after the King assassination—and Chicago!" he recalls. "The southern movement splintered into nonviolent and Black Power components. The SNCC was replaced by the Black Panther party, which grew first in Oakland—I saw the beginnings!—then nationally into a major force in urban ghettoes."

Marv had much sympathy and much in common with the Black Panther movement. The Panthers coupled revolutionary ideas with social assistance programs like their breakfast program for poor kids. He studied the Panther's Ten Point Program for Revolutionary Change and was in total agreement with the manifesto's human rights demands. Had he not marched, gone to jail, and fasted to demand that the oppression of blacks be ended, that they have the freedom to determine their own destiny, and receive access to decent housing, education, and health care? Marv had seen with his own eyes that black people held in United States prisons and jails did not receive fair trials. On the other hand, the militaristic portions of the manifesto left him cold. Nothing in Marv's own history led him to believe that black "Power" could be derived from guns and popular militarization. Nonviolence was the only "force" that could put a spanner in the machinery of violence.

Once back in his home territory, Marv moved to southeast Minneapolis, near the University of Minnesota, which had an active Students for a Democratic Society (SDS) chapter. He wanted to connect with youth and minority movements against the war. Although blacks were a small minority in Minnesota, the state could boast of a socially conscious political tradition extending back to the early political career of Senator Hubert Humphrey, who had brought civil rights measures to the Congress fifteen years before the Kennedy administration introduced the Civil Rights bill. Local concern for Native American rights also had deep roots in the region. "The American Indian Movement," Marv said, "was born in 1968 as Pat Ballenger, Edie Benton, Clyde and Vernon Bellecourt, and Dennis Banks in the Twin Cities and Russell Means and his brothers in South Dakota began to organize."

In October 1968, a Staughton Lynd editorial in *Liberation Magazine* caught Marv's attention. Lynd described the Johnson administration as *imperialist*, in so far as it wanted to extend its authority over other nations in any way it could. Corporate money and power, especially that of defense contractors, aided the administration in these ambitions. Lynd suggested that the anti-war movement consider taking on weapons producers. He held up some criteria for selecting appropriate companies—whether they made weapons systems used in Indochina, whether directors and board members intersected with other corporate power, and whether there was a union history.

Marv had to look no further than a few miles from his Minneapolis apartment to the corporate headquarters of Honeywell, Inc., the state's largest military contractor. Dave Dellinger had already written about Honeywell cluster bombs and the devastation they were creating in Indochina. Marv began to canvas activist organizations in an effort to recruit seasoned leaders and generate interest and support from grass roots and minority groups. He met with Matt Eubanks, a young black leader close to the Panthers, and with Dennis Banks at AIM. Both endorsed an effort at Honeywell, although Dennis, who was a Honeywell "minority recruiter," warned that his priority was helping to put food on the table of Indian people.

Earlier that year, a small group had already demonstrated at the Honeywell plant in Hopkins. Learning that Unitarian minister Bob Lehman was a part of the group, Marv talked to him about what had happened. The plant's management, Lehman told him, brought out coffee and donuts; they had an amicable discussion, and answered protesters' questions. The group hadn't returned to the plant.

Marv knew that taking on a major corporation would require more than a coffee klatch with donuts. On December 4, 1968, he convened an exploratory meeting to talk about forming a serious, sustained project to confront Honeywell's war profiteering. Around twenty-five people participated, among them Evan Stark, an antipoverty worker, and Martha Roth, a writer and draft resistance worker. There were people from the Committee of Returned Volunteers (Peace Corps), Young Socialist Alliance (a youth group sponsored by Socialist Workers Party), SDS, women's groups, and the Progressive Labor Party.

Marv passed around Staughton Lynd's editorial. He told them, "It makes no sense to take on a major multi-national company for a week or a year. Let's not begin unless we are prepared to go at least *five* years. And we should adopt nonviolence as a means of struggle." Most of those attending, witnesses to the unremitting violence of Vietnam and civil rights struggles, agreed.

For the next four months, Project members met weekly, reading about weapons and their use in Indochina, researching Honeywell's operations and directors. It was eye-opening to note how Honeywell's board "interlocked" with the boards of other big companies, foundations, media, and cultural institutions. There were Pillsburys, Daytons, and members of other well-known families that often contributed generously to foundations, charities, and the arts.

During these early months, Marv and the others also tried to meet with workers and union representatives but had little success. The Project needed to get through to workers at the plants, but how to gain support of leadership? Finally, the next spring, a Teamsters Union recording secretary, Marie Nagangast, called to commend their work and agreed to speak to the Project about how to talk to bomb assembly workers.

"Marie spoke at one of our Thursday night meetings, explaining what it was like for a mother of five children to work in the heating control plant, go to the university at night, and lead the rank and file caucus that fought union leadership." The group was impressed, and Marie seemed to be on board with the Project's plans. But after becoming identified with the activists, Marie was harassed by other union leadership and later was forced to resign.

Trying to help her, Marv called Harold Gibbons, international vice president of the Teamsters Union. Gibbons had visited Vietnam and spoken at anti-war rallies. Although Gibbons was sympathetic, he asked where Jack Jorgenson, head Teamster in Minnesota, stood on the matter. When Marv admitted Jorgenson had said nothing about the Project, Gibbons replied "Sorry, I can't do anything for her."

With Marie's assistance, Project members for a time were able to put leaflets in the hands of hundreds of union workers—though only a portion of them got read. Marv received a call from one union leader and veteran, "Yeah, I got your material," he growled, and described what he'd like to do if he had Marv in the sights of his own high-caliber weapon.

The Project was relentless in its efforts to set up meetings with union members and keep the information flowing, but it wasn't easy. At that time antiwar sentiment wasn't strong among blue-collar workers, who saw their labor as essential to the U.S. war effort. Many also believed that the lucrative government contracts kept their jobs safe. "And management lied to workers about how cluster bombs were aimed 'only at conventional military forces' in Vietnam!"

Early in 1969, Ed Anderson, a University of Minnesota Professor of Mechanical Engineering, entered the picture. He had formerly been a Honeywell employee but had resigned in protest over the corporation's weapons production. Anderson succeeded in arranging a meeting with company officials, and in March he, Woods Halley, Associate Professor of Physics at the University, and Marv sat down at the table with Honeywell's chairman Jim Binger and Gerry Moore, vice president in charge of labor negotiations and personnel.

Marv announced that the Project intended to pressure the Honeywell executives until they stopped producing cluster bombs and other war materials. "Our demands are non-negotiable. We *will* work cooperatively, though, by bringing economists, scientists, engineers...who will develop plans for conversion to peaceful and creative products."

Binger was unimpressed; when Marv offered to show him a cluster bomb, he replied, "I have seen many bombs." Following the meeting, the Project requested that four representatives be allowed to speak at the stockholders meeting. The answer came: *one* would be permitted. Honeywell then issued its first public statement about the Project's demands, noting that the company shared the desire of those who wanted to end the war, but supported *government* efforts. Until a solution was found, the company had an obligation to provide American forces "with the equipment they need to maintain a strong military posture."

Evan Stark, a young social worker who had recently received a masters degree in sociology from the University of Wisconsin, spoke for the Project at the shareholders meeting on April 29,1969, framing his statement as a "trial" opening statement against the corporation, with himself in a prosecutorial role. He drew chuckles when he said that the company had done well by him as a stockholder, but when he went on to claim that those same stockholders were no better than war criminals, the friendly smiles stopped. The *Minneapolis Tribune* quoted extensively in the Business section from his statement: "It is undisputed that such weapons...are used most frequently and consistently against the civilian poor. Clearly the men responsible for this production are accomplices to [war] crimes."

In an interview with a TV network reporter, Binger acknowledged that Evan had brought up "matters of grave concern," but that didn't mean Honeywell executives had reached the same conclusion. "Honeywell will continue to meet the needs of the Defense Department."

Meeting with board members separately proved to be equally frustrating. In June, Evan and Marv met with member Bruce Dayton, whose

The early days of organizing the Honeywell Project.

personal fortune derived from the family retail empire. At twenty-three he began a tenure as a life trustee of the Minneapolis Institute of Arts. For Evan, who would go on to become a Rutgers University professor and a leading author and lecturer on domestic violence, the Vietnam War was already having clear and devastating effects on American society and families; he could do no better than work on this campaign to stop it. He called to arrange the meeting with Dayton, convinced that a reasonable person could be made to see he must put an end to such atrocities. Marv would bring his cluster bomb.

After shaking hands, Marv laid the bombshell, together with a photo of a dead Vietnamese baby, on Dayton's desk. Dayton had never seen a cluster bomb nor heard its effects described. He listened gravely as Marv said that he "wanted him to know just what Honeywell was doing," what misery these weapons were causing to civilians, especially children like this one. The bomb was an anti-personnel weapon, Marv told him. It was not designed to damage or destroy a military target.

"This atrocious weapon" (he pounded the mango-sized object, gray and dingy-looking, on the desk) "is only one of about 660 released from the main bomb container. See these little wings?" Several flanges protruded from the shell. "They make the bomblets spin so they stabilize in flight and disperse in a huge area. Each bomblet is filled with small, steel balls so when they explode—'bomblets,' nice name, huh?"

Dayton winced and held out his hand to examine the shell.

"That's what they call them. When they hit, these steel balls whiz out from their shells at tremendous speeds like mechanical banshees going everywhere, killing and maiming..."

Evan interrupted: "They almost define 'indiscriminate,' because they cover such a wide area and have no targeting mechanisms."

"And when they don't explode," Marv added, "and there's lots of duds, little children pick them up... *boom*," he whispered the word, "One dead kid. It's guaranteed that there will be 'unintended' victims. Little children will die or be injured. Can you deny this is the *intention* of your company?"

"Of course not. I mean...." Dayton blustered. "I do deny it. Look, I'm a Democrat, and I support Gene McCarthy." He looked down, then took a breath and slid the bomb and the picture across the desk. His final remark was, "America has always been the hope for peace in the world, always will be, and you can't take the weapons from the troops."

That was to be a theme of the next several meetings with board members and Honeywell management: the troops needed the weapons. Marv later visited Phil Gerot, president of Pillsbury and on the Honeywell board, accompanied by twenty-two-year-old Charles Pillsbury, a senior at Yale and member of the old Minneapolis milling family.

Gerot backed Honeywell's management: "They are tremendous corporate citizens. Besides, our contracts are with the government. *Your* fight is with the government. We need to get good weapons to our boys!"

As the devastation continued in Vietnam and the antiwar movement broadened its constituency, the focus on weapons sharpened. The Honeywell Project was growing in numbers, and some of its members tried a different tack. If Honeywell had first been successful making heating controls, why couldn't the company return to non-lethal products? Woods Halley and Clayton Giese, both physics professors at the University, began studies on peace conversion and brought their ideas to Project meetings. Marv took their arguments to the lion's den:

"On December 2 another Project member and I met with James Binger in his office. We had just lost a friend to a car crash. I asked him,

"If you can guide rockets with Honeywell science, why can't you make guidance controls for cars?"

"We could do it tomorrow," Binger replied, "but there would have to be profit."

Marv looked him in the eye, pressing his point home, "If you think we are saying something which is factually untrue, tell us and we will change our message." He jabbed the air with his finger with each word: "The bombs are used *indiscriminately* against men, women and children."

Binger nodded, "And they are lethal." That was his point. They worked, they were good weapons.

Ten days later, on Friday, December 12, 1969, the Project held its first mass action, moving small groups all over the city to emphasize the Minnesota corporate interlock and the systemic nature of war-making. "We distributed leaflets at all Twin Cities Honeywell plants. At noon Grandmothers for Peace supplied hot soup and sandwiches to the cold demonstrators at the campus YMCA. High school interns and actors from the Guthrie Theater did anti-war skits for the group." They held two-hour demonstrations at Northwest Bell, Northwest Airlines, First National Bank, Northwestern Bank, and Dayton's department store, pointing out the interlocking directorate on the Honeywell board. In downtown Minneapolis, Project members handed out thousands of leaflets to Christmas shoppers. In the late afternoon two hundred people walked onto Honeywell headquarters property for a one-hour demonstration. There were no arrests, but plenty of notice.

In the next few months the Honeywell Project became a coalition. Marv met with Fred Smith and Bill Grace of the Center for Urban Encounter (CUE) to begin Minnesota Proxies for People, a coalition of anti-war and environmental groups. The group included thirty-nine college professors from the University of Minnesota Faculty Action Caucus, thirty-eight clergy and professionals from the Twin Cities, members of the Committee for Returned Volunteers, including members of the Peace Corps and USAID, and many students from college campuses around Minnesota. The idea was that people would pool their resources, canvas their friends, schools, congregations, and organizations, and jointly purchase enough blocks of Honeywell stock to bring representatives into the shareholders meeting as legitimate shareowners. They planned to put resolutions before the stockholders, calling for an end to war products and for conversion to nonmilitary items that could help solve economic and environmental problems.

Charlie Pillsbury owned $45,000 worth of Honeywell stock and joined the plan to buy stock and initiate a reform movement within the corporation. The Project's effort to place resolutions in the proxy statement to shareholders didn't meet Honeywell's deadline, but Marv and Charlie continued to line up speakers for the meeting, thinking it would be several hours long. They targeted April 27, 1970, when shareholders would meet at corporate headquarters, for an action. Activists would be in force inside and outside the meeting; those without proxies would demonstrate outside, but in huge numbers.

In the run-up to the action, Marv made a national speaking tour (in Los Angeles, towns in the Bay Area, Philadelphia, and Washington, D.C.) to encourage simultaneous demonstrations at Honeywell offices and other weapons plants and sales offices. "I spoke to American Friends Service Committee at Pendle Hill Conference Center in Wallingford, PA, where I met with Michael Klare, who even then was the Movement's primary expert on the U.S. military. I met with the economic task force of the New Mobilization Committee against the Vietnam War. They signed on, organizing actions at the spring shareholders meetings of United Aircraft in Connecticut, AT&T in Cleveland, McDonald Douglas, St. Louis."

Smaller "preliminary" actions in Minnesota helped attract national media. In January, after notifying Honeywell executives Jim Binger and Steve Keating, a group demonstrated near their homes on Lake Minnetonka. The same day, a hundred Teamsters held a wildcat walkout as workers were negotiating with their union committee. "So cluster bomb production was stopped for one and a half-hours."

National Mobilization to End the War in Vietnam was helpful to the new campaign. NARMIC (National Action and Research on the Military-Industrial Complex), an American Friends Service Committee project that published materials on the high-technology warfare against Laos and North Vietnam, sent representatives to help out. The Project supplied information and made extensive use of NARMIC materials for education. "Lots of movement groups wrote for our literature and reproduced it in underground newspapers. The Black Panther Party reprinted our leaflet in its February 28, 1970 edition."

In St. Paul, the Macalester College student government pressed their administration and board of trustees for use of the college portfolio at the Honeywell shareholders meeting. When the request was denied, the students seized and held the college's business office for three hours, until they were granted another hearing. The trustees never did endorse the plan, but the widely publicized event energized campuses across the state. Church groups, too, began to buy stock.

The campaign alarmed and excited stockholders around the nation. Many had been unaware "their" corporation was producing such hideous weaponry and were now willing to see the issues debated in stockholders' meetings. Reporters barraged Marv with calls. When they asked, "What are you going to do at the spring Honeywell shareholders meeting?" Marv would reply, "We're going to *demonstrate* inside and outside their meeting." The invitation was clear: reporters should come and see for themselves.

One month before the April action, Marv was invited to speak to seven hundred people from seventy nations at the Fifth International Stockholm Conference on Vietnam. NGOs and antiwar groups from around the world had started the conference to trade information and explore initiatives to end the war. In Stockholm he renewed his friendship with singer Dean Reed.

Dean was an "American idol" in the U.S.S.R. and Latin America, though he had never been so celebrated in the States. During an evening meeting Soviet generals and revolutionaries began shouting for Dean to sing. He jumped onstage and sang partisan songs from World War II to thunderous applause and foot stomping. The Pathet Lao, National Liberation Front (NLF), and Khmer Rouge were all at the conference. Marv recalls, "I met a Mr. Thuy, a main diplomat from North Vietnam and gave him a NARMIC booklet." Marv believed that the booklet would impress the Vietnamese, underscoring U.S. grassroots activists' desire for ending the war.

After his experience in Berkeley, Marv had always worried about factionalism in antiwar groups, especially around issues of nonviolence and direct action. In Stockholm, he could see bitter disputes about strategy and tactics bleed into the U.S. delegation. "I remember apologizing to an NLF agent who said, 'Marv, don't worry. The Swedish government is watching out for us; they permit us a suite of offices here. We'll have a party for the delegation tonight. Everything will be fine.'"

That evening, six U.S. Army deserters who were living in Sweden joined the gathering. They were an uneasy bunch, which Marv describes as "working class guys who found Swedish language difficult and they were unhappy, though grateful to their hosts, to be living there." They were suspicious of the South Vietnamese and international peaceniks. They listened carefully, however, as Vietnamese elders spoke of their lives in the liberation movements, and they gradually warmed to the people and relaxed. "Each man and woman in the group of eight Vietnamese told us in simple terms who they were. They began with the oldest member; the soldiers and our delegation followed, and when we finished the whole group had bonded."

Meanwhile, in Minneapolis, the Proxies for People campaign was busy writing scenarios that covered every concern in a peaceful, rational way. They prepared for welcoming large numbers, made arrangements for meeting and demonstration spaces, found housing for out-of-town proxy holders, protesters, and speakers, and booked entertainment for an evening rally and the demonstration. April 27 would be a historic occasion, with potential to shift public opinion in a significant way and really rock the corporate war makers.

When he returned from Stockholm Marv called Binger, asking him to meet with ten representatives. Binger said, "Too large a group."

Marv replied, "Jim, we are now a coalition of twelve groups."

He sighed, "Okay. Bring them all up."

On April 14, the ten met with Jim Binger and Honeywell head security agent Fred Cary. Marv presented the demands:

1. Let all people into the meeting who have shares or proxies.

2. Move the meeting from the Honeywell lunchroom, which seats 700, to the Minneapolis Auditorium, which can seat everyone.

3. Admit all of the press, so the nation can see how decisions are made.

4. Let there be adequate space in the Honeywell parking lot opposite headquarters for members of the coalition who cannot get into the meeting.

5. The coalition needs electricity for bands. "We need a powerful sound system to reach our people."

6. The coalition needs one hour of time inside the meeting to present the program.

As Marv read the demands in a quiet, deliberate voice, pausing after each point to glance over at Binger, the CEO looked increasingly pained and started shaking his head. His answer came before Marv had finished: "The meeting will be held at Honeywell. We will admit three people for every bloc of stock you have. No parking lot, no sound system. If you bring one, we'll take it. We will choose which members of the press to allow in. No TV. *If* you comport yourself like gentlemen you will get time in the meeting."

The women in the group made no comment but assured Marv later that they'd do the best they could to be "gentlemen." (Of the many women in Proxies for People and the Project, hundreds had been successful in obtaining proxies. Mrs. Laura Lafond of southern Minnesota donated 600 proxies.)

Marv had notified the press of the meeting and several reporters were waiting outside Honeywell headquarters when it was over. "I told them that we found Binger's answer to our demands unsatisfactory. We were *trying* to negotiate to preclude violence. The onus of any violence that occurred as a result of our not being able to effectively organize, reach, and discipline our demonstrators would be on *him*." Binger called the Proxies for People office two days later, capitulating on two points: "You can have the parking lot and adequate time in the meeting."

Nevertheless, a few days later, the *Tribune* reported that Honeywell "confirmed the company would allow no more than three persons per bloc of stock" to attend. Individual shareowners would be prevented from dividing their shares among more than three proxy holders each.

On Monday, April 27, the Honeywell Project held a news conference at Macalester. Among the media organizations present were *Time, Life, Newsweek, Business Week, US News and World Report, Wall Street*

Journal, and the *New York Times.* All three national networks covered the action.

Marv established what became a decades-long tradition of bringing in keynote speakers and performers to jack up the audience so that on the following day hundreds would participate and even consider civil disobedience. Marv's California colleague Jerry Rubin, now famous as one of the Chicago Seven, was the headliner.

The afternoon of the rally, Marv called the airport to announce that "a group of students" would be meeting Rubin and wanted permission to do a brief snake-dance through the terminal to honor the world-famous yippie. Flustered, the representative asked whether they were grade-school or high-school kids; was this some sort of ethnic performance; and would they be in costume? Marv said, with aplomb, that they were Macalester college students, kind of white but very mature, they'd be in tie-dyes, and the event would be festive. Strangely, permission was granted. "Can you imagine such a thing today?" Marv asks with obvious glee. "It was a blast! All these kids, snake-dancing through the crowds, crowds following."

The late Molly Ivins, who was then a *Minneapolis Tribune* reporter, had been following the Project, fascinated by the use of stock-holder proxies and the idea of developing alternate, peaceful products for Honeywell. In her coverage of the rally preceding the stockholders' meeting she wrote:

> More than 3,500 people roared to their feet and cheered last night after Jerry Rubin screamed, "We're gonna make Honeywell stop makin' bombs and go back to makin' honey!"
>
> "A little off, but right on," commented one Honeywell Project leader behind the speaker's stand.
>
> Rubin was the last in a series of rousers at the big yippie-rad-pacifist pep rally last night at Macalester College stadium to get ready for the action at the annual stockholders' meeting today of Honeywell, Inc.

Poet Robert Bly inaugurated his anti-war poem "The Teeth-Mother Naked at Last," a scathing critique of American foreign policy. Bly was a frequent presenter at Project rallies and a defendant or witness at later trials. The Macalester College stadium, joyously raucous during the speeches and music, was hushed as the tall, tousled poet leaned out to the audience, abandoning the podium to bestow this difficult lesson, alternately crooning and shouting the message.

Robert Bly

Between speakers, The Sorry Mothers played and sang; Minnesota musicians Papa John Kolstad, Judy Larson and Bill Hinckley harmonized on folk songs and bluegrass. Barbara Deming, whose writings had motivated and empowered countless women and men in the years since she and Marv had been in jail together, was among the speakers.

Marv later recalled, "I asked Barbara if she would cut her remarks short since it was getting late and lots of kids were waiting to hear Jerry. Thankfully, Barbara said *no*, and proceeded to give the most profound talk of the rally. I realized my own sexism, not for the last time."

Barbara spoke about her trip to Saigon in 1966 with A. J. Muste and about her recent trip to Hanoi, where at the War Museum she saw cluster bomb casings that had Honeywell written on them, as well as dozens of photos of women, children, and men killed by the bombs.

The rally was hugely successful and the coalition raised about $9,000. Marv spoke last, urging everyone to be there next day at the Minneapolis Institute of Art, the gathering space near Honeywell headquarters. He explained the nonviolent discipline, directing the audience, "If you cannot be disciplined, please don't come." Intelligence agents were also at the rally in force. One of Marv's friends took dozens of snapshots. "We could easily identify the government agents, trying to look like us, but looking more like disco freaks of an age to come!"

By the next day, the campaign had registered 860 people on a proxy list. That morning nearly 3,000 people met at the park. Marv and AIM leader Clyde Bellecourt spoke and Marv once more elaborated on the commitment to nonviolence. A committee had met with

Minneapolis police and a representative of mayor Charlie Stenvig, but the demonstrators did not secure a parade permit, so they had to march on the sidewalk. They proceeded solemnly, four abreast, with "proxy people" leading the way. The long line snaked to Honeywell headquarters and onto the property. Despite the announcement about proxies, Honeywell management surprised the protestors by admitting the first 700 people on the list into the building. Honeywell security guards then slammed the glass double doors. Marv remained outside, giving interviews as the crowd filed onto the park-like grounds. Others lined 28th Street, holding signs.

The main goal of the action was to bring pressure on the corporation in a focused, "sanctioned" way, which would effectively move the mainstream to deeper reflection about America's policies in Southeast Asia. To insure that the event held true to this tone, fifty Honeywell Project members had trained for four months in handling crowds, counter-demonstrators (there were none), and a possible police attack. These marshals wore green t-shirts saying "Honeywell Project" on the back. There were doctors and nurses among them. A subcommittee had arranged to bring buckets of water and rags to protect against tear gas.

But they were not prepared for the violence that suddenly erupted, because it came from an unexpected quarter.

Ike Pappas of CBS *Cronkite Nightly News* was interviewing Marv near the door when a group of about twenty people rushed the doors, breaking them open. "They were known radicals," Marv maintained, "some Yippies, and no doubt some police agents. I shouted at Ike, 'I can't talk now, Honeywell guards are going mace them.' I had a bullhorn and was able to back the crowd up, just as a couple dozen people came running out of the building, rubbing their red and sore eyes. Honeywell security guards didn't have any experience with mace! They were spraying each other, and the Honeywell secretaries, and media people."

What happened next was even more bizarre. A bare-chested man Marv had never seen before ran up, brandishing a National Liberation Front flag. He threw the flagpole through the already broken door, shattering more glass and generating a "photo op." Beer bottles were scattered amid the broken glass inside. The Associated Press photo that went around the world was of people that neither Marv nor any of the other organizers had ever seen before. Marv insisted, "We didn't know who threw beer bottles through the broken door. The Minneapolis police tactical squad marched in formation onto the compound. Sixty cops all wearing gas masks stopped 20 feet from us. They laid down a tear gas machine in the street as the inspector said through a sound system, 'I order you to move on! This demonstration is illegal. You have ten minutes to leave.'"

Marv called for the marshals in green t-shirts to form a line facing the police and sent two people to the back of the crowd to "see if the cops meant to catch us in a crunch." No police were behind the crowd and the marshals prepared to take a heavy beating.

Meanwhile, up in the lunchroom meeting area overlooking the main entrance and courtyard, Project people near the window could see what was happening. They began yelling at Jim Binger, "Take your cops away! They're going to injure people!" Dozens of people surged toward the windows or stood facing down the directors onstage and calling for action.

Binger, white-faced, announced, "The directors have been re-elected. This meeting is *over!*" Management and board then began hurrying from the room; coalition people not already standing rose and shouted, "Heil Hitler!" raising their arms in a Nazi salute.

The meeting had lasted about fifteen minutes. A Project member who was inside rushed out to Marv, telling him Fred Cary (the head of security) wanted a meeting and was waiting in the Honeywell garage. "I ran to the garage. I saw Minneapolis police with shotguns there. Cary took hold of my shirt and in a panic screamed, 'Marv, can you control it, can you control it?' We heard 3,000 people shouting. I said, 'Fred, let go of my shirt and I'll try.' I ran outside."

He ran to 28th Street, where dozens of police in riot gear were marching toward a nearby parking lot in a more or less orderly phalanx. The crowd followed them down the street, many with raised fists shouting, "Power to the People!" In a few minutes the protestors drifted back to hold a "people's shareholders meeting" in the middle of the street. Mark Dayton, Charlie Pillsbury, and Project members spoke briefly, and those who had been inside gave their reports. They passed the bullhorn-microphone around to whoever had something to say, "with mixed results," said Marv.

"Later, our FBI files showed this police action was an FBI COIN-TELPRO. The feds wanted to prevent us from gaining publicity and embarrassing Honeywell!"

The *Minneapolis Tribune* published pictures the next day of police with their badges covered with tape, suggesting that they were permitted to act aggressively and not be identified. The national media focused on vandalism. But regardless of the slant or interpretation various media outlets adopted, it was clear that many Minnesota citizens actually opposed the hideous weaponry made at Honeywell in their neighborhood. As Marv put it, "We all believed these were untried war crimes by management who live like kings and queens while making money out of murder."

On April 28 there were antiwar demonstrations in Sweden, England, France, Germany, Brazil and elsewhere, similarly focused on Honeywell offices.

The next morning, as Marv read the newspaper accounts and tried to tune in to national networks for their coverage, the phone kept ringing. The most surprising call was from Jim Binger. "Marv," he began, "I want to commend all of you. We panicked. You saved it." He was going to elaborate, talking about the preparedness, but Marv interrupted. He was seething about something he had just heard on NBC.

"Thanks, Jim. But I got a bone to pick with you. Why did you lie to the national media at your morning press conference? You said, 'Despite what you have heard from Honeywell Project, the cluster bombs are used solely against military forces of the enemy?'"

Binger was silent.

Marv pressed the advantage: "And Jim, you know we are going to keep at it until you and people like you have no power in this society."

It may have been bravado but his statement stemmed from Marv's deepest values and a passionate hope that they would be realized. Binger sighed and replied,

"Yes, I know."

14

The Project and the Minnesota Eight

While the Project was preparing to confront weapons makers at the Honeywell stockholders meeting, President Nixon and his national security advisor, Henry Kissinger, were laying plans for an invasion of Cambodia called Operation Rock Crusher. Ostensibly directed against NVA and Viet Cong forces, the attacks targeted North Vietnamese sanctuaries in Cambodia with massive helicopter and bomber artillery. The operation reflected Nixon's desire to begin troop reductions and Vietnamize the war in Southeast Asia.

The invasion was launched on April 28, the same day the war resisters wound through the streets toward Honeywell. On April 30, Nixon informed the nation of the campaign, claiming that the operation had prevented "the first defeat in a proud U.S. military history." The nation's response was not what he expected; the invasion triggered antiwar protests at college campuses around the nation, including at the University of Minnesota. During a protest at Kent State University a few days later, four students were killed and nine others wounded, one of whom suffered permanent paralysis. Some of the students who were shot were merely walking nearby or observing the protest at a distance. In Mississippi, protesters were killed at Jackson State.

More than 400 campuses were closed over the next weeks and thirty ROTC offices were destroyed, and on May 9 an estimated 75,000 to 100,000 demonstrators gathered in Washington, D.C. to protest the escalation of the war. Kissinger noted in his memoirs: "Campus unrest and violence overtook the Cambodian operation itself as the major issue before the public. Washington took on the character of a besieged city…. The very fabric of government was falling apart."

Worldwide, the emphasis on deadly weapons gave new energy to antiwar activists. If the connections could be made between corporate capitalism, economic oppression, and war, targets for action could be both varied and focused. In London, two delegations—one from the International Confederation for Disarmament and Peace and one from the British Society for Social Responsibility in Science—met with executives of Honeywell LTD in London to protest bomb production. In India, Japan, Germany, and Scandinavia, demonstrations were held at Honeywell plants, and in Boston concerned citizens formed a Honeywell Project affiliate group.

In July 1970 the Project called for a nationwide "anti-corporate" conference to be held at a farm near Connorsville, Wisconsin. A hundred people came from around the country to share information on research, local projects, and ways to network. Marv remembers the retreat as an idyllic coming together of a spirited but besieged movement: "We had a big tent to shelter people from the sun, marvelous meals—corn on the cob, BBQ chicken. There was a sauna and women and men went to sit naked together from time to time. There were northern lights and many of us lay on a hill looking at nature's fireworks. How spectacular!"

Although an effort was made during the retreat to expand the Project to other cities, it was mainly a time for reflection, a respite from the anger kindled by the escalation of the war.

Yet the Project was facing serious issues at the time, such as how to sustain participation without stifling democracy, and how to effectively raise funds. Some participants wanted to formalize and "professionalize" the organizaition and soften its anti-corporate stance.

In late summer 1970, the National Student Association held its annual meeting at Macalester College and invited Marv to present workshops. Marv and the core Project members urged students to demonstrate on campuses when Honeywell and other corporate war producers recruited or spoke there. The Student Association passed a resolution before the entire body, incorporating the Project's three-point program:

1. Stop research, development, and production of weapons.
2. Peace conversion with no loss of jobs.
3. Worker and community control of the nation's corporations.

Despite these public relations successes, Project leaders were becoming both conflicted and exhausted. It seemed as though every mass action that year had ended in violence or police repression. The killings at Kent State and Jackson State shocked the nation and sapped enthusiasm for confrontational styles of civil disobedience. In Minneapolis, too, police had shown themselves willing to use force to break up demonstrations on campus and at the Honeywell doors.

In September 1970 Honeywell held its shareholders meeting for the first time *outside* Minnesota, which Marv took to be a sign that public pressure was having an effect. But there were divisions within the larger group: key members Charlie Pillsbury, Mary Williams, Bill Grace, Fred Smith, and lawyer Bill Mahlum separated from direct action-oriented leaders to form the Council for Corporate Review (CCR) which pursued a more legalistic strategy and targeted a number of local corporations that were involved in military production, including Sperry, FMC, and Control Data. The council publicly rejected Marv's three-point program, advocating "internal changes" to Honeywell corporation instead, such as putting a union or community member on Honeywell's board.

After studying Honeywell's operation, CCR formally requested that five proposals, including having union and community board members, be brought before the next stockholders meeting. Management refused. At the September special meeting, CCR proposed that Honeywell create its *own* committee on corporate responsibility, comprising representatives from labor and management, minorities, environmentalists, and economic conversion specialists. They had the temerity to request funding from the corporation itself for this purpose: $100,000 annually. The shareholders, not surprisingly, voted no. CCR next requested a mediated review by the federal Securities and Exchange Commission, which did affirm three of its proposals—to add corporate board members, establish a corporate responsibility committee, and amend qualifications of board members. At the next shareholders meeting, these "dissident" proposals were soundly rejected, receiving only 1 percent of the vote.

While some Minnesota activists were presenting reformist alternatives to corporate profit from weapons-making, others went underground. The summer of 1970 turned the nation's attention to Minnesota for another reason—raids on draft boards.

Between 1967 and 1971, a wave of draft board raids hit the Selective Service System throughout the country. Primarily a Catholic-based movement of pacifists, the effort included men and women with a variety of motives. Most understood the personal risk of jail and loss of income, and many ended up suffering the consequences.

For some raiders, actions went beyond making a moral statement. They considered destroying draft files as a way to save lives and keep their friends out of Vietnam. According to Molly Ivins, the young men who became the Minnesota Eight had many things in common, but one feature stood out: sensitive and tortured social consciences.

The pre-computer, paper-based offices gave the raiders opportunities to wipe out the records; draft boards rarely kept backup files. The raiders focused on the '1-A' files because those identified young men about to be drafted. Once a file was destroyed, it was up to an individual to make a conscious choice to re-register.

The Berrigan brothers, Daniel and Phillip, set the standard at the Baltimore Customs House raid in October 1967, pouring blood on records. Their federal charges included destroying government property and interfering with the Selective Service System's operation. The Berrigans were also among the Catonsville Nine who, on May 17, 1968, lifted 378 draft files, brought them to the parking lot in wire baskets, poured homemade napalm over them, and set them on fire. The Milwaukee Fourteen performed a raid on September 14, and throughout the next year it seemed as though a raid took place almost once a month. Occasionally, sympathetic authorities did not press charges; more often prosecutors sought and judges meted out harsh sentences.

The Minnesota Eight were more ambitious in their actions, becoming legends of the anti-war movement when, as part of the Beaver 55 raid, they shredded records of forty-five rural boards housed in the U.S. Postal Service towers in downtown St. Paul. Frank Kroncke, one of the Eight, later recalled, "Hundreds upon hundreds of blank draft cards and official Selective Service stamps were seized and destroyed. ...But even better than that... [I] stumbled upon roughly 1,200 draft stamps –official stamps that, once affixed to a draft card, proclaimed that the card holder had completed his service… the stamps were promptly shipped to Canada, which made it possible for hundreds of American refugees to return to the U.S. legally."

Their next raids were not so successful. Movements against the Vietnam War were monitored by local police, the FBI, CIA, IRS, the National Security Agency, and military intelligence. The young men who became the Minnesota Eight were part of a larger group called The Minnesota Conspiracy to Save Lives, who plotted to raid several draft boards in Minnesota on July 10, 1970. In three of those locations, at Alexandria, Little Falls, and Winona, the FBI lay in wait and arrested a total of eight men, including Frank. One other draft raid was success-fully conducted that night, and one raid was aborted.

It's likely that by that time, informants had been planted inside many peace groups, including the Project.

Following the arrests of the Eight, federal trials were held. Six of the men—Bill Tilton, Brad Beneke, Don Olson, Pete Simmons, Chuck Turchick and Cliff Ulen—were tried before Nixon appointee Ed Devitt. Mike Therriault and Frank Kroncke were tried by federal judge Philip Neville in Minneapolis. Ken Tilsen defended all eight men. Marv remembered, "Judge Neville promised he would allow a defense of 'necessity,' which we have sometimes used in our trials—that means it's necessary to do these actions to save lives."

Not all of the eight had made a study of nonviolent theo-ry or of the legal principles surrounding a defense of necessity. All of the "co-conspirators" were bright, academically gifted, and driven by their ideals. Charles Turchick, 23, was a philosophy major who had worked for VISTA, in a Job Corps camp, and on housing issues in Mil-waukee. Pete Simmons, the youngest of the group at 19, had been politi-cized by working on community organizing projects, and tried to turn in his draft card during the 1969 Moratorium. Brad Beneke, 21, from a rural area in southern Minnesota, had received conscientious objector status from his local board. He worked with mentally disturbed teenag-ers and at a Big Brother camp. Mike Therriault was a psychology major and had attended seminary. He was a draft counselor who knew from experience that the draft fell most heavily on rural areas and small towns.

Cliff Ulen, who dreamed of being a people's lawyer, was reflective, and described his position as carefully reasoned rather than "radical."

Don Olson was a major in international relations. He planned a career in diplomacy, but at the time of the arrests described himself as "a full-time radical" and a pacifist. He worked at the Draft Information Center and taught at the Free University. Still active in the Minnesota peace community, he hosts a weekly radio show on Pacifica radio. Bill Tilton was well known at the University of Minnesota, serving in student government and as a leader in antiwar activities on campus. He was known as a person who could cool tempers.

Kroncke emphasized the religious motivation for his actions, based in his moral training as a Catholic. He had been in the Franciscan novitiate for a time and had graduated with honors from the University of St. John's in Collegeville. His honors thesis was on Pierre Teilhard de Chardin, from whose theology his beliefs in nonviolence stemmed. He described the draft board raids as "consciously and intentionally illegal acts but, equally, symbolic nonviolent acts." The trials offered a microcosm of the great divide between those who were willing to sacrifice their futures for a chance to stop war on such grounds, and those who supported the war for one reason or another.

Emotions among Minneapolis activists ran high that summer. Immediately after the draft board arrests, a demonstration brought a hundred people to the Hennepin County Courthouse. One young woman rammed a flagstaff through the glass doors of the building in a scene reminiscent of the demonstration at Honeywell, and Minneapolis police rushed to the scene and arrested fourteen demonstrators.

Community activists including Marv got on the phone to their networks: a Committee to Defend the Minnesota Eight was quickly formed. The American Friends Service Committee assisted in producing educational literature and brainstorming possible actions; several members planned a week-long vigil and public fast. An AFSC leaflet declared: "We hope by our vigil and fast to communicate the need for concern for life over property...we are here denying the normal hungers of our bodies to show that no one should surrender his will and conscience to the authority of any government." The leaflet closed with a plea to join the vigil and protest the exorbitant bail ($50,000 for each defendant).

The peace and justice community had differing opinions about the raids—especially over whether they fit into the nonviolence category. At a fundraiser, liberal Senator Hubert Humphrey decried what he called the raids' "violence" and concluded that the actions were counterproductive in their effects on war policy. Letters to the editor in Twin Cities papers praised or condemned the young men in equally fervent terms. A John Berryman poem, "The MN 8 and the Letter-writers," contrasting the gentleness of the young men with the vitriolic attacks in the papers, was published in the July 21 *Minneapolis Tribune.*

The executive board of Clergy and Laity Concerned also weighed in: "Violence on persons and property should be abhorred but ... violence on persons is far worse than violence on property." "Some property has no right to exist," the board cautioned, referring to the draft files, and "At times, in order to save lives, one must resort to destruction of property." Marv remembers, "The D.A. thought the guys were part of an international Catholic conspiracy fomented by the Berrigan brothers and funded by Castro!"

Worries that the supporting demonstrations themselves might spawn violence were not unfounded: "Free the eight, smash the state" was the loudest chant from three hundred youthful demonstrators marching down Nicollet Mall on July 16. The march climaxed with a fight, after a veteran roughly seized a Viet Cong flag. Mayor Stenvig soon denied parade permits to any march sponsored by the Committee to Defend the Minnesota Eight.

During the first trial (of Bill Tilton, Chuck Turchick and Cliff Ulen) it became clear that the Nixon government took antiwar actions very seriously. FBI agents testified that they had received tips about the raids, had a list of cars to watch, and had been staking out draft boards for some time. Tilsen questioned the agents, probing for names of informants. To each such question the prosecutor objected and Judge Devitt sustained the objection.

The atmosphere of suspicion, mistrust, and despair deepened as the trial proceeded. For the defendants, who had not held out much hope for an acquittal, the repression that came at every turn was spiritually bruising. But they were not silenced. Marv wanted to cheer when Bill Tilton stood at the end of his trial to face the bench: "Bill expressed his sentiments for all of us when he looked at the head federal marshal and said, 'Harry, you would have made a fine S.S. Officer,' and to the judge, 'Devitt, you are a good German.'"

Before the second trial (of Brad Beneke, Don Olson, and Pete Simmons), Father Bill Teska sought a means of bringing reconciliation to the divided community. He organized a service of blessing at the U.S. Federal Building in St. Paul that featured readings, peace songs, incense, and a call-and-response reading of a Dylan song.

But the acrimony remained: a bomb threat delayed the trial and several days later, Devitt declared a mistrial after five jurors were overheard in the courthouse cafeteria excoriating the defendants. When the trial finally got underway again, the attorneys requested defendants' FBI files; Devitt eventually ruled that the lawyers would get the relevant information by cross-examination.

For the final trial (of Mike Therriault and Frank Kronke), the defense committee worked to bring in expert witnesses to put the focus on the reason for the action. And since the attorneys had less freedom than their clients to testify about motivation, Frank acted as his own lawyer. He offered testimony that "breaking into a draft board office was a Christian act, one consistent with the teachings of Christ." Two of the documents he entered as the foundation for this motivation were "The Documents of Vatican Council II" and Pope John's 1963 encyclical "Pacem in Terris."

The attorneys hoped that Judge Neville would be more open than Devitt, but he, too, steered testimony away from the war. The expert witnesses' testimony and struggles with the judge made the papers. Marv listened closely to his friend, history professor Staughton Lynd, as he talked about the use of civil disobedience in history. Lynd was forbidden to relate contemporary acts of civil disobedience to events like Boston Tea Party or the Abolitionist movement. "Exactly what I didn't want to get into," declared the judge. He also refused to allow Father Al Janicke, who had served a year in jail for a Milwaukee raid, to testify: "We are not trying that one!" he said.

The prize witness, Marv said, "was a handsome man with a brilliant background, Dan Ellsberg." At the time Ellsberg was a research associate with the Center for International Studies at MIT. But in a strange turn of events, his plane was late, and to drive home the point that the raids *did* have a context in foreign policy, Ken Tilsen called Marv Davidov as the next witness: "He used me as a filler for over one hour!"

Frank and Mike knew Marv by reputation and understood that his testimony about antipersonnel weapons could be important to their case. The supporters in court, if not Judge Neville, hung on Marv's words. Without notes, he addressed the jury and the judge, declaring that profit-taking from the war was spilling across the American landscape like a "toxic wave, lapping even at the doors of Minneapolis." Ignoring the prosecutor's restiveness, Marv accepted Ken Tilsen's nod to continue. He laid out the necessity of interrupting Honeywell's quest for profits and power.

The Honeywell Corporation, he said, "while this court was busy trying guys who cared only about saving lives," was constructing nightmarish, anti-*civilian* weaponry. "The fragmentation bombs are *designed* to shatter into tens of thousands of fragments that would kill or maim those in the way—not soldiers." He paused, letting the words sink in. The prosecutor was glaring at Neville, who raised his gavel as Marv shouted: "Honeywell not only operates above the law—the law itself guards that exalted position zealously!"

Neville was furious. "We are not here trying Minneapolis Honeywell," the judge snapped, "Whether they are just or unjust or proper or improper in what their Board of Directors do." Marv tried to answer but couldn't utter a syllable before Neville thundered: "You are not to talk! You are not to talk! You are a witness to be asked questions of and to give answers!"

The judge reserved his special ire for Marv but continued to suppress any references to the war. Ellsberg finally arrived, and when he had taken the stand, Tilsen led him via questioning through his impressive vita. Then Ellsberg said, "I have information in my possession to prove presidents from Kennedy on have lied to Congress and the American people about the nature and conduct of the Vietnam war."

Before the defense prosecutor could even rise to object, the judge said, "I will not have that in my courtroom!" Ken Tilsen nodded, then switched questions, focusing more on the effect that the nationwide protests, and the defendants' actions in particular, might have on the administration's policy.

In response Ellsberg provided details of how acts of draft resistance had 'very explicitly' affected government war policy. Judge Neville interrupted, noting that "this gets us a long ways from Little Falls on July 10" but allowed some comments on those aspects that bore on the defendants' acts. Ellsberg was not allowed to elaborate on what he said was a pattern characteristic of the past five administrations that kept the war going. The judge sustained objections to *any* criticisms of the administration or Congress. He did allow the jury to see color slides on the effect of American "herbicidal" practices on the terrain, though not pictures of fragmentation bomb wounds or bodies.

Finally, Ellsberg declared, "the chief argument against sending 206,000 *more* American soldiers to Vietnam in the spring of 1968 was that domestic unrest, particularly the draft resistance, would be overwhelming." Clark Clifford, then secretary of defense, "seceded" from that policy. "Even people who fail to sympathize with such acts [as the raids] have to adapt to them," Ellsberg continued, "as a cost of carrying on the war."

The courtroom was silent, and Tilsen allowed Ellsberg to remain on the stand for a moment before dismissing him. He was the last expert defense witness.

After two hours of deliberation, the jurors returned and asked whether they could read the documents that Frank had referred to ("Pacem in Terris" and "The Documents of Vatican Council II"). "The judge had to say, quite vociferously and sternly, 'No! You cannot!'" The jurors returned, many with tears in their eyes, and gave the verdict of guilty.

Mike Therriault and Frank Kroncke both received five year sentences, the same as the reactionary judge had given the other defendants.

That night, Ellsberg attended a party for the defendants at Tilsen's house, and "spoke with great authority about some secret information revealing conduct of the war."

During the trial, he had referred to a ten-thousand-page document, the product of a Department of Defense study group set up to study decision-making about Vietnam from 1940 to 1968. He had

Marv and Bill Tilton at a rally

participated in the study and authored part of the report himself. That document later came to be known as the Pentagon Papers, "the colossal litany of lies soon to be known to the world about the war—its pretexts, its precipitation, its perpetuation."

Although Marv understood the substance of Ellsberg's references, he did not know the true significance of the "document" until several weeks later. He was preparing to board a plane for the Bay Area with Karl Vohs, a friend from the Project, to attend a conference on organizing being held by Joan Baez and Ira Sandperl. Ellsberg was to be one of the featured speakers. As they passed a newsstand, Marv spotted a headline in a late edition of the *New York Times*: "Unknown gives Pentagon Papers to the NY Times" and underneath, "FBI seeks the person."

Marv said to Karl, "It's got to be Ellsberg. I bet he won't be at Palo Alto. He'd have to go underground," which proved to be true. The implications of the documents Ellsberg released to *New York Times* correspondent Neil Sheehan were enormous. They showed that the administration knew the war would not likely be won and would lead to many times more casualties than was ever admitted. The level of cynicism and disregard for human life that Ellsberg saw in the Pentagon Papers compelled him, after a period of intense reflection, to search for a way to make them public. He wanted to persuade a sympathetic U.S. senator to release the

Papers on the Senate floor, because a senator could not be prosecuted for anything said before the Senate on the record. He failed to find anyone to cooperate but found a courageous reporter in Sheehan.

Ellsberg went underground for sixteen days. He decided to turn himself in on June 28, well aware that he might spend the rest of his life in prison. He was charged with theft, conspiracy, and espionage. The Nixon administration also began a campaign to discredit him. Nixon's "plumbers" broke into Ellsberg's psychiatrist's office in September 1971 in an attempt to find damaging information, and the break-in became part of the Watergate scandal.

In light of the Minnesota Eight trials, the literature that the Honeywell Project developed that year focused on contrasting the power and prestige of Honeywell's corporate leaders with the plight of the oppressed including devastated Indochinese citizens, American soldiers, and resisters like the draft board raiders. Marv also included in this category the American taxpayer who was financing the war.

Following the same lines, an editorial in *North Country Press* named eight prestigious business leaders, four of them from Honeywell corporation, and compared them with the "other" Minnesota Eight. The article characterized these businessmen as members of the ruling class elite who determined the objectives of power; their interests often "merged with the military to perpetuate a permanent war economy that benefited only them [the elite]," not the majority. The editorial described these men as war criminals.

The draft board raiders, on the other hand, were part of a new generation for whom it was obvious that the Vietnam War was not in their best interest, nor in the interest of people around the world who wanted only to live in peace and meet the needs of their families. Most Americans, the piece concluded, share such modest needs with "the Vietnamese, the Black Panthers and other insurgent peoples around the world... who are rising up to declare their independence."

This identification with oppressed people around the world was a common theme in a reinvigorated Honeywell Project. Around the country, small groups were focusing on Honeywell's production of antipersonnel bombs; in Honolulu, eight people were arrested during a sit-in in a sales office; that trial ended in a hung jury. Two national groups, Clergy and Laity Concerned about the War in Vietnam and the American Friends Service Committee, joined the effort against cluster bombs. By the summer of 1971, with a roster of twenty new people joining four old-timers, the Project's leadership began planning a "corporate war crimes investigation." Val Woodward, a professor of genetics at the U of M, traveled to Hanoi with a mission of bringing a message of solidarity to the Vietnamese people. From a peace organization there, Woodward obtained more photos of cluster bomb victims to use in educational materials.

Minnesota Clergy and Laity Concerned "wanted to go its own way without consultation with the national coalition," Marv said, and dissension and an eventual rupture in the organization followed. That same year the Project joined the New American Movement, a Socialist organization of the New Left. Marv was elected to its interim committee. In England, the Campaign for Nuclear Disarmament also began to publicize the Project's activities.

During the second week of February 1972, a series of public events called the "Corporate War Crimes Investigation" was the Project's major initiative. It began at Augsburg College, where Daniel Ellsberg spoke before nearly four thousand people. By this time, Ellsberg was a household name.

The Honeywell Project took out ads in suburban papers, alerting people who might otherwise be unfamiliar with the Project. "Half of the people who came we had never seen before. And Dan gave *all* the money raised from his talk to help us fund the corporate war crimes investigation." Despite his exposure and the demands on his time, the former government worker was generous with his attention to peace groups. Nearly sixty news people attended the lunch for media that the Project set up.

"What shall I emphasize to the press?" Dan asked Marv.

"Tell them why you came to Minnesota last year—to release the papers, under oath, at the draft board raiders trial. They'll get it! And tell them Federal Judge Neville would not let you do it."

During the six-day event, more than twenty witnesses, including Noam Chomsky, testified before local panels about the war. James

Binger and Steve Keating of Honeywell were invited but didn't come. Minnesota Public Radio won a national award for documentary coverage of the event. "The U of M's *Minnesota Daily* reporter did some nice stories about us," Marv said, then added, "He was later hired by Honeywell as a technical writer!"

As was the Project's usual practice, the lectures and panels were interwoven with poetry and music. Meridel LeSueur and Robert Bly read poetry. Bly's "Teeth Mother Naked at Last" so upset two women on a panel that they threatened to leave the conference. Bly and Marv met with them privately and straightened out the problem.

In March of 1972 Marv learned that the *New Scientist* magazine, a prestigious British journal, had severed its ties to Honeywell Ltd., England, because of information the Project sent the magazine. *New Scientist* printed information about Honeywell antipersonnel weaponry, and *The London Times* and *Manchester Guardian* covered the story with a headline that read "The Honeymoon is Over." A flood of letters from scientists all over the world followed, asking for further information.

National CALC, AFSC, the Council for Corporate Review, and the Honeywell Project began organizing for the spring shareholders meeting. Although this broadening of participation pleased Marv, he was still upset that the national campaigns approached the event conservatively; he grumbled that leaders were apparently ignorant of what the Honeywell Project had accomplished. "They didn't bother in any serious way to find out what we achieved, where we were, or establish a decent relationship." The national organizers had extensive resources and a budget Marv could only envy. They were able to draw support from mainline religious bodies and the moral outrage of a war-weary public.

Despite the tensions, the Project gained extensive local support around the issues of worker control and the unjust elite profiteering from weapons and war. At the stockholder's meeting, the Project led a demonstration of 1,000 people at Honeywell headquarters, while dozens of people, including well-known members of the clergy such as Sister Luke Mary Luke Tobin and Robert McAfee Brown, spoke before the shareholders, who were meeting at another location.

CALC organized proxy holders who presented more than two

hours of testimony critical of arms production. But no amount of reasoning or moral appeal seemed to alter the opinions of stockholders who controlled 98 percent of the shares. On the resolutions CALC and CCR submitted, to disclose military contracts and organize a committee on peacetime conversion, the "vote was 15.2 million shares against the resolutions, and 200,000 shares in favor."

Meanwhile, Honeywell began to respond more vigorously to the attacks on its image. That spring it stuffed a four-page flyer into the pay envelopes of 110,000 employees worldwide, purporting to answer questions "being circulated in the campaign against Honeywell" concerning weapons production, business in South Africa, hiring of minorities, employment of women, and pollution. The corporation also took out full-page ads in Twin Cities newspapers asserting that their cluster bombs were more effective weapons than hand grenades or conventional bombs "because they cover a wider area than conventional explosives." They rejected the charge that producing the weapons "makes Honeywell people war criminals. This is a slanderous charge that is utterly devoid of merit."

The University of Minnesota campus, not far from Honeywell's headquarters, was the scene of intensified antiwar protests that spring. In early May, the Nixon administration announced mining the harbors of Hanoi and Haiphong. Carpet bombing of both cities began soon after, and antiwar activity exploded on hundreds of campuses across the country. "It began small at the U of M," Marv remembers. "Perhaps a hundred people invaded an Air Force recruiting office in Dinkytown, throwing files out the window. The group marched down to the U of M Armory and the iron fences around the building were uprooted and tossed into the street."

Riot squads of the Minneapolis police responded with force, attacking students with clubs and throwing tear gas. University officials were appalled. "This is not really a politically charged campus," University vice president Al Badiner moaned to the *Minneapolis Star*. On the contrary, said Marv, "police beat the students into political awareness. That built the movement on campus into a few thousand!"

Activist students occupied the student center at the U and used it as headquarters during the next few weeks. People barricaded

Washington Avenue with bicycle racks and fence pickets. "The last night of the school year, people we didn't know [a familiar phrase during the Vietnam phase of the Honeywell Project] backed a pickup truck to the barricades and unloaded dozens of iron bars, shouting 'Defend yourselves against the pigs!'"

Marv watched as high school kids began picking up the improvised clubs, and he quickly called together some of the more experienced demonstrators. Project and CALC volunteers moved in to talk to the students: "We confiscated all the clubs and called a news conference the next morning, exposing that activity as obviously done by provocateurs—cops or intelligence agencies."

As dozens of Minneapolis police in riot gear marched down Washington Avenue, hundreds of students poured onto the two bridge walkways over Washington Avenue, jamming every space. Marv sprinted through the crowd, shouting, "There are no neutral observers, get off—the cops will attack you, too!"

A few moved but most did not, wanting to stand their ground or protect their buddies. Police ran up the walkways screaming at people, "Move, move" and whacking anyone who dallied or moved too slowly. When the bridges were cleared, according to Marv, police gassed people in Dinkytown from helicopters.

Hundreds of students, faculty and staff, along with local peace activists, were meeting daily in front of Coffman Union. During one meeting, Marv guided them in forming affinity groups of 25 or so, suggesting that each group select a man and woman to represent them in a leadership council. The protests continued daily until Governor Anderson called in the Minnesota National Guard to patrol the campus. "The war had come home!" Marv said. "Next, we organized for a march from the campus to the state capitol. Perhaps twelve thousand people participated."

Through the rest of 1972, the Project was active in organizing local antiwar rallies and demonstrations, producing literature about the war and Honeywell weapons, and attempting to meet with Honeywell corporation executives. A small ad hoc group passed out flyers at the Honeywell plants in St. Louis Park and Hopkins describing the variety of actions people were taking to end the war and bring troops home.

"We urged bomb production workers to consider taking actions of their own."

They even tried to engage the legislature. On May 9, Project supporters met with Governor Wendell Anderson to recommend calling a special session. The governor agreed with the proposition calling for a withdrawal from the war and said that he would consider the Project's proposal for conversion of the economy to peacetime production, to be supervised by elected councils of workers and community representatives. In Minnesota, propositions could be placed on the ballot by approval of the state legislature. In December, a legislative panel heard testimony from peace and consumer groups, but did not finish its work until after the election, and failed to recommend the Project's proposals. When the government signed a peace agreement with North Vietnam in early 1973, public interest in the war waned, making corporate campaigns even more difficult.

The peace agreements signed with Vietnam were as "ambiguous as the conflict," according to Flora Lewis of the *New York Times*. There was "no clear victory or defeat for either side." The signing ceremony was muted, with little celebration to mark the relief of stopping the bloody war. The U.S. involvement began before France left Indochina in 1954, but January 1, 1961, is considered the starting date for the U.S. role and casualties became official at that point. By the end of the war the United States dead had surpassed forty-five thousand. Vietnam released figures in April 1995 claiming one million Vietnamese combatants and four million civilians killed.

With the peace agreement signed, anti-corporate activity waned and Honeywell Project energies dissipated. A small core group carried on Project work but by 1974, Marv said, "most people went back to their own lives. Former project members became active in the Women's Movement, battered women's movement (with Sharon Vaughn starting the first shelter in the state), tenants' unions and anti-imperialist work. Eight of us remained."

15

Suit against "The Suits"

Although the Honeywell Project as an entity was withering, Marv and Karl Vohs continued to work on antiwar projects, producing literature and organizing small demonstrations at Honeywell and at "corporate interlock" or government sites until the last Americans—ten Marines from the U.S. Embassy—left Saigon on April 30, 1975. Marv was convinced that the United States had a permanent war economy and that he should continue organizing to shed light on the destructive nature of corporate power. Other peace activists were insisting that the Vietnamese people had won the war, but Marv echoed Noam Chomsky in contending that "nobody won. We set Vietnam back perhaps a hundred years. The message has *always* been that if you get out of line and attempt to control your own resources, the U.S. will murder your people and decimate your land."

The Vietnam "syndrome" and the successful resistance of the Indochinese people should give Americans pause, he said: we ought to examine our own bloody history. "America had never been what my generation had been indoctrinated to believe it was. Vietnam was only the continuation of a history that began with the slaughter of native people, slavery, and the exploitation of women and working people."

Though his message was growing tiresome to many, Marv knew that he wasn't alone in his radicalism, and he was pleased to discover a keen awareness in the younger activists who now surrounded him.

"Youth came up with the idea of participatory democracy in the 1960s and strove with hearts and mind to make it so. We believed the operative factor that ended the war was *our* street action, our organizing, the disruption of social peace!" The phrase *participatory democracy* appeared in the 1962 Port Huron statement, and it was once again on the lips of the left in the mid-1970s, as student leaders revitalized Students for a Democratic Society. They sought to broaden decision-making within their own groups with the belief that they were also making common cause with oppressed peoples.

Nixon and Agnew had resigned. The Watergate trials opened for the American people and the world a window on the secret police operation the FBI and CIA had run against the Civil Rights Movement and antiwar groups. In the 1975-76 investigation into the abuses, the Senate Intelligence Committee opened a window, too, for Marv. When the Committee released its report on FBI abuse of citizens' rights on April 26, 1976, Marv found a memo on page 28 concerning the Honeywell Project. The FBI had launched a counter-operation on April 28, 1970, the day of the Project's demonstration, *"just to stop us* from gaining publicity, and to keep us from embarrassing corporate officials."

Marv gathered his own committee to make calls on the staff of Senators Hubert Humphrey and Walter Mondale and Congressman Don Fraser. Fraser responded: he wrote to U.S. Attorney General Edward Levi asking about FBI infiltration of the Honeywell Project. Levi passed the inquiry on to FBI director Clarence Kelly, who confirmed that the FBI *had* been alerted to the "organization, the objective of which was to counter the national defense effort by attacking national defense contractors... this information was received from officials of the Honeywell Corporation *who had been contacted by individuals affiliated with the organization."*

Director Kelly identified Marv as the chief organizer, describing him as "a self-professed instructor of revolutionary nonviolence." Stunned, Marv decided to talk with lawyers about possibility of a lawsuit. Finally, Jack Novick, a lawyer with the American Civil Liberties Union, agreed to look into the case.

Meanwhile, local peace and human rights groups sought to bring their own case before the people in a "Minnesota Citizens' Review Commission" of the FBI's abuse of civil liberties. A diverse panel of feminists, peace activists, and Native American people held five days of hearings with extensive testimony from historians, attorneys, labor and, especially, Lakota people of Pine Ridge about FBI attacks on peoples' rights. It was an electrifying education for the audience, who made their way downtown on some of the coldest days in winter, February 2-6, 1977, and crowded into a small courtroom in the Hennepin County Government Center, stuffing their bulky coats under the seats. During the hearings they heard about the Hoover COINTELPRO focus on blacks, the attempts to discredit Martin Luther King, the raids on the Panthers, the planned killing of Panther leader Fred Hampton. There were, witnesses claimed, extensive efforts to neutralize the American Indian Movement during the late 1960s, including a search by a hundred agents of spiritual leader Leonard Crow Dog's home. Feminists testified that from 1969 to 1973, the FBI compiled an astounding 1,377 pages on women's organizations. The Honeywell Project leaders told of their recent discoveries and learned more about FBI practices of recording license plates, creating files on individuals, wiretapping, and surveillance. It was all of a piece—each group had evidence or knowledge of harassment.

Later that spring, the ACLU agreed to file the suit against Honeywell Corporation and the FBI. Marv and six other plaintiffs joined the civil suit charging Honeywell, CEOs Binger and Keating, the FBI, and the U.S. Attorney General with engaging in a conspiracy to breach their civil liberties. The seven gave the *New York Times* an exclusive story, which appeared in a 1,500-word piece on the front page of the business section. Marv was ecstatic, and set up a local news conference: "The major local news media had to show up!"

He prepared his own statement on behalf of the Project: "From 1968, the Project tried to do three things: Stop Honeywell from producing anti-personnel weapons and all weapons and weapons systems; convert production to goods that people need; and move toward worker and community control of the nation's corporations." He knew the Project's program was radical and was not surprised the administration tried to stop it. "In our country, when anyone organizes a mass movement around such a political program, the government and its police agencies react…. It is our contention," he wrote, "that the FBI has been used since its inception to protect the corporate rich against the interests of minority people and working men and women."

Finally, he repeated his charge that Honeywell management and board members and officers were war criminals. But true to his egalitarian, class-analysis principles, he insisted that "we never charged the working men and women at Honeywell with war crimes, just the corporate management; and those decision makers, even today, still continue weapons production."

The depositions dragged on—for eight years. ACLU's Jack Novick and local attorney Ken Tilsen gave FBI and Honeywell lawyers a box of notes and flyers from the Project, CALC, and AFSC. The U.S. Attorney's office turned over eight large file cabinet boxes with 6,000 pages of FBI documents on the three groups, much of it on the Honeywell Project.

Summaries of the FBI's surveillance reports and notes are revealing less for their relevance to the trial's outcome than for glimpses into Marv's character and the tenor of the times. To judge from the documents, during the early 1970s the atmosphere in Minneapolis was almost McCarthy-esque and disillusionment with authorities was widespread.

An FBI agent included in his report in April 1971 that Marv was having considerable difficulty raising support for the Project. "More militant followers have apparently left him as he has not resorted to more violent tactics. The more conservative following likewise is failing to support him, in that he has not appeared to be effective in his work." In October 1971, an informant reported that "Davidov was becoming increasingly isolated because of the conflict over whether violence should be used." The FBI apparently did not know what to make of Marv, who pressured groups to be confrontational while maintaining strict nonviolent discipline. At a December 1971 meeting, an agent claimed, Marv had insisted that it was necessary to "force" a physical confrontation at Honeywell, perhaps by walking into the building with media present, so that they could show security personnel "pepper-spraying everybody, even their own workers."

An agent reported that in 1972 he found "Davidov so thoroughly disillusioned with the local political climate that he has given thought to entering the priesthood." When he read that particular note, Marv erupted into laughter: "What I *said* was, things are very confused. It's depressing right now. Maybe I should become a priest, drive around in a big car, drink good wine, meet some nuns!"

When ACLU's Jack Novick died of lung cancer, attorney Susan Shaffer took over the case. In Ken Tilsen's small St. Paul law office, figuring that the venue would bring them in more intimate contact, the plaintiffs' representative (often Marv) and lawyers chose to depose Binger, Keating, and Fred Cary, the Security head at Honeywell. Cary turned out to be the most active go-between and supplier of information between the FBI and Honeywell. (Of the sixty-six contacts recorded between the FBI and Honeywell, Cary took part in thirty-five.)

The team interviewed Jim Binger separate from Keating and Cary. Binger said Honeywell had asked for help from the FBI right after the meeting in April 1969 between Binger and Project members; Honeywell had a task force that met periodically for the sole purpose of dealing with the Project. Binger's answers to questions about Keating, who ran the company in tandem with Binger during the war, were revealing, Marv thought. Binger said that they were social friends only "on occasion." But Keating responded to the same question, "Of course." Marv judged Keating to be a poor but talented young man from a small Minnesota farming community who had been co-opted into the local elite by people like Binger, while remaining on the fringe of their world socially.

The ACLU also deposed Richard Held, former Special Agent in Charge (SAC) of the Twin Cities FBI. Marv had never met Held, but when he walked into Ken's office the agent beamed as though he'd known him all his life, booming, "Marv, how the hell are you?" Marv did know of Held's reputation, however, and a chill went through him. He could not respond to the effusive greeting.

Richard Held had come to the Minneapolis FBI from Chicago. He was the Chicago SAC when, with information from an FBI spy, Chicago police raided an apartment and murdered young Panther leaders Fred Hampton and Mark Clark. In repeated directives, J. Edgar Hoover had demanded that COINTELPRO personnel "destroy what the [Black Panther Party] stands for" and "eradicate its 'serve the people' programs." Ninety-nine police bullets were fired into the apartment.

Honeywell head of security Fred Cary testified that Honeywell had

a young woman employee who joined the Project and gave information about the Project's plans. He said he "didn't know her name" but
used to meet her in Bridgeman's near Uptown where she delivered reports in a brown paper bag. Federal Magistrate Brian Short ordered the
FBI and Honeywell to give the lawyers the names of informers so that
they might be deposed. U.S. Attorney General Griffin Bell refused the
order, risking contempt of court. The FBI was not about to divulge
names of its informants and risk breaking their spy system. If they did
that, how would they ever recruit again?

The difficulties and successes of this historic Honeywell Inc. vs
Honeywell Project match were the talk of civil rights litigation for
years to come. Attorney Susan Shaffer spoke later at a Conference on
Surveillance Litigation, analyzing the strategies. This small group of
human rights activists had taken on a major war contractor *and* the
government that had ensured their profits. The activists asserted that
rights of free speech and assembly were violated—that the government,
with Honeywell's help, had created files, recorded license plates, and
generally harassed the Project members. But the depositions, Shaffer
said, unfortunately (but not surprisingly) showed that none of the field
agents remembered anything.

After the Attorney General and the FBI Director refused the magistrate's order, plaintiffs' lawyers convinced federal Judge Alsop that
the informants' names should be revealed, if only to the judge and
attorneys: the lawyers would not be allowed to share the names. Tilsen
thought the suit would still be a long, uphill battle and that the government would assert informants' privilege. The plaintiffs then moved to
sanction Honeywell, but the judge didn't seem inclined to offer sanctions; the corporation and the agents, he said, were not responsible for
the *government's* refusal to supply the names.

At this point, the idea of a settlement came up. Marv and Ken
Tilsen had always believed that monetary awards should somehow be
directed to the victims of Honeywell's antipersonnel weapons: "Our
side, after much agonizing, offered the settlement," Marv said. "If
Honeywell and the government would each give us $35,000 we would
end the lawsuit. We did not have the smoking gun (because we were
not permitted to depose the FBI informants)."

Within three days the government and Honeywell agreed, and on April 26, 1985, the agreement was signed. Ken Tilsen, after all these years working pro bono as a consultant, was gratified. However, as he told the *Mankato Free Press*, the resolution was inadequate to the charges: "It's clearly a violation of rights to take steps that prevent people from being heard."

Karen Bachman, public relations spokesperson for Honeywell, contended that the settlement did *not* mean the company was admitting guilt. "Our desire is to dispose of the case." David White, attorney for the U.S. Justice Department, did not return the paper's phone calls.

The individual plaintiffs received $1,000 to $2,000 each. The ACLU received about $20,000 for part of their expenses; Honeywell Project received about $10,000, a much-needed boost that would help in organizing the next phase of the Project. During the long suit, the Honeywell Project, though dormant, gained nourishment from grass-roots struggles locally and around the world.

The bulk of the settlement—$35,000 from Honeywell, Inc.— went to the Philadelphia-based American Friends Service Committee for their "shovels for Laos" project, a program dedicated to removing unexploded fragmentation bombs. Since the war, Laotian farmers had frequently hit unexploded Honeywell cluster bombs. The death toll was enormous. With a special shovel, they could dig slowly in the earth, removing and defusing the bombs, to avoid death or maiming.

The AFSC was delighted. In their news release of May 1, they pointed out that the bombing in Laos left more than two tons of bombs *per person*, and at least some lives would be saved. Moreover, the lawsuit was "the first to tie a major corporation into the FBI's operations against the antiwar movement." It was fitting that Honeywell was paying $35,000 to help the victims of its own weapons.

Marv was not willing to give the corporation even that ironic credit. He said, "*We* saved some lives with the Honeywell money with no help whatsoever from Honeywell management … but since Honeywell is paying out [the money] … that should be counted a great victory for the Honeywell Project."

16

Marv Goes Green

With the end of US involvement in Southeast Asia, the Honeywell Project went into hiatus during the late 1970s, though there were plenty of political issues to keep Marv busy between courthouse appearances and depositions. And in 1976 the nuclear power movement burst on the scene with the Clamshell Alliance, which generated militant, nonviolent actions at the construction site of a plant in Seabrook, New Hampshire, some forty miles north of Boston.

The Alliance had its beginnings in a traditional small-town democratic process, when the town of Seabrook voted four times against construction of a twin reactor complex at salt marshes along the Atlantic coast east of town. The utilities company offered major economic incentives, but forward-looking local people would have none of it, and environmentalists, fishers, and antiwar activists from nearby rural communities rose up to form an unlikely but effective coalition. The coalition began small-scale civil disobedience at the Seabrook site and on August 1, 1976, eighteen people were arrested; on August 22, a hundred and eighty more volunteered.

On April 30, 1977, about two thousand protestors once again occupied the Seabrook site. Months of preparation had gone into training small "affinity groups" in the theory of non-violence and in role-playing for various scenarios of arrest and jailings. This was the kind of training and action that Marv could get behind. He was excited to read about the events of the next several days.

Typically, protestors were ticketed and released on their own recognizance. But New Hampshire's governor demanded that out-of-state protestors be detained and pay bail; most of them refused and in solidarity so did the local protesters. By morning more than a thousand protesters were being held in National Guard armories around the state. National and international media seized on the story, eventually the governor reversed his position, and the remaining Clams, pledging to return for trial, were released without bail.

The standoff revived the antinuclear movement and sparked a national movement for green energy. In Minnesota, Marv, George Crocker, and Don Olson began Northern Sun Alliance to bring public attention to the dangers of nuclear power. They visited CEOs of utility companies and engaged public agencies, researching and publishing information about nuclear power. "We quickly had a group of twenty men and women, and together with comrades from Wisconsin we put such organized pressure on the Wisconsin Public Service Commission that it voted to refuse a license for Northern States Power to build a nuclear power plant in Tyrone, Wisconsin."

Another "power" issue involved the historically conservative farm country of west central Minnesota. In 1978, Marv and the Northern Sun Alliance became aware that Minnesota dairy farmers were making frequent appearances at the state capitol. Dozens, then hundreds came to complain about high voltage power lines being forced through their farms. "We weren't quite sure what it meant until Will Mische wrote me from rural Minnesota, 'You all have got to take note of this populist struggle: it really grips the people in Western and Central Minnesota. They meet above a fire station in Lowry, Minnesota.'"

Farmers wanted to stop construction of a 400-mile-long transmission line that would cross private land from the North Dakota border to the Twin Cities. The Alliance sent member Danny Tilsen (Ken's son) to Lowry to take a look. He reported, "There are a couple hundred farmers, men and women. They meet and sing satirical songs about the Republican and Democrat governors." His voice was worried. "And they talk about stopping *anyone* who threatens to destroy their farms."

For Marv, the power line dispute was a justice issue, again pitting corporate power against the little guy. The farmers were convinced that the power company wanted to cross small farmers' land because the big, irrigated farms wouldn't have the line on their own land. According to farmer Virgil Fuchs, corporate farms told the power company that lines would interfere with their huge irrigation rigs. He had heard the plan was to run the power line through land that was "less productive"—in other words, small family farms!

Counties passed resolutions against the lines; the Environmental Quality Council held numerous hearings; various agencies brought the matter to court. Farmers were assured that they would receive a notice if the power company received permission to begin work. But according to Fuchs, one day the surveyors just showed up in his fields.

The farmers got organized—and creative. When surveyors came to a site, a ditch across the road would block them. The farmers had obtained legal permission to dig, claiming they'd had to fix a bridge. Another tactic was to start up farm machinery close to the surveyors, "so they couldn't talk."

Marv tells a story he claims originated with Fuchs: "A survey team came onto a farmer's land. They saw the farmer jumping up and down on a raised platform shouting '31, 31, 31.' They asked the farmer why he was shouting '31.' The farmer asked one of the surveyors to step up and see. The farmer then jumped off and pulled the wood slats off the platform; the surveyor fell into the well below. The farmer put the planks back on, jumped on top, and shouted, '32, 32, 32.'"

County authorities were in a bind. They were sympathetic to their friends and neighbors but companies and state agencies brought immense pressure. Local sheriffs and law enforcement officials, as well as the farmers, took their grievances to the capitol but Governor Wendell Anderson declined to intervene. At that point Pope County Democrats turned to Alice Tripp, who had been active along with her husband John in earlier anti-nuclear activities, to run for governor.

"I was so astonished, but I thought, sure, why not?" she said. "And then Mike Casper, a local physics professor, agreed to be on the ticket as lieutenant governor, and he wrote the press releases, and he fixed up a solar loudspeaker... so that we wouldn't be wasting energy!" Peace activist Russ Packard wrote the campaign song:

Where you going to be on election day?
Are we going to let them have their way?
Pushing farmers off the fields to big power lines.
Nuclear plants are their big design. Vote for Alice! Vote for Alice!

Alice Tripp's showing in the election was impressive. To no one's surprise, Iron Range liberal Rudy Perpich won the endorsement, but in the primary Alice Tripp gained 97,000 votes statewide and in Pope County won 44% of the vote.

Marv watched with interest as the anti-power line campaign escalated. Masked riders on horseback would drive survey crews away. "The REAs were laying $250,000 lawsuits on farmers who resisted, effectively silencing them," Marv remembered. "So, we asked the Tripps, 'What if we came up and blocked surveying with our bodies? They can't lay big lawsuits on us. We don't own anything.'"

It took several weeks to make the arrangements, but finally both Tripps were on the phone, taking turns and swapping stories with Marv. Alice was weary of the battle. She was still out and about, too often away from their land, in her opinion; there were too many meetings to attend. The tiredness showed in the shadows around her eyes, but was belied in her abrupt laughter when her eyes would suddenly light up behind her rimless glasses. John felt the strain, too, his mild good humor tempered with disappointment. It seemed as though none of the battles had gone the farmers' way.

"Oh, I guess I was sort of pleased at how people could get together and offer resistance to something like that," John said in an interview on MPR. "Politicians are probably going to be a lot more careful about how they go about doing something like this, and not just say, 'Get out of the way, we're coming through.'"

Alice informed Marv when the surveyors were on their way, saying straight out that about twenty-five farmers planned to meet at their place when the surveyors came. A dozen of the Northern Sun Alliance people, including Don Olson and George Crocker, an antiwar activist who had spent a year and a half in prison for refusing to serve in Vietnam, drove up to Pope County in late October. A cold sleet dotted the frozen stubble after weeks of drought. Alice had given them good directions and they arrived shortly after noon, feeling determined but "slightly anxious. We didn't really know anyone well. We walked into the Tripps' house to find the farmers drinking hot chocolate, eating egg salad sandwiches. It was like no one acknowledged our presence at all."

They sat, listened to the conversations when possible, smiled and waited. The atmosphere was relaxed. An hour later, a farmer announced, "They're coming on the property." Don and four others went out into the frozen fields, just covered with slushy snow, and stood in front of the survey equipment so the surveyors could not begin their work. The supervisor called the sheriff's office; a half hour later a couple of deputies arrested the Alliance people and drove them to the St. Cloud jail.

"We bailed them out and everyone met in George Mische's bar. George had been one of the Catonsville Nine, a draft raider who did two years in prison. He also had been elected to the St. Cloud City Council, knew the Tripps and other farmers. We all began to circulate among the farmers then, and they gave us noticeable respect."

Alice and John Tripp, hearing about the 'Georges' and Marv's experience with active non-violence, convinced their neighbors to listen, saying "These young people know something valuable for us." By then, farmers were willing to listen to activists they might have formerly disregarded, people like George Mische, who in pictures of the Catonsville Nine looked like a disguised cherub, bandito dark mustache and scrubby beard hiding his youth; and George Crocker, looking like a 1950s blue-eyed Jesus with his long blond hair and air of mild rebellion. Alice later remembered sitting in a meeting next to a farmer's wife from north of Sauk Center, when "George Crocker and about four or five other people walked in, wearing their red bandannas. And this woman turned to me and said, 'Are they going to meet in the same room with us?'"

"She later became quite an admirer of Crocker's," Alice said. Crocker moved from the Twin Cities to work full time on the protest.

The struggle continued through the fall of 1978. Farmers would blast visible fixtures on the line with their shotguns. Masked young men, crawling through the fields next to the towers cradling the lines, "began to topple these $250,000 steel blots on their landscape. They would saw the legs with hacksaws, saying it was 'bolt weevils.' Fifteen to twenty of these monsters were knocked over and no one was ever caught."

Governor Rudy Perpich, who had paid a number of surprise visits to farmers around the state, was sympathetic for a time, but the intense and widespread resistance wore him down. "He called out the largest operation of state police in Minnesota history to put down this populist farm revolt," Marv said. The state police "stayed a few months. At one point farmers massed 6,000 people in Lowry to protest the line."

Always determined to link people engaged in similar activities, Marv had just returned from a speaking tour to Upstate New York, where Indians, farmers, and city radicals were resisting another high voltage line. He spoke to members of that coalition about the Minnesota struggle. "The people there gave me a precious photo to bring back: two Iroquois women with their arms around an old tree. High up in the tree was a 70-year-old grandmother, Stella, on whose land the power line people meant to down the old tree."

Native Americans had asked to join the New York coalition earlier and had been refused. But when power line people came to cut Stella's tree, the two Indian women came to help. Police beat them up, "which catapulted Indians into the coalition. Stella came back with me to speak at the huge Lowry, Minnesota rally."

That winter Marv's friend, actor/singer Dean Reed, also entered the story. Marv had invited Dean to stay with him during a premiere of Dean's film *El Cantor* for a U Film Society-sponsored screening. Reed wrote and directed the biographic film about murdered Chilean folk singer and revolutionary Victor Jara; he also starred in the title role. Reed was aware that to many Americans he was unpatriotic, having crossed a line that most celebrities would not dare. In an interview with the *Minneapolis Tribune* he said, "People will accept a Joan Baez or a Jane Fonda.... But not a Marxist living in East Germany. I'll come to America when I can help fight for a movement that needs me. But I'm not going to come to the U.S. to sit on my ass." Reed thought that he could help out his old friend in the radicalized rural Midwest.

The Northern Sun Alliance declared its intention to do a civil disobedience action, gathering a broad coalition of farmers, AIM activists, and politicians to demonstrate at Buffalo's utility station. Reed was delighted at this small-town insurrection. The program was spirited and the singer captivated the crowd with the broad golden voice that had been likened to the younger Elvis's. "Seventeen of us were arrested including Dean," Marv remembered. "Four pled guilty and paid fines.

The rest of us, eight men and five women, remained in the small Buffalo jail, all in the same cellblock, awaiting trial."

The individual cells would be opened early every morning, so that the group could gather in a common room until nightfall. Spirits were high: the group was tight, talking and plotting nonviolent strategies that might influence public opinion. They started fasting the first day. All refused to post the $300 bail. Reed joined the hunger strike and announced, "I consider myself a political prisoner."

Reed was uncommonly happy; he awakened early every morning and at the top of his voice would sing, "Oh what a beautiful morning, Oh, what a beautiful day" from the musical *Oklahoma*. The other inmates were not quite so bubbly: they would scream "Shut up, man, we are trying to sleep!" and the ebullient singer would comply—for awhile.

Dean Reed and Marv were radicals with some similar personality traits; they were both idealists with strong egos and leadership qualities hiding vulnerabilities that haunted them. Dean shone when he found a place congruent with his beliefs and a young audience like the one he'd had in the Soviet Union that lionized him as a typical American rebellious rocker—which he wasn't.

Charles Laszewski, a *Pioneer Press* reporter who became aware of Reed during the power line struggles, wrote a biography called *Rock 'n' Roll Radical: The Life and Mysterious Death of Dean Reed* (Beaver's Pond Press, 2005). "You can't read this guy's life story, ... without coming away really impressed at his courage," said Laszewski, before doing a reading from *Radical* at Marv's apartment building. "Not many people ever put their lives on the line for anything. And he was doing it routinely."

On the fourth day of their jailing, Dean told the Alliance prisoners, "We can make this struggle visible worldwide. If I call friends around the world asking for support, I bet it will happen!" Marv knew that Dean wasn't bullshitting, but suggested they call the farmers first. "I called Alice and explained what Dean wanted. Alice said, 'We're having a meeting right now. I'll tell people and get their input.'" In a moment, Marv could hear raucous laughter. Then Alice came back on the line. "We agree. Tell him to go ahead, we have nothing to lose."

The jailers wheeled around a pay phone on a cart every day. The inmates were able to call (collect) anywhere in the world. Dean called John Randolph, president of the Screen Actors Guild. He called Jean-Paul Sartre in Paris and friends in Moscow and Eastern Europe. Dean had told Marv early on that if they called Dean's teacher and mentor Paton Price, he'd be there the next day. "Sure enough, he was," Marv said. "He visited us and persuaded us all to drink plenty of juices while fasting, which we did. About the seventh day both the Associated Press and United Press came out to the jail to interview Dean."

The story was a major news feature in Moscow. School children from the Urals sent letters to the jail demanding "U.S. authorities release our good friend Dean Reed and his comrades."

The sheriff's department could listen in to Dean's phone conversations; "they must have found it interesting because they never shut us down," Marv said. Letters and telegrams were coming in from all over the world. *Time Magazine* (November 27, 1978) reported, in a tongue in cheek critique of Soviet hyperbole,

The newspaper Komsomolskaya Pravda *reported that telegrams "expressing wrath and indignation at the arbitrary rule of U.S. authorities" were pouring in. A quartet of Soviet classical composers fired off a message to the White House prodding President Jimmy Carter to "urgently intervene to put an end to arbitrary action and ensure the release of Dean Reed." Finally, the Carter White House called the jail, "trying to find out the source of this tumult on the plains."*

After thirteen days of fasting, the Alliance group was set for their three-day trial. Attorney Ken Tilsen once again took the activists' case *pro bono* and the thirteen were released from jail on their own recognizance. The group chose about eight people to testify, including a young Indian woman, several farmers, men and women from the jailed group, and Dean. The Democratic Republic of Germany sent a television crew from Washington, D.C. TASS, the news agency of the Soviet Union, also sent a reporter from their D.C. bureau.

"Ken gave a marvelous summation of why we would risk arrest and what we felt were the serious changes to human and animal life caused by this power line," Marv recalled. The jury, made up of local people, farmers and rural business people, deliberated for six hours and came in with a verdict of not guilty.

"We had won the World Series of Trespass!"

Although the farmers ultimately lost the power line battle, the Alliance, Marv, George Crocker, and more famously a young politician named Paul Wellstone were able to make connections between the power line protest and other grassroots struggles.

"Having people like Paul there and the students that he brought along was a very empowering thing for the communities.... you know how Paul can talk," George Crocker said later in an interview on MPR. "You know how he can go to the heart of a matter and help people understand not only what's wrong but what's right and where there's hope and why it's important to do the right thing."

The Northern Sun Alliance sowed seeds among rural people that bore fruit in the decades to come. They listened to the farmers, heard their love of the land and commitment to their communities, and responded by putting their bodies on the line. Marv and his friends illustrated for the embattled farmers the power of nonviolence in such a situation, not only as a strategy that brought world attention to an issue, but as a force that created bonds between people and the strength to "do the right thing."

17

The Nukes, the Sacred, the Profane

In 1979 Marv was again invited to take on corporate despoilers in coalition with Native groups and local farmers. This time the issue was land that indigenous peoples held sacred, Paha Sapa—the Lakota name for the Black Hills. One of the oldest geological formations in the Western hemisphere, the doorway to the Great Plains, Paha Sapa is also the center of the Lakota Nation, who believe they have a sacred charge to protect it for future generations.

The global energy crisis of the 1970s led to a rekindling of the historic conflict over minerals in the Black Hills. Multinational mining companies looked to the Black Hills for energy resources, including uranium mines. A coalition of Native Americans, environmentalists, and farmers came together to protest the proposed exploitation.

In April 1977, Union Carbide announced it had located a significant uranium deposit in Craven Canyon, Black Hills National Forest. But before the year was out, thousands of people were marching through the Black Hills, concerts were organized featuring artists such as Bonnie Raitt and Jackson Browne, and ranchers, churches, chambers of commerce and citizens entered into an alliance to protect a treasured environment and a way of life. (Along with several other corporations and even the Department of Defense, Union Carbide continued in their bid in the late 1970s and 80s to carve out pieces of the Black Hills both for mining and for places to test bombs and other munitions—including some from Honeywell, Inc.)

In 1979, a registered nurse at the Pine Ridge hospital started noticing a dramatic increase in spontaneous abortions among the women. She and other medical people who had suspicions were told to "Leave it alone." The Alliance initiated their own research study. During a one-month period in 1979, they found, 38 percent of women in Pine Ridge had spontaneous abortions. Out of the live birth children of that same time, 50 to 60 percent of them suffered some type of birth defect; most were respiratory ailments, some were liver or kidney ailments.

The American Indian Movement began to organize a massive rally and conference of nearly two weeks in the foothills of the Black Hills, called the International Survival Gathering and billed as a rally to save the Black Hills from coal- and uranium-greedy energy companies. It was a grand experiment to see if students, radicals, environmentalists, farmers and Indians could get along together. Marv was brought on board to do logistical work on the Peace and Justice panels.

A white rancher, Marvin Kammerer, lent his abundant land in the foothills for the event. "He was a generous 'cowboy'," Marv recalls, "who pitched his lot with the Indians and activists."

Marv's team joined several groups to build wooden structures from local resources, with roofs of parachute cloth to provide sorely needed protection from the sun. In July the temperature hit 100 degrees in Rapid City every day. Everyone looked forward to the evening concerts, when heavenly cool—65 degrees—descended. "Local carpenters built an enormous stage and the very best sound equipment was brought in. Tom Campbell, a professional, produced the concerts."

During the days, panels were held on a variety of energy issues. Evening sessions featured speakers like AIM's former chair John Trudell. "After hearing John illuminate the values imposed on us by the 'corporate Reich,' as he called it, I would have followed him anywhere."

The grounds were vibrant with color, with a village of teepees sharing spaces with multicolored tents for the 'non-Indians.' Water wagons kept the people hydrated and vendors sold hot food and sandwiches. The Alliance had decided that no alcohol or drugs would be allowed in the area, and AIM security enforced the policy. Tribes from all over the globe were represented, "all describing the common problem: greed taken to the highest level by the homegrown corporate leeches, as indigenous peoples were stripped of their cultures and put on reservations while the whites stole the resources."

Jackson Browne, Bonnie Raitt, and/or Danny O'Keefe played

nightly. Relieved from the daylight hours' withering heat, Marv, along with thousands of conferees, lay on sleeping bags under brilliantly starry skies "with an occasional B-52 from Ellsworth Air Force Base roaring overhead, reminding us the U.S. had an empire to defend from mostly imaginary enemies."

The effort of such a gathering slowed the uranium exploration, Marv believes, because the thousands of people exerted pressure on federal and local agencies, and on the corporate powers that ran them. The Black Hills Alliance could claim victory in the mobilization that Marv helped generate. It was a model for alliance building through-out "Indian country," with events spilling onto campuses and national gatherings of other movements and concerns of the 1970s and 80s.

The Black Hills Alliance understood that the nuclear fuel cycle in the United States began on Indian homelands. When the mining companies dug, they contaminated the countryside and the aquifers. Marv also realized that the nuclear cycle ends on Indian homelands. "I'm here to tell you that now they're looking at Indian lands because they can't find any place to store the damned stuff forever."

"I remember Dr. Sam Epstein giving a talk on how cancer is polit-ical; that is, the epidemic is caused by corporate pollution and toxicity chemicals in the water, food and air. For years now I have asked classes and people I talk to, 'How many of you know friends or family that either have cancer now or have died from it?' Eighty to ninety-five per-cent typically raise their hands. 'By the way,' as poet Kenneth Patchen said, 'they mean to kill us all.'"

In the next few years such issues were seldom far from Marv's at-tention. "We saw the connections between exploiting poor people for resources like uranium and military posturing for power. The rich got richer while the working poor slid backwards, while the arms race threatened unimaginable disaster for humans, plants and animals."

Minneapolis Tribune writer Steve Berg (August 3, 1979) asked whether people might be beginning to see Marv as a "burnt-out, pa-thetic figure, jumping from cause to cause." Marv's answer to such criticisms was consistent with the unitary vision that sustained him through the decades.

"I don't jump between causes because there is only one cause, they're all tied together," he said. "That's what true radicalism is."

At the time, millions of West Europeans were taking to the streets, alarmed by the planned shipment of short-range U.S. Cruise and Pershing nuclear missiles to Italy, France, Belgium, Great Britain and Germany, to counter Soviet SS 20s aimed at Western Europe. The European nuclear disarmament campaigns awakened a U.S. movement, and another cycle of national and local collective action got underway.

In 1980 Ronald Reagan became president. He had gotten his start in politics, Marv reminds people, as an FBI informer against progressive trade unionists. He was a "friendly witness" (stoolpigeon) before the House Un-American Activities Committee in 1947, informing on fellow actors and screenwriters whose careers were destroyed by the Hollywood blacklist. Now the "most powerful man on earth," he proceeded to ratchet up Cold War rhetoric to the point where many middle-class Americans were alarmed, and more than a few felt compelled to take action. Most of Minnesota's congressmen opposed the military buildup but seemed reluctant to criticize it. (As Minneapolis mayor Don Fraser said, "When the government puts out bids, it doesn't bother me that Minnesota gets the work.")

Marv knew that Honeywell, Inc. was sensitive to these political postures; the weapons lobby in Washington was powerful, sending contributions through political action committees (PACs). The moment was coming to bring attention to the skewed role local contractors played in the nation's war economy.

In September of 1980 an event took place at General Electric Nuclear Missile Division in King of Prussia, Pennsylvania, that would have a great impact on Marv's career as an activist. On September 9, Dan and Phil Berrigan; Molly Rush, a mother of seven; Ann Montgomery, Religious of the Sacred Heart sister and teacher; Carl Kabat, Oblate priest and missionary; and Catholic lay people Dean Hammer, Elmer Maas, and John Schuchardt became the Plowshares Eight. "They cased the joint," Marv said, "and carefully planned this first act of creative nuclear sabotage." Father Carl Kabat put the guard in a nonviolent bear hug while Sister Ann Montgomery sat on the phone. The others rushed in and "providentially" found a crate containing a freshly made nuclear rocket nose cone for the Mark 12A first-strike nuclear warheads. They removed it, hammered dents and poured their own blood on it, and stood praying and singing while they waited for the authorities.

They were arrested and charged with ten different felony and misdemeanor counts. During their trial they were denied a "justification defense" and could not present expert testimony. They were found guilty, but the action and the trial caught the imagination of the media and a wide segment of society.

In early 1981 Carl Kabat came to Minneapolis to speak about the action at Newman Center at the University of Minnesota. In his talk, Kabat stressed the link between global militarism and poverty. "Knowing Phil and Dan Berrigan, I naturally went to hear Carl," Marv said. "That action shook up the church and helped move us out of our sleepwalk about the nukes. The King of Prussia Plowshares action led to revival of the Honeywell Project as an activist group."

During that same period a group of Sisters of St. Joseph of Carondelet in Minneapolis, including Char Madigan and Rita Foster, were also in contact with Catholics doing Plowshares actions and vigils at the Pentagon. The Plowshares' long-range plan was to bring people from Catholic Worker houses and other communities to Washington to spend a week-long vigil at the Pentagon.

Char and Rita talked about the rebirth of the Project at their new HOPE center (Homes on Portland Enterprises), a two-block-square campus offering housing and social services for a flourishing multicultural community. "Six of us went to Washington in November 1980 from our St. Joseph's house, a shelter for women and children," said Char. "We packed our sleeping bags, traveled all night in an old van, slept in a church basement, and handed out leaflets. Other groups took charge of other actions, blockaded streets or entrances to the Pentagon, did civil disobedience." At the time, neither Char nor Sister Rita Foster could imagine doing such a thing as "c.d.," waiting for arrest and possible imprisonment.

The sisters had plenty of work to do—the work of justice and mercy. "Dorothy Day, my mentor, said you spend most of your time on works of mercy," Char remembered. "But you also *have* to speak out against

systems of injustice, resist systems of domination that take money away from the needy and spend it on war." The actions in Washington were compelling, "standing in that place of war-making, saying *no*." During the week, the recruits tried to connect with the Pentagon workers and visitors, and those connections and acts of sharing were empowering. At the end of the week, Char said, "We were given 'homework,' to bring the message somehow to our own towns and cities." She shook her head, bemused. "We were unsure of how to do it."

During the question and answer time after Carl Kabat's speech at Newman, Char Madigan stood up. "We have been to actions at the Pentagon, but we are not sure what to do here at home, where to go!"

Marv sprang to his feet, "I know a place! How about Honeywell? They make guidance systems for first-strike nukes and cruise missiles."

"Five days later," Marv declared, "eleven nuns and I, one Jew, met in the attic of St. Joseph's House, a Catholic Worker home for battered women and children."

Char recalled that the early group "wasn't all nuns, though it's true there were a lot of us, religious, lay Catholics. But later, in the meetings about trials, we made efforts 'not to be so Catholic.'"

Whatever the motivation, the meetings in the attic grew larger through the winter and on into spring, as concerned men and women met to decide on the focus for action.

The Twin Cities participants were inspired, if not directed, by the Catholic Worker movement and the Atlantic Life Community, and these "religious" brought a vision and spirituality to the anti-weapons movement. In opposing the war economy, St. Joseph's House sisters were also working to alleviate poverty and homelessness near at hand, on Franklin Avenue, "… issues of safety, homelessness, poverty—Gospel matters," Char said. "This became part of spirituality for us, doing the works of mercy *and* works of resistance." The sisters had been doing such works of mercy at Portland and Franklin Avenues for many decades, and St. Joseph's House, a respite from the pain of homelessness and abuse for many women and children, became Homes on Portland Enterprises, a multi-site housing conglomerate that has changed thousands of lives in South Minneapolis.

"Dorothy Day, founder of the Catholic Worker Movement, knew that her work involved 'comforting the afflicted and afflicting the comfortable," Char said. "The weapons makers said that the strength of arms is calcium building our nation up; we said no, it's a cancer eating our souls."

A weekly vigil at Honeywell headquarters began on Good Friday 1981 and became the focus for action and community formation. Over the next year, the revived Project had three dozen people coming to weekly meetings, and many of them shared the weekly vigil at Honeywell headquarters. Char remembered, "We'd have it in our weekly calendar to go to that place—we intended to have a little prayer and we'd bring along meditations or selections from the Bible to read." At Christmastime, the sisters sent out a news release that a "Peace on Earth" rally would be held at Honeywell, calling on "members of churches, peace organization, anti-nuclear groups, sympathizers with the Polish Solidarity union and other concerned individuals… [to join] a nationwide effort to challenge the assumption that nuclear strength means national security."

Such weekly vigils helped maintain a shared identity for thousands who worried about the arms race but needed a place to put their ideas into action. "After we had been there about a year," Char said, "we heard via the grapevine that Edson Spencer, CEO at Honeywell, had said we could 'stand there until hell freezes over as long as we did not cause trouble.'"

In Marv's opinion it was time to choose trouble. He threw down the gauntlet publicly in an April 21, 1982, editorial titled "The nuclear freeze and beyond." He praised the freeze movement for helping to raise mass consciousness, but emphasized that a single-issue campaign was inadequate. He spoke of racism, and of the plight of Native peoples who were dying of uranium poisoning, "the first phase of the nuclear cycle." Disenfranchised people of color who did connect with the peace movement came "as warriors from people battered daily by the violence of the status quo." In an eleven-point critique of the movement and suggestions for movement building, he named again the permanent war economy that was devastating the country; he said class consciousness was a necessary tool because the ruling class and the working class would "blow up together, but the American ruling class *does* administer the nuclear arms race and does profit enormously from it, taking us on its death trip."

"The movement must stand against production and use of conventional weapons like those made at Honeywell and used against Third World peoples in such countries as Vietnam and Angola." He issued the challenge that had made him an FBI target: "the movement must support those...like the Berrigans...who participate in acts of nonviolent civil disobedience, including sabotage of war material." Finally, "thousands of us must be prepared under certain circumstances to go to jail, as our brothers and sisters did in the civil rights, Vietnam, and nuclear power/environmental movements."

In June of 1982 Cruise and Pershing II missiles were on their way to Europe and people were moving to the streets: peace and anti-war groups traveled to New York to protest the nuclear arms race. Close to a thousand people came from Minneapolis for the June 12 peace rally in Central Park.

"This was the largest demonstration I had ever been in," Marv said. "I think about a million people marched from various points around New York to Central Park. Police reported no serious incidents of violence and most observers seemed enormously sympathetic." Two days later, the "Blockade the Bombmakers" nonviolent civil disobedience action confronted the U.N. missions of the five major nuclear powers. *Time* magazine writer Kurt Andersen reported, "All afternoon, righteous speech making was interspersed with big-time pop-music making … by Linda Ronstadt, Bruce Springsteen, and Jackson Browne; tweedy and middle-aged folk singers Peter, Paul and Mary; politically insistent balladeers Joan Baez and Pete Seeger." Then on Monday "a small, willful faction of Saturday's crowd planned to 'blockade the bombmakers,' shutting down for a day the U.N. offices of major nuclear powers. More typical … were concerned mainstreamers like New York Mayor Edward Koch. Said he: 'It's terrific to try to affect the conscience of the world. It's just regrettable they don't have a similar demonstration in Moscow.'" During the event 1,653 people were arrested.

Encouraged by this national example of mass resistance, Marv suggested that summer that "*we* begin a campaign of non-violent civil disobedience. I was the only one in the group who had extensive experience with this, but everyone was eager to try."

Within a few days of the June action, the *Washington Post* broke the story that Israel was using cluster bombs in Lebanon, and civilians, including children, were the targets. In the next weeks, Marv and the community made the link to Honeywell.

He outlined his process in a letter to potential supporters: to open "a small office and do day-to-day work on Honeywell. In the past two weeks I have spent $200 on phone calls nationwide and in Xerox. I went to the *Minneapolis Tribune* at least ten times trying to get them to cover a story that the *Times, Post, Philadelphia Inquirer, Village Voice, London Times*, television networks and others were covering, all without naming that these were *Honeywell* bombs…" The *Times* article had included a diagram of the cluster bomb and Marv believed the weapon was the type he carried with him. The *Tribune* put a reporter on the story, but the *Trib* editors stopped him. When Marv called, the editors said there was no proof the bombs were Honeywell's. Other local papers would not print the story.

Next, he went to the offices of Minneapolis Mayor Don Fraser, St. Paul's George Latimer, Senators Durenberger and Boschwitz, and Congressmen Sabo and Frenzel. Only Latimer seemed to be listening.

He called Congressman Lee Hamilton, chair of the House Mid-East Committee, about to begin hearings on Israeli use of U.S. weapons, and shared the evidence he had. Finally, on July 17, the Minneapolis paper carried a *New York Times* piece by Hedrick Smith, stating "members of Congress have warned that the use of cluster bombs, *primarily manufactured by Minneapolis-based Honeywell,* could be a politically sensitive issue because of widespread concern over civilian casualties in Lebanon." Not unreasonably, Marv credited his own tireless pursuit and pressure for the story's coming to light. He held up the timely "opportunity to get these damn terrorist bombs outlawed and banned."

Although first denying that the bombs were sold to Israel, Honeywell CEO Edson Spencer later admitted, "The U.S. government apparently provided Israel munitions which are manufactured, in part, by Honeywell." Honeywell spokespeople echoed the position the company took during the Vietnam war: "We think it proper that American companies like ours respond to the needs of our nation for defense."

In the next weeks, Marv learned of a chance to advance their cause; Film In the City and University Community Video were going to co-sponsor the U.S. premiere of Emile de Antonio's docudrama *In the King of Prussia,* which dramatized the trial of the Plowshares Eight. In the film, the Plowshares Eight portrayed themselves and, after finishing taping, reported to court for their imprisonment. It was a tremendous opportunity to witness nonviolent action as it happened and to be inspired by the example of people like the Berrigans.

"Our friend Neil Sieling worked with UCV and he invited us to collaborate in the film showing. We did outreach into the justice and peace community statewide. I called Dan Berrigan and told him we were working on the premiere." Dan said the reason the filmmakers chose Minneapolis for the opening was *because* of the Honeywell Project, even though it had been quiescent for a few years. Marv was delighted and lined up the guests for the showing and a Project rally: Berrigan himself, director de Antonio, and actor Martin Sheen, who played the trial judge in the film. Fame was just around the corner. Once again, Minneapolis and Marv would be center stage in the annals of activism.

18

You can't do that!

The Project undertook meticulous preparations for the world premiere of *In the King of Prussia*. At the same time, they made arrangements for the nonviolent civil disobedience that was to take place the following day. Marv knew he could recruit for the action during the evening program, and Project members contacted corporations, the police, the press, and the members of the peace and justice communities throughout the state, to let everyone know what was being planned. Sister Char Madigan later recalled, "I think we spent at least three months trying to pay attention to details."

The Project held a day-long retreat with nonviolence training sessions at a retreat center in western Wisconsin to promote bonding and to allow participants who wanted to risk arrest time to get to know and trust one another. "We drew a map of the Honeywell headquarters compound," Marv said, "and looked over all the entrances. We mused over what it would take to provoke an arrest in a disciplined and nonviolent fashion." The group did role-playing to simulate a blockade, "everyone taking turns playing cops, Honeywell security, and demonstrators."

For St. Joseph's House Sister Rita Foster, this retreat, more than the Washington Pentagon vigil, was a turning point. "What I mostly remember about my first action was that retreat ... the discussion of nonviolence was all very compelling, moving, but when Marv asked at the end: 'How many are willing to risk arrest?' I didn't raise my hand." She looked around at those faces, young, old, scared. She drove home quietly with Char, pondering the question. "I went home and thought. I recalled the Pentagon experience, that as I was leafleting I couldn't imagine doing anything more risky. Suddenly I thought, 'Of course I am [willing].' I surprised myself. It seemed so clear, such an appropriate thing to do and it was just fine."

The day of the premiere, November 3, finally arrived. "It was easy to get a full house," Marv said, with Martin Sheen attending. He played the Pennsylvania state judge who stacks the case in favor of the prosecution, and had also put some money into the film.

The Plowshares Eight were also well known to activists and a significant number of the Catholic faithful who kept abreast of their social action initiatives. Another activist "star"—Bernadette Devlin—would also be in town for the premiere. A former member of the British Parliament and fiery opponent of the British occupation of Northern Ireland, Devlin had taken many bullets in her body earlier in the year. Armed members of a Protestant paramilitary group had burst into her home near Belfast and seriously wounded both Devlin and her husband, Michael. Bernadette had recovered and was touring the United States, to enthusiastic responses from Catholic and Irish audiences. Marv proposed that she do a "walk-on and brief statement" of support and she had agreed. "We told her we were going to pass the hat at the performance for the Plowshares Eight Defense Committee."

Before the show the Project held a news conference with Dan, Martin Sheen, and Carl Kabat, and Marv gave out packets about the next day's action to media. He wasn't daunted when controversy reared its head: A co-sponsor, the president of Film in the City, spotted material in the packet about the Honeywell Project. Alarmed, he rushed to collect the packets back from reporters, saying to the co-sponsors, "We can't make announcements about the Honeywell Project action!" He insisted that they could not pass the hat for the Plowshares Defense either. He declared that Bernadette could not speak.

"I took him outside the room and said, 'What the hell is bugging you, man?' He said that film is *art* and has nothing to do with Honeywell and policy, and so forth. I said, 'Who the hell do you think Berrigan, de Antonio, and Sheen are? They chose Minneapolis because of the Honeywell Project, and all of them will join us at Honeywell in the morning. Relax.'" To encourage him to relax, Marv threatened to expose his fearfulness if he persisted with this behavior. "As one co-chair of this event I will get up on the stage and tell over a thousand people what you have done," he said. Somehow, a clash was averted and the program and media promotion went forward.

Honeywell, Marv later found out, had given money to Film in the City. "Top people from the corporation contacted the group, hysterically complaining about the connection of HP with the film premiere."

The premiere attracted 1,200 people to the Willey Hall Auditorium. Amid the buzz of conversation, an air of suppressed excitement vied with tension and worry about the event's success and the uncertainties of the next day's planned events. The showing didn't begin auspiciously. The 35-millimeter projector wasn't framed properly on the screen and there was a 45-minute delay. "It was so electrifying in the auditorium you could have put a blank image up there."

Then Marv walked Bernadette, limping, onto the stage. "When people began to recognize her they went nuts and gave her a standing ovation. She said her people supported our action at Honeywell and the 'Plowshares action done by the U.S. Irish-Catholic branch of the family.'" She ended with a brief statement about the struggle in Northern Ireland, many of whose members learned tactics from the U.S. Civil Rights Movement. "If you want to help our struggle in Northern Ireland," Bernadette concluded, in her warm Irish lilt, "make a revolution in the U.S. and get the bomb off *everyone's* back!"

Sheen, Berrigan, and de Antonio introduced the film, Berrigan outlining the reasons for the General Electric invasion the audience was about to see. "Being a moral person today involves some resistance," he said, "as it would have, say, if you'd lived next door to a crematorium under Hitler." The crackle of excitement in the capacious auditorium hushed. "We didn't want to be judged by history as 'good Germans' who were complicit in crime."

Theater professionals Martha and Paul Boesing sang a Bertoldt Brecht song. And after the film the Project did an hour of questions and answers, passed the buckets for donations, and explained the plan of action for the next day.

Dozens of wool-clad, hardy Minnesotans were at Honeywell headquarters by six a.m. the next morning. Marv was not an early riser but if he had to go out at that hour, he preferred it to be for breakfast! Still, he was usually one of the first at Honeywell vigils.

The day was exceptionally cold for early November, in the post-Halloween "thin" time, when traditionally spirits are near the border between the living and the dead. The barren trees seemed to cast ghostly shadows over the Honeywell parkland even as the dawn rose and the compound lights dimmed. Gigantic puppets from Sandy Spieler's In the Heart of the Beast Puppet and Mask Theater added to the eerie scene, looming like specters over the company plaza. Representing Prairie, Sky, River, and Forest, the figures symbolized the protesters' concern that "all of creation is held hostage to the arms race."

With mittened hands, the early group leafleted employees arriving for work. Larry Dunham, a railroad worker, passed out flyers that included photos of cluster bomb victims. One man wearing an expensive suit and driving a luxury car snatched the leaflet, glanced at it, then began to read. He looked at Larry, and with emotion welling in his voice said, "This is the horrible thing that my company does."

Daniel Berrigan soon joined the group outside Honeywell's front door. "It's only the people that are going to save the people," he said. "Our leadership is absolutely corrupt, they're in league with this" (pointing at the Honeywell tower). Honeywell management had decided to wait the protestors out and did not call the police. Martin Sheen spoke through a bullhorn to Honeywell employees inside, none of whom seemed to be working. Sheen turned to Marv saying, 'It's a wonderful demonstration of very alive people against these hideous weapons. My only problem is it's so damned cold here.' Someone rushed to get him a parka, hood, hat and leather mittens, making him look like a real Minnesotan.

On into the evening, the vigilers took turns occupying an annex leading from Honeywell's parking lot into the main building, where those who had been standing in the cold could escape from the biting wind. Marv left the protest about 6:00 pm for a second showing of the film at the University of Minnesota. About 600 people attended, and Marv updated the audience about what was going down at Honeywell.

Char and Rita were among the three dozen overnighters. They had left the main entrance, a mall extension of Fourth Avenue, and set up camp at the corridor entrance at Fifth Avenue. This annex was unheated, offering relief from the wind but little else. "Our supporters brought us sleeping bags and food for a long stay. Martha Boesing was there, so we had some singing, lots of talking. Ken Tilsen was there, and also his mother-in-law, Meridel [Le Sueur]," Char said.

"They didn't stay the whole time," Rita remembered. "Meridel was a grand activist and a trooper, but she was probably in her eighties then. She needed a cane, she was kind of heavy…"

Char demurred. "We all had our needs. There was plenty of food, even hot soup! But you know, mostly junk food." She broke into laughter, recalling: "No facilities! This freezing cement floor, we hardly slept, and down some stairs … we put two cans side by side and labeled them "His" and "Hers."

The long winter night passed, and in the bitter cold of the next morning, at 7:00 am, thirty-six activists walked to the front door of Honeywell headquarters. They wrapped a chain around the door handles and padlocked it; someone held a homemade sign that read "The Bomb Factory is Closed." Rita laughed, "They locked the inside doors against us, of course; so we locked them in, too."

A hundred-odd people returned in the morning to aid the overnighters by blocking other doors until the police arrived. Honeywell management had lost patience and security guards arrived to explain that the demonstrators were illegally occupying private property, inhibiting their employees from entering work. Minneapolis police arrested the thirty-six at the front doors, put them in squad cars, and took them downtown. After a couple of hours in holding cells, the group was relieved when sheriff's bailiffs herded them into an arraignment courtroom. "I was handcuffed to Father Harvey Egan, Pastor of St. Joan of Arc Catholic Church," Marv said. "I looked up at tall, aristocratic Harvey: 'Harvey,' I asked, 'Does this mean we're going steady?'" Harvey said, "Sure. I will announce it at Mass on Sunday.'"

Harvey Egan had been a Catholic Worker as a young priest, and in the years to come would conduct an early morning mass before actions, at St. Stephen's Catholic Church, a few blocks away from the Honeywell campus.

"Harvey preached the Social Gospel," said Marv, and sometimes called God "she." He did a scathing indictment from the pulpit of U.S. foreign and domestic policy. He brought vibrant music and song

into the mass, and in the eighties built St. Joan's into a thriving community. Father Egan offered the pulpit on occasion to people the likes of Marv to give a social justice homily. In fact, Marv claimed, Gloria Steinem had even done a homily once, "which upset the diocesan bishop greatly."

For the local media, the arrests did not cause much of a stir. *Star/ Tribune* newsman Jay Weiner wrote to his publisher, copying Frank Wright, complaining that "The S & T ... covered the demonstration with six paragraphs buried on the last page of the Shelter section," whereas the *New York Times* "must have considered it nationally significant" because it gave the arrests some space, and the British lefty weekly *The Guardian* devoted a large piece to it, headed "Bomb factory blockaded; Trident foes arrested." "If this paper wants to be a good local paper, it's going to have to realize that people other than state senators and Pillsbury execs live here. ... People demonstrate because issues affect their lives, issues that affect the lives of many of our readers... . When 36 people in our city get busted for trespassing on the grounds of a local corporation tied into a war machine, that's news. And you don't have to be an Einstein to know that." The publisher's response is not recorded, but for a time the local coverage improved.

The arrestees came to trial in February 1983 before Judge Michael Davis, a newcomer to the bench, presiding over his second criminal trial. Davis was a good friend of Linda Gallant, one of the Project's pro bono attorneys along with Ken Tilsen and Mark Wernick.

In front of a courtroom packed with supporters and media people, the six-person jury, though not unmoved by the testimony of eloquent religious and committed defendants, found them guilty as charged. Even the prosecutors were disappointed: Surrounded during the trial by so many nuns, assistant city attorney Peter Ginder said that he felt like "the lion being thrown to the Christians."

Judge Davis sentenced the defendants to pay a $100 fine or collect an equal amount worth of groceries for food shelves or perform 20 hours of other community service. Most gave to food shelves, pleased with the creative sentence. However, Harvey Egan refused the sentence, saying his life—indeed, the ideal life—*was* one of community service. His decision was based on moral principles and he "had not committed a crime." It was Honeywell Corporate management that should be in the dock on war crimes charges. "The judge sweated but did not send him to jail on contempt," Marv said. "We paid the $100 for Harvey" and he had to accept the community decision.

Worldwide, the calls for nuclear disarmament grew louder, but U.S. policymakers were unmoved. New forms of protest were needed, Marv thought. Vietnam-era demonstrations and proxy initiatives had been effective to a degree, but the time had come to "up the ante." Yes, but how?

Organized religious channels, though not the institutional hierarchies, were developing networks of activists who saw the need for self-discipline and sacrifice. Harvey Egan, Dave Dellinger, the Berrigans, sisters of St. Joseph of Carondelet, and Franciscan sisters fired up parishioners in Minneapolis and St. Paul. This new movement was not wholly Catholic: Local Quakers, CALC pastors and lay leaders, Wiccans and other activists with spiritual roots were also involved.

The peace movement in the Twin Cities was also gaining support from Women against Military Madness, a feminist anti-war group that joined forces with the Project in 1982. Because it was a tax-exempt group, it could not sponsor civil disobedience, but some members were also strong Project supporters. "The Honeywell Project *was* the peace movement in the middle 1980s," Char Madigan recalls. "Many groups began to form around such issues as poverty, racism, Central America, police brutality. The Project was able to harness energies of people across groups—not only us nuns."

Rita Foster agreed, "There was George Crocker and the farmers on the power line issues, Prairie Island nuclear issues, Native Americans, the AIM people."

"Back then Marv impressed people with the idea of diversity," Char added. "For the rallies he'd bring in national figures to show how oppression tied in with corporate greed and bad policy. Dennis Banks came, Vernon and Clyde Bellecourt." So many peace workers were involved for spiritual reasons in the eighties—doctors, teachers, housing and women's advocates like Char and Rita, Rita Steinhagen, and Sharon Rice Vaughan; Esther and Jim Ouray of Heart of the Beast; Native American leaders like Bea Swanson and Larry Cloud Morgan.

The catalyst was Marv, Char emphasizes: "I think the whole thing, the whole period of arrests and trials, comes down to Marv's leadership, inspiration, and vision. The idea of training people for nonviolence, figure out what to do in changing situations, to remain nonviolent, that took work."

Marv organized the rallies as well as the resistance actions, bringing in national figures to encourage and inspire people. "And always music, people singing, the arts—that was important to him," Rita said. "And education was essential, to show, as he said, the corporate evil and what we should do about it."

Evil? Marv never minced words in describing Honeywell's corporate behavior. "Oh, the language!" Char shook her head, "It was clear. And it was consistent. The name-calling sometimes went too far for me ..." Marv's more polite epithets were descriptive: Honeywell officers were "murderers, liars and thieves." Char and Marv had a running battle over the name-calling, trying to differentiate between what was accurate if indecorous, and what was out of bounds.

Nonviolence trainings for the next action began in March of 1983. On Friday, March 18, Robert Bly did a benefit poetry reading at St. Stephen's Catholic Church in Minneapolis. A second orientation on April 7 preceded the April 10-14 showings of *In the King of Prussia*. On

Martha Boesing and Meridel LeSueur. (Photo by Mark Jensen.)

Saturday, April 16, Project members conducted a larger training session at the Peoples' Center on Riverside Avenue, on the West Bank campus of the University of Minnesota, for more than a hundred people who were considering risking arrest.

This time around, both national and local papers covered the preparations and training for the action. *Nuclear Times,* a Midwest publication, carried a feature article "Behind the Honeywell Blockade," with an "arresting" photo of Marv. The article's descriptions of the meticulous planning, contingency discussion, wardrobe questions, and scenarios for arrest had a tongue-in-cheek tone: "The audience watched intently as a discussion leader pointed with her stick to each entrance and outlined the tactics of 'Plan A.' There was also Plan B, Plan C, and Plan D." The last paragraph was more serious: "But mostly the talk was of finding the best way to challenge the weapons work…, of raising the consciousness of Minneapolis, of connecting the next day's action to civil disobedience movements around the country, and above all, of carrying off the action in a spirit of nonviolence."

On April 18, 1983, the mass demonstration at Honeywell vied with European protests for turnout. The previous evening's program had featured poetry by Meridel LeSueur, who claimed, "You couldn't live in this century and be for anything that is true and just and not go to jail occasionally." Folk musicians Judy Larson and Bill Hinkley performed as they had done in April 1970. Phillip Berrigan, recently released from prison for his part in the King of Prussia action, exhorted the audience to "lead the retreat from the nuclear brink, or otherwise we must question our very worthiness to live."

In the course of this action, another gentle but outspoken woman, a member of Women against Military Madness, came to the attention of local and national media. Minneapolis Police Chief Tony Bouza's English-born wife Erica had decided to risk arrest. "I never did protest against the Vietnam war," she said, "and I should have." Like Erica, most of those arrested on April 18 had never been arrested before.

The night before the action, Marv remembered, Tony Bouza had a dinner for his command structure. After dinner, Erica announced that she intended to risk arrest with the Honeywell Project in the morning. "This must have shocked the officers," Marv crowed, "though Bouza had done other shocking things since Mayor Fraser had appointed him, like marching with Erica in the Gay Pride Parade."

Tony by all reports was intensely proud of his wife, but he could not refrain from his signature unconventional comments and jibes. During the arrests, a reporter rushed to the chief, shouting "Your cops have just arrested your wife."

"Yes, yes, I know. I want that one taken away for years. She is dangerous."

Nonplussed, the newsman added, "Chief, there seems to be a friendly relationship between the cops and protesters."

"That's because the police dogs and cattle prods didn't arrive on time. I'm just another manifestation of mindless fascist repression. The dogs will devour all of them, including Erica."

That morning, several people were moved to risk arrest by stepping over a yellow rope, for the first time: Gloria Cushing, mother and freelance writer, was interviewing a woman who planned to risk arrest and suddenly wondered, "What am I doing here? The interview is not enough. I must join them." Bea Swanson, an Anishinabe grandmother who did anti-poverty work, came to observe and was so impressed with the demeanor of the participants she decided on the spot to join them.

Marv remembered, too, being arrested with "Moira Moga, a good friend of the Berrigans. Moira had been arrested at the Pentagon and was exceptionally clear-thinking and eloquent about why she did civil disobedience. We were released a couple of hours later on our own recognizance from booking and returned to Honeywell. Moira's eyes lit up as she said to a small group of us, 'We can do it again. Let's go.' I saw this phosphorescent light in Moira's eyes and followed her."

Other notables arrested that day were Meridel LeSueur, "who arrived in scarlet slippers, clutching a rose and walking with a cane"; and 14-year old Jennifer Boesing, who had parental permission, since her mother, playwright Martha Boesing, was arrested with her. Jennifer was not the youngest, though; Sasha Isaacs-Andrusko was 11.

Marv was usually the first to offer himself for arrest, Sisters Char and Rita often the last, to "sort of keep tabs on people," Char said, as well as on the numbers and the demeanor of both the participants and the police. "Oh, sure, the arrests were coordinated, as much as we could. Honeywell Project began to have an office, where the Core Group, the coordinating committee, would plan the actions and trials." For a time the office was at 33rd and Hennepin, then at 1929 Riverside on the West Bank, the building known as the Meridel LeSueur Center.

The nightly television news and papers the next day highlighted the arrest of the wife of the Minneapolis police chief along with 138 others and that Chief Bouza had administered the arrests.

At a mass arraignment, the demonstrators came before Judge Robert Forsyth, former Republican State Chair. When Erica Bouza's name was called, the judge remarked that they had recently been to a dinner party together. Erica acknowledged that she would not expect any special treatment: "I'm here because I *have* to save your children and mine, not because I want to but because I *had* to. The arms build-up between the U.S. and Russia has got to stop. It's crazy. Protesting at Honeywell is not un-American. It's trying to save the world from nuclear destruction."

Erica, Karen Hanson, and other women from their WAMM affinity group who pled guilty, refused to pay the small fine assessed; rather than jail them on contempt the judge said, "If you return to Honeywell next time, I will send all of you to jail."

On June 3, the first thirty-six who had pled not guilty came up for trial. "Fathers and sons, mothers and daughters gave testimony that read like Zen poetry; people condensed their lives and motivation to ten minutes!" Marv said.

During the trial, attorney Ken Tilsen put Marv on the witness stand for more than half an hour, displaying his cluster bomb. At the end of the testimony, the judge recessed the trial and ordered Ken and Marv into his chambers. "Marv," the judge ordered, "I want you to take that bomb out of my courtroom. There's no way to tell if it's armed."

"Judge, I glued the two halves of the bomblet together myself. There is no fuse inside. I have boarded planes with this bomb."

The judge shuddered. "Either give it to the bailiff or leave the building."

"Okay, if he returns it to me at the end of the trial."

The agreement was made—but not kept.

The jury deliberated for four hours. As the verdict "not guilty" was announced, the courtroom erupted into unabashed cheers and crying. "We had cast a reasonable doubt concerning guilt, in light of a phrase in the Minnesota trespass law about 'claim of right.'" The city prosecutor asserted that the claim of right provision referred to a belief that a person has the owners' permission to be on a certain property. Defense attorneys and several defendants argued that Honeywell's production of cluster bombs and parts for nuclear weapons provided a good-faith claim of right to sit down in front of the Honeywell doors.

"I was awed by people's total commitment," said the jury forewoman, a retail buyer. "I gave them a lot of credit for standing by their beliefs."

The bailiff disappeared right after the verdict, Marv complained, and no one seemed to know how to reclaim Marv's property. The next day, President Reagan spoke at a fundraiser for Senator Rudy Boschwitz at the Lexington Hotel in Minneapolis. "We were mounting a large demonstration expressing many grievances," Marv said. "So that morning I decided to go to the sheriff's department to get my bomb. They would not return it. I then went to the Lexington, cursing, one hour early. I saw two Secret Service agents standing in front of the hotel looking at me. They crossed the street. 'Marv, I am Major so and so.

This is Captain so and so. Do you have your cluster bomb on you?'"

Exasperated, Marv growled, "No, the bailiff took it from me and the sheriff's department won't give it back."

Unconvinced, the major persisted, "Would you mind emptying out your pockets for us?"

"Unless I have exceptionally large testicles, you can see I don't have a bomblet in my pants pocket." But he complied. "They cordially thanked me. I said, 'Gentlemen, there seems to be excessive concern about this empty bomb. Don't you have any concern about the live ones that have been going off every day all over Indochina, killing men, women and children, and it's eight years after the war ended?'"

"Sorry, Marv, we can't comment about that. Have a nice day."

But the contretemps wasn't over. "Next a Minneapolis cop crossed the street with a dog, a bomb-sniffing German Shepherd. I knew some Germans hated Jews and was on my guard. The dog, too, could not locate a bomb on me."

Six thousand people demonstrated that afternoon in front of the Lexington. The next day, Marv returned to the sheriff's office, and once again the sheriff would not return the bomb. "I then went to the head judge and told her my sorry story. She wrote a letter to the sheriff ordering him to return my property. He would not. My only recourse was to walk right past the secretary in the office of U.S. Federal Attorney Jim Rosenbaum, whose brother Ron had been in Honeywell Project during Vietnam.

"Jim, the m--f--rs stole my cluster bomb and I want it back. Help me."

"What the hell are you talking about?"

Marv explained. Jim then called an FBI agent into his office, and told him the story, emphasizing that "everyone knows Marv carries empty cluster bombs with him to show people. Get it back for him." The agent explained that he was aware there was an ongoing "little investigation" of the incident.

Two weeks later, Jim called Marv to tell him he had terrible news. "The sheriff's department blew up your bomb, they dynamited it."

"They dynamited the empty bomb?"

"Yes, I'm sorry."

Five years later, the American Civil Liberties Union sent him "ten whole pages on this wild scene from my FBI file."

The organization around arrests and trials was not hierarchical. "The Core Committee collected names and contact information, arranged legal support, and made suggestions to the arrestees," Char Madigan recalled, "but each affinity group, each individual, made decisions about strategies regarding arrests, arraignments, and pretrials. Affinity groups often formed at the point of arrest, sometimes in a paddy wagon or holding cell. Friends were encouraged to stay close by to keep track of one another. The Project urged, but could not direct, protestors to participate in jury trials, give personal witness, and seek to sway juries. The National Lawyers Guild and *pro bono* lawyers met with Project members to assist in preparations for court appearances and jury selection.

Marv and Richard Seymour strategize, 1983. (photo by Mark Jensen.)

Sometimes the actions themselves took hours. In the early demonstrations, "Richard Seymour rode his bike around, remember?" Rita offered, "he was our communication system, he biked between groups when people sat at different doors, to help us make changes in plans."

Richard also helped computerize the office. Char remembered that in the early 1980s he would put statements at the head of computer screens like "the 719th day of Leonard Peltier's imprisonment."

During the summer of 1983, the Livermore Action Group called for an International Day of Nuclear Disarmament; more than 1,200 arrests were made at nuclear sites and weapons companies around the country. Honeywell Project members Marian Mollin and Richard

Seymour took part in the mass protest at Lawrence Livermore Laboratory in Livermore, California, and were detained in tents for two weeks with their fellow protestors. Hundreds of committed, diverse activists lived in close quarters preparing for trials and possible jail time, an experience that provided intensive training in forbearance and in affinity group organization. When they returned, Richard and Marian designed a Project handbook modeled after the Livermore Action Group and the Women's Peace Encampment at the Seneca Army Depot in New York, where Marian had been an organizer.

The handbook gave a history of the Project, a brief description of Honeywell's weapons, and the goals of the October 1983 action. The book noted that supporters differed in their motivations for understandings of nonviolence: for some, it was a political tactic that could give strategic advantages against an opponent; for others, nonviolence was inherent in "a way of life" or a system of beliefs. But all were welcome to participate in this nonviolent confrontation of Honeywell's murderous enterprise.

The Project began organizing for the October 1983 action in mid-May of that year, even before the trials for the previous action had been held. The core goals remained the same: 1) Stop research, development, production, and use of anti-personnel cluster bombs and land mines and guidance systems for nuclear rockets and all other weapons of war. 2) Develop peace conversion, without loss of jobs, to goods and services necessary for human survival. 3) Build a force for worker and community control of Honeywell and the nation's corporations.

The fall focus that year was on guidance systems for Pershing and Cruise nuclear short-range missiles; in October the U.S. was to ship these weapons to Western Europe. Nonviolence training workshops were held in early September. Marv and Project members gave the recruits a synopsis of the fourteen-year history (from Vietnam War days to 1983), and laid out the scenario for the day's action and what its legal implications would be. Increasing numbers were coming to training sessions and Marv believed the demonstration would be large and powerful. Ninety-five percent of the workshop attendees had never been arrested. "When I asked them why they might risk arrest, the answer was 'my children and the children of the earth are in danger.'"

More than 2,000 men, women, and children were at the Honeywell campus at dawn on October 24. A ritual began that day, a spiral dance that participants found appealing and worth repeating: People joined hands and slowly walked from 28th Street to 26th Street and then doubled back; every demonstrator at some point would face every other.

"We cautioned people, 'Don't lock arms. If an employee comes your way, be friendly and firm: Make them step over you." The idea was that employees might understand the subliminal message that "management steps over human life by making these weapons." The Project invariably chose corporate headquarters or a stockholder's meeting for their action, so that they would not come into direct conflict with union members. The bulk of responsibility lay on management, who made the major decisions and profited highly.

Tony Bouza was on the scene, with Lieutenant Bob Lutz as main commander of street officers. As in April, Tony drove Erica to corporate headquarters. Just as the action was about to begin, Erica came to Marv and declared, "I'm going to risk arrest."

"I embraced her," Marv said. "I knew Judge Forsyth would send her and her WAMM friends to jail."

The protests that day by the Project took place in conjunction with more than 140 antinuclear protests in other places around the country spearheaded by a Philadelphia group, October Actions to stop Euromissiles; at the same time, a million Europeans were protesting the NATO deployment of Pershing II and Cruise missiles.

Members of the Project prepared a sturdy ladder and an efficient process for helping people over the fence. More than two thousand people showed up, forming a human chain around the Honeywell building in south Minneapolis; the arrests lasted well into the afternoon, surprising both the organizers and the police. Most people lined up to be placed in vans or buses, though more than a few expressed their beliefs by "noncooperation" with the police and were dragged or carried. Five hundred seventy-seven people, the largest mass arrest in Minnesota history, was the tally by late afternoon.

Robert Bly was present, as was Mark Paquette, a young man who had directed Honeywell's production of guidance systems for Pershing

II nuclear missiles. Mark had attended a workshop after seeing a powerful documentary film on the U.S. bombing of Hiroshima and Nagasaki. He'd asked himself "Why do I participate in this nuclear madness?" He quit his job just before the action and spoke to Marv about his decision. Marv asked that he speak to reporters, and a Minneapolis paper did a short piece on Mark's motivation for risking arrest. "While I can't hope to change the world unilaterally... I can take the first step by withdrawing my support from the system of wars which ensnares all countries," he wrote in his resignation letter. His conscience had prompted him to "research the impact of a nuclear explosion, and he became horrified by what he read."

Ruth Youngdahl Nelson, religious author and member of an influential Lutheran family of pastors and politicians, came with her son Jon. A peace and justice advocate, she had been arrested the previous year with her son, Jonathan, while trying to block the first Trident submarine docking in Bangor, Washington. Standing atop a small rubber raft in the direct aim of a water cannon, she confronted the seaman pointing it, "Oh, no, young man! Not in *my* America!"

Though she had undergone cancer surgery a few days earlier, Ruth arrived at Honeywell in a wheelchair pushed by her son Jon. She apologized for not having the strength to be arrested.

Chief Bouza believed in going slow. By 10:00 am, police had made perhaps 250 arrests, taking people in rented city buses to the Minneapolis Convention Center, where Bouza had hot coffee and donuts for demonstrators *and* police, contrary to later critical reports. "He paid for them out of his speaking fees," Marv said. "I saw him sitting at the bus stop alone, legs crossed, looking like General Kutuzov from Tolstoy's *War and Peace* asleep on his horse at the battle of Borodino, nothing left to do—the forces were in motion and would play themselves out. I felt the same way."

Marv walked over to Tony, mindful of the reporters watching. As soon as the two were spotted chatting amicably, several media people "ran over popping light bulbs and shooting their TV cameras." Marv pointed out a young woman carrying a baby, standing by the chainlink fence. He told Tony, "She is 26. Her child's name is David, 18 months old. They were the first two to be arrested." Without missing a

beat, Bouza replied, "That's not a baby. That's a midget. We have been looking for him for ten years." A lot of people criticized the chief for his irrepressible one-liners, Marv remembered, "but the media lapped it up. I thought he was the Lenny Bruce of cops."

Marv was arrested about 10:30 a.m., confident that the steering committee could lead the rest of the day. Tony Bouza left at noon. Late in the afternoon, Lieutenant Lutz ordered the main gate opened; a phalanx of police rushed out and maced the crowd sitting in front of the fence. An affinity group including many children from the Children's Theater "ran into the heavily trafficked street rubbing their eyes. Char Madigan lay on the ground like a spread-eagled angel," Marv said. "A cop stood over her and shot a stream of mace into her face. Another cop knocked the glasses off a sister and deliberately stepped on them, crushing them. The cops cleared a path" through the demonstrators so that a waiting group of remaining executives could enter the compound.

The action was over by 3:30 p.m. "We learned later that only 15 percent of Honeywell headquarters personnel ever made it into work. We had closed down their nerve center for an entire day."

The media covered the protest, although they concentrated their attention on the second arrest of the "chief's wife" and the acerbic humor of her husband. Reporters followed Erica and Tony through her plea, conviction, and jailing. Not everyone in the public arena was sympathetic: Erica was put into solitary confinement because of telephoned death threats. Apparently unfazed, Tony told the papers that he had inspected her cell, ordering it to be "painted lavender with chintz curtains hung," that he was "humiliated by my wife's lawlessness," and that he would "change his name, disavow her and escape to Mato Grosso of the Amazon jungle in Brazil."

The mass arrests received notice in other official quarters; Attorney Elliot Rothenberg, a former Republican State Department official and executive of a legal foundation, filed a $500,000 suit against the Project, WAMM, the Minnesota Women's Peace Encampment, and Minnesota SANE Freeze. Rothenberg deplored the money being spent on the demonstrations (and trials and prison) and claimed the protesters had abandoned democracy. The suit eventually was rejected, a Hennepin County judge stating that it was not based on valid legal theory.

The literature distributed by the Project during the protest focused on the fallacy of calling defense contracts an economic boon. It quoted from U.S. Department of Labor Statistics to the effect that almost any category of civilian employment would produce more work than defense production. Action goals remained the same, but a further objective was added—to raise contributions for medical care of cluster bomb victims in Lebanon and Indochina.

The Honeywell public relations department struck back. The company put out a full page ad in the *Star Tribune* depicting a high fence emblazoned with a No Trespassing sign; a sad little caption read: "We didn't want to build this fence." The text defended the military contractor, stating that nuclear weapons constituted a 'political' question ("It is getting the most serious attention in Washington and other political capitals") and that question should be addressed to elected officials, not the company.

19

Trials and Tribulation

For the faith-based wing of the Project, the rhythm of demonstrations was like that of a liturgical year. Once each spring and fall, and at other special times commemorating a religious holiday or iconic day like Martin Luther King's or Gandhi's birthday, people came together for education, then action. Marv and the core committee planned pre-action rallies to pull together streams and strains of the movement. Rallies highlighted education, inspiration, and cultural engagement through films, music, and entertainment—often satirical comedy.

At the demonstration site, whether at Honeywell or a stockholders' meeting, protesters would be ticketed or arrested, but Tony Bouza's department soon decided that issuing tickets was futile in stemming the tide of demonstrators, who might return to blockade or become a nuisance. After the numbers swelled in the 1983 protests, the Project encouraged demonstrators to walk with the police instead of remaining seated or going limp, out of consideration for the officers' (and the protestors') backs.

The trials became another hub of activity and an organizing tool. Not every affinity group was as lucky as the first set to be tried. If they were acquitted, Project members made the event an occasion for celebration, but verdicts of "guilty" soon came to be an expected part of the struggle. Marv advised nonviolent trainees, "If you can't do the time, don't do the crime."

Strategies around pleas, arraignments, jury selection, and engagement in the process differed. Most hoped to use the court as a public forum to put on trial Honeywell's profiting by deadly weapons and to gain broader support for disarmament. Guilty pleas at arraignment meant that the arrestees waived their rights to a jury trial and would be sentenced by a judge. Some chose to witness to their beliefs by exercising their right to make a statement before sentencing.

Not everyone wanted to plead their case before a jury; not everyone believed that a legal case was possible; and not everyone was willing to offer himself or herself for prison witness. The differences made for lively and intense debate. But in the mainstream, knowledge about the corporation and its moneymaking products grew with the trials and publicity. In her first trial, Char said, the judge asked the jury pool if anyone had heard of the Honeywell Project. No one had. "When they were asked the same question at the third trial, the entire jury pool laughed."

The Project initially drew supporters from broad networks of religious and secular pacifists and feminist peace activists, many of whom were inspired by women's peace camp movements and cultural collectives. But with the spread of information about the danger of nuclear annihilation and increased nervousness about Reagan's Star Wars policy, the anti-weapons movement grew. Writers such as Richard Falk, Joanna Macy, and Jonathan Schell gave technical analysis and cultural context to the arms race, sometimes in excruciating detail, and a new generation of films—*War Games, Testament,* and *The Day After,* for example—provided graphic scenarios that went well beyond *Fail-Safe, Dr. Strangelove,* and other films on similar themes from earlier times.

The Day After, a made-for-TV effort, portrayed a fictional nuclear war between the United States/NATO and the Soviet Union/Warsaw Pact, with technical realism and emotional content unmatched in its time. The film, seen by at least half the U.S. population, provoked a good deal of controversy and brought a new wave of recruits to the antinuclear movement. President Reagan was reported to have written in his diary that the film depressed him, and in 1987, during the era of Gorbachev's *glasnost* and *perestroika* reforms, it was shown on Soviet television. The filmmaker later received a note from the Reagan administration suggesting that the movie had played a part in the Reykjavik treaty.

Meanwhile, scientist Carl Sagan and conservative pundit William F. Buckley debated on a *Nightline* show, Sagan offering the famous lines that the U.S. and Soviet Union were like two adversaries waist deep in gasoline, one holding five matches and one with three.

W hen Marv talked about nuclear disarmament, he emphatically linked weapons production and the Reagan administration's escalating militarism to issues of poverty, homelessness, and urban decay. "Location, location"—a mantra not only for real estate—guided the Project's work for peace and justice in the neighborhood. Honeywell's headquarters in south Minneapolis was only a few blocks away from St. Joseph's house, sandwiched between busy freeways and crumbling, run-down buildings. The Sisters of St. Joseph of Carondelet tried to focus on relationships between local/global poverty and the war machine's destructive profit taking. Marv's friendship with Native American activists, many of whom lived in the nearby Phillips neighborhood, and his emphasis on expanding the diversity of the movement were similarly interrelated.

Not all of the demonstrators were attuned to the justice-peace linkage, but most of those who stood for trial were anxious to make a moral witness. Pro bono lawyers like Ken Tilsen and Peter Thompson and their offices provided invaluable resources and education in collective action.

Seventy percent of the trials ended with convictions, but the hung juries, suspended sentences, and the rare acquittals were occasions for celebration. If they hadn't previously joined affinity groups, as people prepared for trials they formed themselves into groups. The Sisters were one of the earliest sets and comprised the central group holding weekly vigils at Honeywell Plaza. Another collective called "Water on the Moon," a mysterious metaphor for something desired but not existing, was made up of Project organizers, core supporters, and office staff. A third, larger affinity group that generated later subgroups were women who were part of Women against Military Madness and their partners or spouses. To distinguish themselves from WAMM and to be inclusive, they called themselves People against Military Madness.

The affinity groups did not always disband once the trials were over; the "big three" mentioned above continued or reformed throughout the 1980s and beyond, morphing into working collectives, political campaigns, and social sets that helped to sustain the spirit of activism in Minnesota.

Groups usually went their own ways in deciding how trials should be conducted and actions planned. These decentralized configurations sometimes threatened Project cohesion. For example, feminist and faith-based affinity groups rejected hierarchical decision-making, and they suspected most of the decisions were Marv's. Again, while Marv favored mass, coordinated demonstrations to maximize the pressure on Honeywell, Christian faith-based groups wished to schedule actions according to the liturgical calendar and favored small-group actions of witness.

Marv sought representation from as many groups as possible on the Honeywell Project Council, which would make decisions by consensus. The loose organizational structure worked well during the initial mobilization of the Honeywell protests, but in later stages disagreements were more likely to emerge. Char Madigan put it succinctly: "With every action, there were some fights, some power struggles—then peace would come—we were all haunted."

Other troubles hounded the Project. There were disputes over strategies, the quality of nonviolence, and the delicate balance of disruption and effectiveness. Fears of provocateurs, FBI infiltration, repression, and reactive violence were rife. Many complained of the decision-making structure, with Marv and a committee of cronies in front and a diverse collection of small affinity groups tagging along.

The Project decided to have two monthly meetings, one for "process," during which the organization's own structure and methods would be scrutinized and discussed by the members themselves, and the other for planning specific events and actions. (Across town, in a longhouse constructed beside war contractor Sperry Corporation, the Minnesota Women's Peace Encampment, a 'sister' project targeting Sperry, had recently adopted a similar meeting structure.)

Marv took the brunt of criticism about leadership styles and financial support. Following the large demonstrations of 1983, the Project cut its office staff to two part-time workers owing to a lack of funding, and moved its office to a supporter's basement. At this point, emotionally drained by the turmoil and fighting depression, Marv temporarily stepped back.

Richard Seymour remained as staff, producing a newsletter (*The Circulator*) and organizing small vigils and demonstrations. He also worked with a legal collective to convince Project members and the courts to arrange conjoined rather than individual trials, to clear the logjam of cases in Hennepin county. A year after the demonstration of October 1983, forty-one protesters had been convicted, forty-five had been acquitted, and nearly five hundred individuals remained in the system. Under the collective plan, affinity groups would name representatives to testify, select a jury, and present opening or closing statements in a group trial. All defendants would abide by the jury's decision. The courts accepted this plan of action, and the affinity groups were pleased with a strategy that seemed to allow both participation and solidarity.

The Sisters of St. Joseph continued to lead weekly vigils, attended by the faithful as well as the strategically minded, who believed that consistent pressure, even if small, was a moral necessity. On December 29, 1984, to commemorate the Feast of Holy Innocents, protestors walked onto the Honeywell Plaza and decorated a tree with pictures of mothers and children. Fifteen were arrested. Earlier in the day, six women poured their own blood on baby clothing in the lobby of the federal building. Federal Judge Miles Lord refused to order an arrest but sent federal marshals to protect them from harassment.

Affinity groups like PAMM grew stronger internally, enjoying an independence of action though they relied on Marv for information and analysis. For these groups, religious symbolism, such as pouring blood, displaying crosses, digging graves, and commemorating holy days continued to be important. A commitment to 'way of life' nonviolence pulled in many who could no longer sit on the sidelines of the arms race. Small group actions were numerous, many organized by PAMM groups. Hennepin county judges began to dismiss cases and in bench trials acquit defendants on technicalities. To save court time and perhaps discourage "moral witness" devotees, prosecutors began to reduce the charges from a misdemeanor to a petty misdemeanor, which did not entail jail time and excluded trial by jury. By May of the next year, the backlog had been reduced through group trials, with eight group acquittals, fourteen convictions, and twenty-eight dismissals.

Though Marv himself was less often on trial, he was often in the courtroom. In his darkest times, he could not withdraw completely. He considered that his work of stinging the corporate and ruling class was bound to continue through the judicial system. His ethos *was* on trial in the witness of each of his friends. Besides, "the scene fascinated me. The testimony was always riveting, people expressing their core beliefs. The judge, the prosecutors, the jury—they had to be affected by what they heard."

I first encountered Marv at the Sperry Women's Peace Camp in the spring of 1984. The weather was bearable and we were outside without parkas. The occasion was a group community meeting; Marv was recruiting and advising. People sat on folding chairs and someone's discarded couch in the open field, a property adjacent to Highway 5 that belonged to the highway department. The area, about the size of a football field, was high on a bluff overlooking the confluence of the Minnesota and Minnesota Rivers. We had the Minnesota Department of Transportation's permission to "camp" there, between the weapons corporation and the highway, after our headquarters teepee had been ejected from Sperry's property.

Because the overlook was a native sacred site, we had also secured permission from Women of All Red Nations, which was more important to us. The Peace Camp founders concentrated on Sperry because Marv and the Project had Honeywell "under control." There were crossover people: Some of the camp women went to Honeywell demonstrations, and during 1984 a few Project women attended Sperry protests. The camp endured for one calendar year, from October 1, 1983 to October 1, 1984, and during that brief but intense period women who had been excluded from mainstream and activist leadership were empowered. When the camp finally closed, for a variety of reasons (not the least of which were Sperry-Unisys negotiations with Honeywell), many women were already working with the Project.

Marv seemed to draw energy from the camp's lively rituals, adopted from Native American, Jewish, and "earth-centered" or pagan spiritual traditions. He also attended larger camp events and discussions and would update people and recruit for Honeywell actions, though he wasn't involved in our planning or decision making.

Before the camp closed, a pair of Catholics came on the scene

in spectacular fashion. On August 10, Plowshares action volunteers John LaForge and Barbara Katt, disguised as quality control inspectors, entered Sperry Corporation. They poured blood and hammered on two computers designed to provide navigation information for Trident submarines and F4G fighter-bombers. While awaiting arrest, they presented a citizens' indictment of Sperry officers for war crimes. They had acted without the prior knowledge of Peace Camp leaders, but after the event they had our enthusiastic support: founder Nancy Mosier exclaimed, "I have to meet this *woman*!"

In a packed courtroom, after some preliminary singing (with occasional song duels between Christian hymns and Peace Camp favorites), Katt and LaForge were allowed to present a defense of necessity. They argued that they were faced with a choice of evils, whether to obey the letter of the law, or try to prevent a more egregious violation—nuclear annihilation. The jury convicted them of destruction of government property. To everyone's astonishment, Judge Miles Lord imposed a six month *suspended* sentence and "used the occasion to criticize the arms industry, and to cite Sperry's corporate corruption."

It was not the first time that Judge Lord had hinted where his sympathies lay. In December of 1983, about the time that Pershing and MX missiles were being shipped to Europe, Minnesota newspapers had published charges of corruption against Sperry for large cost over-runs on Department of Defense contracts. The Minnesota Women's Peace Camp made the most of this publicity: in July 1984, we held a protest sit-in at Sperry corporate headquarters in Eagan, attempting to inform workers of the cost overrun and corruption charges. In the lobby/atrium, we made paper airplanes of our statements and news articles and sailed them to waiting hands on the balcony. We were ar-rested; Nancy Mosier, Mary Spiering, and I were jailed. Believing we were doing a public service in informing workers, we'd refused the sen-tence of community service and were charged with contempt of court. We had begun serving our indeterminate sentence—my first jail expe-rience—when we received a letter from Judge Lord: "I always thought someone should go to jail for the corruption at Sperry; I just didn't think it would be you three women!"

Marv and the Camp women began calling our Dakota County sentencing judge; after several days he relented and released us, saying he was "seared by the experience."

In an article commemorating the Peace Camp at its closing in October 1984, *St. Paul Pioneer Press* reporter Jacqui Banaszynski in-terviewed camp leaders and heads of Minnesota peace organizations, including Marv and Ginger Ehrman, about the camp's effectiveness. Ginger was coordinator for the Minnesota Peace and Justice Coali-tion, the coalition of 100 civic, congregational, and activist groups scattered around the state, including WAMM and the Project. Ginger, who Marv claimed "walked on eggs all the time" to keep the diverse coalition together during the tumultuous 1980s, said, "It's really useful to have groups out there who *aren't* willing to make compromises and are willing to stand on their beliefs.... they served as the conscience for all of us."

The small group of women involved with the Minnesota Women's Camp for Peace and Justice had, during a single year, had a profound effect on the local community. "They built much more than a base from which to protest nuclear weapons," Banaszynski wrote. "The camp became a gathering place for women of different races, religions and sexual orientations—women who were trying to create a peaceful, just community in the midst of what they saw as a violent, oppressive world." The numbers engaged were much smaller than those of which the Honeywell Project could boast, but numbers aren't the only thing that counts. "More significant," Marv told the reporter, "is the degree of commitment and the understanding that this work of ours will take a lifetime."

For many activists who received jail sentences during the 80s, the experience was life changing, whether or not they continued to protest. Careers shifted to work with social services or nonprofits; relationships deepened or, less often, foundered. Minnesota peace organizations clarified or questioned their missions. But the Honeywell Project faithfully insisted on its one target.

Public and media attention to the Project dwindled during 1984. Reporters covered the larger demonstrations and noted arrests, acquittals and convictions, but began to relegate the stories to back pages. In spring of that year, five hundred demonstrators gathered in a cold April drizzle; 284 were arrested, apparently haphazardly, because 68 of the men and women who were rounded up, including Ken Tilsen, had no intention of risking arrest. Chief Bouza, who had not supervised the arrests that day, publicly apologized. His lieutenant then accused the chief of "listening to his wife."

During the high point of the Project's second campaign, Honeywell employed about 79,000 people worldwide, with a quarter of them employed in the Twin Cities. The company's annual payroll was $648 million, a significant addition to the city tax base, and its generous donations to non-profits in the Twin Cities—almost $4 million in the mid-1980s—were well-known. "This did account for the reluctance of the local community to confront Honeywell's murderous military production," Marv said.

The Project knew it had to talk about the way the corporation made its money. As the company history applauds, "Honeywell consistently won military contracts in the millions of dollars, making torpedoes, guidance systems, and ammunition for the nation's defense." Honeywell credited its 24% increase in 1987 sales to the acquisition of the Sperry Aerospace Group, uniting Honeywell's guidance and navigation systems with Sperry's flight controls. Marv adds, "The salary of

Honeywell CEO Edson Spencer was over one million dollars." At a 1987 stockholder's meeting, Spencer was asked what accounted for his exorbitant salary. He reportedly said, "I'm like Kirby Puckett. If you want the results, you have to pay the player."

According to its 1986 annual report, "[Honeywell is] capitalizing on the potential growth in conventional weapons with our mine, ammunition and smart munitions programs, such as SADARM and Combined-Effects Munitions." Marv knew that the public was most interested—and frightened—by nuclear arms, but conventional weapons had to be included in an anti-weapons campaign. The Project proceeded to educate itself and its audience on the latest in weapon-euphemisms and on the weapons' cost in human lives.

SADARM, the newest generation of cluster bombs, was acronymic for Sense and Destroy Armor submunitions, which had miniature radar sensors to search for tanks. When the sensor passed over a tank, it told the computer about the target below. The explosives struck the tank from the top, its most vulnerable position. "They sprayed the inside with molten metal, incinerating the crew," Marv said. If the metal was too thick to penetrate, the impact would send a shock wave through the wall, causing the inside surface to fly off at terrific speeds. "The jagged metal fragments ricocheting inside the tank has a lethal effect on human bodies."

In the mid-1980s Honeywell also earned $25 million a year in revenues from Star Wars contracts, a small chunk of the "billions wasted on a system that does not work," Marv reported in Project leaflets. The Project's literature also emphasized that although Honeywell defended itself by observing that it did not make defense policy, but merely served the defense needs of America, in fact the company commonly used loopholes in campaign financing laws and political action committees to *influence* legislators in Congress.

In 1984, the reelection of Ronald Reagan added to the peace and anti-nuclear movements' malaise. Reagan's Star Wars initiative was a public relations program intended to calm America's fears by touting a nuclear "defense" that would render the Soviet Union's intercontinental ballistic missile system obsolete. Whether reassured, as much of the public was, or dismayed at this national rejection of arms control, as activists were, people began to drop away from demonstrations.

Minnesota activist groups began to focus on other policy issues, like the U.S. role in Central America. Knowledge about the CIA's involvement in the Contras civil war against the Nicaraguan government spread. In 1985, when the House of Representatives approved a hundred million dollars in aid to the Contras, three hundred demonstrators blockaded the Federal Building in Minneapolis. Forty-five were arrested.

Project leaders did not abandon the tactic of nonviolent civil disobedience at Honeywell, believing that consistent, creative actions would maintain maximum pressure on the corporation. Marv was much in evidence, organizing and advising affinity groups and bringing in new troops to demonstrate regularly.

On Good Friday, 1985, about fifty protestors erected a 12-foot cross—a Christ image hanging from a replica of an MX missile—and poured blood at Honeywell's front doors. On Mother's Day, a collection of mothers and children began to dig mock graves on the 28th Street boulevard; thirteen of them, including myself and my 18-year-old son Carl, were arrested. Our shovels were arrested, too; we had as hard a time getting them back as Marv did in reclaiming his cluster bomb.

At the annual spring action in 1985, protestors scaled a ladder over the security fence; 135 were arrested, including Erica Bouza, who had been reluctant to risk arrest but couldn't bear the sight of her friends once again going over the fence.

"Peace negotiations" within the Project began when some supporters questioned the strategies of nonviolent civil disobedience. Younger activists, reflecting on the violence in Central America and around the world, criticized what they took to be a dearth of strategic thinking among the Project's leaders, which they typified as the "moral witness syndrome: an Evangelical approach to change." They felt that more disruptive and perhaps more covert tactics were called for in a society that accepted as legitimate but could *afford* to ignore civil disobedience.

Responding to these internal tensions, the Project published another mission statement in its *Circulator* newsletter, reiterating the commitment to nonviolence:

The Honeywell Project believes that existing multinational corporations are the primary cause of war, oppression, and the pollution of our earth. We focus our energies on Honeywell, Inc., because it is a leading example of such an institution in our community. We advocate tactics of nonviolence to insure its conversion to peaceful, just, and environmentally sound practices.

The newsletter said that cards containing the statement would be issued for members to sign, but the core committee later dropped that idea, since membership and action had always been voluntary. Commitment to nonviolence as a requirement, however, would remain an issue in the tense years ahead.

The resistance at Honeywell headquarters helped spur creation of the Minnesota Economic Conversion Task Force, an effort at the legislature to create pilot projects for military-dependent businesses that wanted to convert to alternative production. In an editorial to the *New York Times*, Mel Duncan echoed corporate concerns when he predicted that the shrinking military pie would create a more competitive, less lucrative industry that would cost jobs. He proposed an alternative to avoid the unemployment and community disruption: economic conversion, a planned shifting of resources from military-dependent businesses into more stable and productive work.

State Representative Karen Clark, representing an inner city constituency, chaired the Task Force, which Honeywell fought hard. The Task Force researched the amount of money Minnesota taxpayers paid to the Pentagon and found that "The average Minnesota family is taxed about $3,400 a year for the US military budget. Those dollars would create more security," said Representative Clark, "assisting laid off workers, foreclosed farmers, and the families and children in our state who don't have the basic opportunities and necessities."

Elected officials were responsive to the Project and, like Karen Clark, to the Economic Conversion Task Force. Many of Minnesota's congressional delegation were opposed to the Reagan military build-up. Martin Sabo at least once introduced an amendment to freeze defense spending overall, and Representative Gerry Sikorski criticized officials who gave lenient sentences to Sperry Corporation for defense contract fraud. But Minnesota weapons contractors, including

Honeywell, Control Data, Sperry, and FMC, stood to benefit greatly from Reagan's military budget.

"Honeywell really had no interest in peace or economic conversion," Marv emphasized, "but after twenty years of organizing, agitating and resisting, we empowered hundreds of Project members to do more than protest a few times a year. They started battered women's shelters, did tenant organizing, joined active gay and lesbian groups, did other foreign policy work, and so on."

The 'empowered' included former Honeywell marketing writer Bill Weinstein, who quit his job in June 1984, sending a letter and a contribution to the Project. The letter had a cheering influence on the planners and demonstrators and was included in the Project's anniversary publication (1988). In part it read, "By your protests … you make the company acknowledge that their business may be considered morally repugnant…I have quit for this reason; others have quit for the same; more will, for I have never talked with anyone at Honeywell who hasn't volunteered that he or she found the work sordid, sustained only by some mesh of rationalization. … Your work has a profound effect."

Marv has seen the individual effects time and time again: "People are always asking me why are people smiling when they're getting busted for social change or against war or for peace. I think the answer is that for a few minutes, privately and publicly, we're one person, acting out our deepest spiritual political humanitarian insights and that makes you a whole person."

20

Cold War/Hot Wars

Harvey Egan, the Catholic priest, called him the "sidewalk Socrates." And Barb Mishler observed, "Marv is always out on the streets, talking to people, educating people," somehow convincing them they had to act on "their deepest most private spiritual, humanitarian instincts."

Marv talked to everyone, not only activists. In the 1980s he spent a good deal of time besieging Honeywell CEOs James Binger and James Renier, corporate and church leaders, foundation heads, and bankers. If he thought that these men of influence didn't have their finger on the pulse of public opinion, he would let them know it. In late 1984 he received a surprising response from Norwest Bank Senior Vice President David Nash. "Dear Marv," Nash wrote familiarly, "some time ago we met with you to hear your thoughts about nuclear weapons issues and corporate responsibility." Nash went on to say he wanted to begin "dialogue about our role as lenders to companies having defense business." Good business practices, the letter went on, dictated that bankers be attuned to public opinion, *"which can precede political change."* Furthermore, in addition to fiduciary responsibility to customers, the bank had ethical responsibilities, and Nash drew attention to Norwest's refusal to invest in the government of South Africa.

The report he enclosed, "Norwest Bank and Nuclear Weapons," echoed Nash's main points, saying that the nuclear weapons issue was currently the most dangerous one; that the arms buildup was ethically wrong and strategically unnecessary; that defense outlays took funds that could be used on human needs; and that banks had a role in directing funds for a more positive effect on the economy. Whether these considerations were reflected in Norwest's relations with Honeywell the report didn't say, but it left Marv with the impression that serious conversations were taking place in the halls of Minnesota finance.

Within Honeywell Corporation the story was much the same, whether or not the corporation admitted it. Among Marv's clippings is a *Newsweek* piece headed "A New Antinuclear Strategy" written by Edson Spencer, Honeywell CEO. Marv's note on the top identified the clipping as "1984, after 1,100 arrests at Honeywell." Spencer proposed that the U.S. and NATO should offer to remove all tactical nuclear weapons from Europe. "The risks inherent in nuclear proliferation do not permit us to continue on the same tedious path of negotiations we have followed for the past 20 years." Why would a businessman take this approach? Spencer asked. He insisted that many in the defense industry were thinking this way: they were proud to supply the means for a strong defense *and would continue to do so*, but that didn't prevent defense contractors "from hoping as ardently as any nuclear-freeze proponent that the United States and the Soviet Union will find a way to wind down the arms race."

Marv was heartened by such theoretical discussions, though they didn't blind him to the critical difference between "hoping" for an end to the arms race and ceasing to manufacture bombs. In the "big business of death," as one of the Sisters once put it during her arraignment, corporate officers "are part of a long chain of individuals; each can feel himself absolved from responsibility, each can salve his conscience" by contributing a more scrupulous effort, or an exculpatory theory, for the massive operation of murder.

As the Project reached its fifteenth year, the moral dimensions of the weapons-making business were hotly debated in the media and the courts. *Star/Tribune* columnist Bob Ebert likened the conflict to a "war … supposed to be all about peace. But there are prisoners taken, bodies counted, blood spilled, graves dug—all on a symbolic level." It was a war, he said, that the Project was losing; after fifteen years "few of the protesters' goals have been realized," whereas the corporation's defense contracts exceeded a billion dollars.

Company public relations spokesperson Karen Bachman insisted that the protests had minimal effect on Honeywell's policies or products. The corporation continued to exercise its "corporate con-science in carefully measured, thoughtful ways." But at the same time, she added, "obviously we wish they would just go away."

Going away was not an option for Marv or for other activists, whether newly recruited or old-hand Project members. And awareness about the arms race and its perils was growing, as articles and editorials about the Star Wars shield and European deployment became more common. Solidarity groups sprang up to make common cause with disenfranchised groups in the United States and in other nations, in-cluding countries in Europe, Africa, and the Middle East. Many trav-eled with delegations or as families to work on hunger, building, or political projects in far-flung places. "Dellinger told us the Movement wasn't dying," Marv said, "it was being reborn—only now people were active on fifty different issues!"

On Good Friday 1985, PAMM groups of Honeywell Project held a vigil under the banner "Nuclear Preparation is Global Crucifixion," emphasizing the worldwide nature of oppression and militarism. And another demonstration took place that summer closely tied to U.S. policy in Latin America, which had became a special focus for religious and social justice organizations.

Following the 1979 Sandinista revolution that deposed the dictator Antonio Somoza, a group of exiles began paramilitary operations in Nicaragua with support of the CIA. Throughout the 1980s, Presi-dent Reagan and Congress fought over the policy of giving these coun-ter-revolutionaries financial and technical support. Reagan called them Freedom Fighters and associated the Nicaraguan revolution with a "red tide" washing over Central and South America. Congress didn't think so highly of the Contras and sometimes voted to withhold funds.

In late July 1985 the U.S. House of Representatives voted for a bill that would give $100 million in aid to the Contras, and following the vote demonstrators blocked the front entrance of the Federal Building in downtown Minneapolis. Forty-five people, including Marv, were ar-rested. Project members were also involved in subsequent actions, but Marv and the core committee insisted on maintaining their focus on Honeywell Corporation.

Rally at the capitol, late 1980s, for peace in Central America. Note Paul Wellstone, center right.

In the spring of 1986, the night before the annual Honeywell stockholders meeting, the Project held a fundraiser with author Margaret Randall. Randall was an outspoken critic of U.S. policy toward Central America and was facing deportation—she was married to a Mexican citizen—because of her positions. Randall had written dozens of books, chiefly on politics and women's lives in North, Central, and South America.

At the next day's stockholders meeting, Marv took the microphone at a question and answer period. He lambasted company leadership for a recent scandal over improper audits and overestimates on defense contracts, much like the scandals that had embarrassed Sperry in 1983: "How can you guys sit there, praising yourselves while you're feeding at the public trough, diverting funds from poor people? Your weapons kill people around the world, and you arrest *us* for trying to stop it. We go to jail and you get a slap on the wrist!"

Later that same day, Jobs with Peace director Mel Duncan explained to a rally crowd how Honeywell's power worked in public policy. He told them how hard Honeywell lobbyists had worked to undermine the Peace Conversion Bill currently at the legislature. Much of the information shared at the rally, however, was never broadcast beyond those who were already converted, because the mainstream media chose to focus on the dwindling number of arrests rather than the broader goals of the movement.

That summer a refurbished two-story building, the Meridel LeSueur Peace and Justice Center, opened its doors to peace group offices. Located near the University of Minnesota and Augsburg College, it was the site for much interchange and organizing work. Also that summer, the Central America groups, the Project, and others sponsored a major national conference called "International Law: the Case against U.S. Policy Toward Nicaragua," bringing in ex-CIA analyst David MacMichael. MacMichael had resigned from the CIA in 1983, claiming the agency was misrepresenting intelligence for political reasons. He was considered the key witness in *Nicaragua v. United States*, an International Court of Justice case (1986), which found that the United States had violated international law by mining Nicaragua's harbors and by supporting Contra guerrillas. (MacMichael stayed with our family during the conference—our closest contact with the CIA.) He told the conference attendees that his recent mission to Nicaragua was to document arms smuggling by the Sandinistas, but he found that just the opposite was true. The Contras were smuggling the arms and drugs, and U.S. government agencies were benefitting.

Other speakers were Witness for Peace representative Jean Abbott and lawyer Reed Brody, both of whom documented Contra atrocities, and historian Howard Zinn, author of *A People's History of the United States*. This event was one of Zinn's early associations with the Project and Twin Cities educators. Since that time his perspective and critical pedagogy has informed and inspired Twin Citians for more than two decades. Marv and Zinn remain in contact, and Marv takes delight in their mail and phone correspondence.

In the fall action of 1986, seventy-eight of several hundred Honeywell demonstrators were arrested. The city attorney dismissed these cases after the arrestees requested individual trials. Hennepin County judges that year, however, were giving harsher sentences, particularly to repeat trespass offenders.

Project activists were deeply engaged in campaigns protesting the U.S.-supported violence in Central America. Judges tended to combine sentences with probation that forbade "any similar offense" within the year—not making distinctions about the target of the protest. The sentencing strategy was putting a strain not only on the court system but also on activists. By the fall, echoes of "issue overload" were heard in movement newsletters: "It feels as if we are trying to extinguish a raging fire with thimbles of water," wrote WAMM member Carol Ryberg. "We focus our thimblefuls on the Contra aid corner, douse that flame, and turn toward budget cuts, SDI, Libya, only to find that Contra aid flames again demand attention."

The Honeywell Project *Circulator* kept members apprised of court dates, sentences, and addresses for those incarcerated, while also keeping tabs on protestors of Central America policy and those involved in the Wisconsin nuclear submarine communications protests. A Catholic Worker collective based at Anathoth farm near Luck, Wisconsin, initiated these antinuclear actions. Barb Katt and John LaForge, the "Sperry software pair" prosecuted for damaging nuclear-trigger computers, were members of both the Anathoth farm and the Honeywell Project.

Through 1986 and into 1987, the Central American Resource Center, housed at the Newman Center at the University of Minnesota, fed the resistance with information absent from mainstream media. WAMM member Pam Costain learned that the Minnesota National Guard had been conducting what they called "embassy supply missions" to Panama and Central America since 1979; she believed that the maneuvers were "part of an overall strategy for building the infrastructure of war and as such, must be stopped."

In December 1986 WAMM and Project members crowded into Governor Rudy Perpich's outer office to express opposition to the deployment. They urged the governor to challenge the new federal law prohibiting governors from interfering with Pentagon assignments for National Guard units. The governor later spearheaded a challenge to the law, though the courts did not immediately take up the case. In the meantime, three Guard units were set to carry supplies and engineers to Honduras in December 1986 and early January 1987. Activists from local solidarity groups, WAMM, and the Project hastily formed "The Coalition to Stop Local Complicity in the War in Central America."

Marv and I were part of plans for a mass rally at the Guard Base and a series of actions to call media attention to the missions. WAMM and other peace groups that had a nonprofit (501C3) tax status were in a sensitive situation in regard to civil disobedience. WAMM could not sponsor civil disobedience as an organization but it did encourage individual members to follow their conscience in acting nonviolently in ways that would promote peace and justice.

In the first engagement of the campaign, I joined a small group of vigilers who planned to kneel on the runway when the planes were scheduled to leave. Marv, a leader in the Coalition but safely warm on a travel-banned trip to Cuba, was to organize a trial support system if we were arrested. He believed the charges would be federal.

The plans were semi-secretive but widely discussed and endorsed; most of us had received nonviolence training as part of the Honeywell project. We lined up transportation within affinity groups and stayed overnight in South Minneapolis near the National Guard base. We carried "An Open Letter to Members of the National Guard." Marv's insertions focused on the ordinary guys the protesters were likely to encounter, emphasizing nonviolence:

"We come here with conviction but without hostility…in complete nonviolence. We understand that you have reasons for being a part of the National Guard. We ask that you understand our reasons for protesting the way the Guard is being used in Central America." Only then did the letter talk about policy: "Our government's policy in Central America is based increasingly on encouraging warfare and violence in the region… To support the war against Nicaragua, our government is turning the neighboring country of Honduras into a U.S. military outpost. It is in this effort that the National Guard is being used."

The winter of 1986-87 was bitter, but the snow by January was scarce and mean, lending no softening or light to guide the protesters. In the predawn darkness of January 3, 1987, a dozen men and women huddled on the frozen mud outside the air base. We had to scale a five-foot chain-link fence near 34th Avenue and hustle about a quarter of a mile to reach the airstrip. The ground in many places was swept bare, especially around the airfield runways, but encrusted snow and ice-blocks were piled high at a convenient place against the fence.

A dozen or so of us scrambled over, not the most agile of adventurers in our parkas and wool mittens. It was hard to find toeholds with boots or galoshes. Sue Ann Martinson, Project office coordinator, made it over the fence but lost her footing and crashed on her shoulder but insisted that we continue. ("I still feel it every January!" she says today.)

We regrouped and stumped slowly forward by twos and threes— we had agreed on this nonthreatening posture. Ten minutes later, two hundred yards into the base, we met the first M.P.s. We sat down. It seemed pointless to kneel at the nervous M.P.s, nowhere near the planes. We tried to explain where we were going and why, and why the Guard flights were probably the unconstitutional offshoot of a deadly policy. Our audience politely asked us to refrain from talking. They had no political position; they were waiting for orders. Within an hour we were herded into a personnel carrier and driven to a gate, where we waited a longer time while the authorities decided how we could be processed.

It was another hour and a half in the cold but occasionally engine-warmed carrier, thanks to the benevolence of the M.P.s set to mind us. Finally we were each handed a personalized copy of a 'ban-and-bar' letter: The "Order Not To Enter or Reenter Military Reservation," stated that we were being removed as trespassers from the 934th Tactical Airlift Group Air Force Reserve Base. We were ordered not to enter the confines of the installation without written permission of the commander. That was it: we were ushered out of the base, luckily not too far from our cars.

The next rally, on January 22, was a different story.

It was my husband Ken's sixty-third birthday and the temperature had dropped well below zero by 6:00 pm. Out of deference to his birthday wishes—we had already spent a good portion of the evening outdoors at a rally at the capitol—we agreed that I would not climb the ladders into the base that night. The planners had chosen a spot that allowed nearly four hundred demonstrators to assemble. Erecting two Honeywell protest-type hinged ladders, the demonstrators prepared to scale the fence, which was seven feet high and topped with barbed wire. The site was near the junction of highways 55 and 62, outside the Air Force Reserve base but adjacent to the National Guard area, the object of the protest. The precise location became a focus of dispute because of what happened next.

As the crowd drew closer to the fence and about a dozen people were climbing the ladders, two military fire trucks pulled up and began shooting water through the fence, drenching everyone within reach. The Air Force Reserve officers who ordered the dousing later claimed that security personnel were heavily outnumbered and were concerned about "insurgents destroying military property," and that the spray was directed only at those climbing the fence. (Photos exhibited at a press conference the next day showed heavy jets of water arcing over and through the fence, drenching the crowd.)

The Guard's adjutant general, through Governor Perpich's office, distanced himself from the incident, saying the dousing "was not initiated or ordered by the National Guard." That the protesters had assembled near Air Reserve property, "just happened," Marv said. "There wasn't any clear demarcation between the bases. This was public land near the highways and federal authorities have permitted rallies there in the past." Project member Maynard Jones had just reached the top of the ladder when the water jets came at him. Looking down, he saw that the military police had removed the ladder from the other side. He didn't know what to do. "I made the choice to jump. I landed on both feet and broke both ankles."

The spraying seemed to go on and on. Those who could move back did so, including media camera crews, protecting their equipment. No one seemed to know what was happening for several minutes. Air Force police kept spraying water over Jones and other demonstrators until they realized he was injured. Then they "were very courteous," he said, and provided emergency medical aid.

Outside the fence, Maynard's wife Nancy had been knocked down by the force of the water. Nancy, a microphone thrust at her, water visibly icing her hair, was not so generous: "Shades of Bull Connor!" she sputtered and the comment led the evening news.

Usually pleased by media attention, Marv decried the media's portrayal of the issue as a battle between military police and the "chosen frozen." "It's a wonder we all didn't get pneumonia," Marv growled, "but our policies are killing people in Central America, and that's why we were there."

Daniel Berrigan brought renewed inspiration to the Project in spring

1987 by appearing at a sold-out fundraiser at Willey Hall at the University of Minnesota, which motivated more than a thousand people to turn out the next day to protest the Honeywell stockholder's meeting. The issues cited were Star Wars, nuclear weapons, peace conversion, *and* stopping production of Honeywell fuses, land mines, and cluster bombs being used in Central America and elsewhere. Berrigan wrote a special essay, "The Hole in the Ground: A Parable for Peacemakers," which the Project published in booklet form and sold for a dollar.

The thinly veiled allegory for Star Wars told of a president who commissioned a mighty project to allay people's fears and boredom: a giant "deconstruction" that would dig the biggest, deepest hole in the world. The president's religious guru (a Billy Graham stand-in) blessed the abyss, which widened and deepened until it sucked in entire cities and populations; neither corporate nor government power could stop the drain on life.

The eighth mass demonstration in the decade resulted in 177 arrests; once again, the beleaguered public relations department at Honeywell defended the company in the *Star Tribune*. More difficulties were in store for the company in 1987 as it tried to open testing sites for its ordnance division in Morrison County, Minnesota, and near Hot Springs, South Dakota. Local groups resisted with the aid of the Project, and the company withdrew its proposals.

In December of 1987 Ronald Reagan and Mikhail Gorbachev signed the INF missile treaty. Under the treaty, both sides agreed to eliminate all missiles with ranges between 625 and 3,500 miles by June 1, 1991, and all missiles with ranges between 300 and 625 miles within 18 months. It was a turning point for peace activists, who held a press conference at the state capitol to celebrate their success after decades of pressure on government. Honeywell Project spokesperson Richard Seymour expressed the cautious opinion of most, however, when he said that the agreement covered only five percent of the nuclear arsenals. Marv agreed: despite an apparent easing of the Cold War, he said, "we know that the U.S. military stance in much of the world, especially in the Middle East and Central America, shows no iota of moderation."

A new chapter in the ongoing internal critique of the Honeywell

Project's motives and methods opened when two members of the Project's core committee, Brad Harper and Leah Rogne, both of whom were sociology graduate students, undertook a study of local activists. About half of the Project members had been arrested for civil disobedience, and half of those surveyed gave their motivations as "raising moral awareness." One quarter were concerned with raising societal awareness, as opposed to strategic effectiveness. Rogne and Harper concluded that the focus on "individual transformations of consciousness located [these Project members] on a dimension that is incompatible with many others in the peace movement."

Younger activists, including many in the Central America solidarity groups, criticized Honeywell Project strategies. Former Project member Kris Gunderson joined with student groups like the University of Minnesota's Progressive Student Organization in advocating "mobile tactics" and direct action. Examples were covert spray painting; rescues of detained protestors by surrounding them and moving them away from police; street theatre; and various "disorderly" but agile and fluid demonstrations. The Project had called for creative actions to win media attention, but these young people differed from the Project veterans by being less willing to subject themselves to arrest.

An urban punk and youth counterculture fed a new wing of the Coalition to Stop Local Complicity with the War in Central America. Known for their striking clothes (ranging from grunge t-shirts with political slogans to black leather, spikes, and chains) and hairstyles (Mohawks or dreadlocks), these politicized youth hung around Uptown, which soon became a center of resistance activities. "A core met as Backroom Anarchists," Marv recalls, operating a bookstore near the Uptown area. In late 1987 they formed a group called the Revolutionary Anarchist Bowling League (RABL), to become briefly famous for disrupting both the civil peace and the nonviolent peace movement.

"I'm an anarchist!" Marv said, "I don't object to the name. But they degrade the name; I don't like their philosophy." In a *Star Tribune* interview, Kris Gunderson said the group intended to participate in the struggles of oppressed peoples through local acts of revolt, "to encourage existing movements to take more effective direct action." He described the youth philosophy as "antiwar, anti-draft, pro-ecology, pro-feminist, and punk." Marv disputed whether those ideals matched the group's operational strategies: "I met with them a couple times— we just don't agree. I'm not going to waste our time. What they're doing has less to do with anarchism than with somebody's overactive hormones—though I do admire their courage," he added.

In March of 1988 the conflicts over government policies in Central America, between local authorities and activists, and within the peace movement, hit the streets of uptown and downtown Minneapolis.

As part of President Reagan's effort to oust the Sandinista government, on March 16 he ordered more than 3,200 U.S. troops to Honduras on the pretext that Nicaraguan soldiers had crossed the border. The administration had been pouring millions of dollars in military aid into the anti-Sandinista rebels, the Contras, but the program was coming under fire from Congress. Trying to circumvent Congress, the Reagan administration engaged in illegal and covert sales of arms to Iran to fund the Contras in what came to be known as the Iran-Contra Affair.

"Vice President George Bush and his staff were building a network of operatives working outside official channels to train, arm, and support the Contras," Marv said. Bush family friend Felix Rodríguez was a CIA agent directing Contra supply. Documented in the CBS program "West 57th Street," a supply pilot flew a DC-6 loaded with guns in March 1986, to Aguacate, the U.S.-controlled air base in Honduras. Contras unloaded the guns and the pilot was paid about $70,000. After a layover, the aircraft was reloaded with more than twenty-five thousand pounds of marijuana and directed as a "nonscheduled military flight" into Homestead Air Force Base near Miami.

"West 57th" traced this plane to Vortex, one of four airlines the U.S. State Department hired to supply the Contras using money Congress designated as "humanitarian aid." Testimony of the Christic Institute (a Washington, D.C., interfaith legal foundation) before congressional committees provided a horrific picture of large-scale drug trafficking with the knowledge and assistance of the CIA. Contra narcotics smuggling stretched from cocaine plantations in Colombia to dirt airstrips in Costa Rica to seafood companies in Miami, and finally, to the drug-ridden streets of the United States.

"So the U.S. government is helping drown our kids with coke.

It's no wonder that young people are seething," Marv said. Many concluded that traditional forms of protest were ineffective against such base and clandestine programs.

Nevertheless, hundreds of activists responded when the Project, WAMM, and the Pledge of Resistance called a mass protest in the Uptown neighborhood. The Project assisted the Minnesota Peace and Justice Coalition in building a phone tree. Callers were able to mobilize more than six hundred people on short notice on Thursday, March 17. As rush hour approached, protesters with signs and banners lined the streets near the intersection of Lake and Hennepin, chanting antiwar slogans and passing out leaflets to motorists backed up for blocks. As darkness fell, people poured into the intersection, forming a massive circle blocking the two main arteries. Police monitored the action but did not attempt to make arrests that evening, allowing the demonstration to continue for five hours. Some direct action groups wanted to do more: they spray painted buildings, burned a flag, overturned trash containers, and climbed atop stalled cars and a bus. "Eat the rich," they shouted at hapless shoppers in the district, as retailers closed the entrances to Calhoun Square shopping center and other businesses.

At 8:30 pm, Deputy Police Chief Bob Lutz met with Marv and other organizers, who said they would stay to ensure the safety of some of the "younger protesters, who may have been novices at demonstrations." They convinced the police to continue exercising restraint, and by 9:00 pm, most of the crowd had dispersed. Marv did not endorse the direct actions, but told police, reporters, and anyone who would listen, that the anger coming out was justified: "What the administration is doing is totally outrageous. Reagan's foreign policy is to make a torture chamber out of Central America."

The next day, a second protest was held in the same area but the outcome was more controversial. A bowling ball smashed into the Army Recruitment Center on Lake Street, presumably launched by a member of the Revolutionary Anarchist Bowling League. Police later reported dozens of calls from irate citizens demanding that officers take a more aggressive stance toward demonstrators.

Honeywell Project and WAMM representatives decided to meet with someone from the Backroom Anarchists and try to hammer out nonviolent guidelines for the next demonstration. The undertaking was not successful, as the RABL rep insisted that instructions be inserted advising those who could not agree to the guidelines to leave the demonstration and assemble in another area. A WAMM steering committee co-chair said, "This language is not acceptable—this is no compromise." We passed out guidelines without the wording or sponsorship of the Backroom Anarchists; volunteers from other activist groups would serve as marshals.

At the third protest on Monday afternoon, well over a thousand people gathered at the intersection of Washington and Hennepin in downtown Minneapolis and marched to the federal courthouse during rush hour. As the first group of marchers approached the courthouse's main entrance, police cars and a phalanx of Minneapolis police in full riot gear appeared from around a corner. Deputy Chief Lutz warned over a loudspeaker that the assembly was illegal and should disperse. The police, accompanied by dogs, marched directly at the protesters, splitting into two lines and hemming in the crowd. Several dozen demonstrators immediately sat down and police began hitting them with riot sticks: "They were hitting people to get them to move, but they couldn't move," said one of the young protestors. "There was no place to go because there were people sitting and standing in back." A glass door of the Federal Building was smashed.

Police began hauling off seated protestors and shoving those who could move back onto the sidewalks. Marv knew we had to regroup, to avoid "a massacre like 1968 at the Democratic Convention." He stood up and with other organizers led the marchers away from the center toward Peavey Plaza at 12th and Nicollet to gather and raise bail money. RABL members stayed back and distributed fliers at the Federal Building; they defended their actions, saying it was obvious the movement needed new tactics: "civil disobedience is for upper-middle class adults who can afford to be arrested a lot."

Shaken but undeterred, most affinity groups at Peavey Plaza wanted to keep marching. They moved back toward City Hall, the site of the jail, shouting "Troops out! No Contra Aid!" When a supporter inside opened the doors, discipline broke down and half the excited crowd swarmed inside before officers could stop them. After some confusion and demands to bail out the prisoners, the demonstrators sat down. Another squad of riot police appeared and ushered them outside, where most dispersed. In the days before cell phones, waits were long, but by morning, all who had been arrested had been released or booked.

WAMM's steering committee held an emergency meeting the next day. Should they continue sponsoring marches? The group reached an impasse. In keeping with the organization's self-perception as feminist and nonhierarchical, the steering committee announced that the meeting would be open to all, and the office at 3301 Hennepin was overflowing. At that time the Project's PAMM affinity groups were well represented among WAMM's leadership, and everyone who wanted to speak was given an opportunity. The meeting dragged on until it was clear that a consensus would be impossible. For the first time in its history, WAMM decided to vote on whether to participate in the next Coalition march. An alternative plan was proposed; a WAMM contingent would vigil at Senator Durenburger's office. "It was doomed from the start," Marv mourned, "of course you let people air their views, but you've got anybody and everybody putting their two cents in when you should be doing serious organizing—a steering committee should steer!"

Marv was a WAMM member, but did not attend that meeting. "We had our own worries," he said. The next day, a feature story ran on the front page of the *Star/Tribune* carrying the headline, "WAMM Quits!" Explanations and repeated calls to inform the editors that WAMM had called an *alternate* demonstration at Senator Durenberger's office did nothing to undo the damage. Key activists resigned their membership or withdrew from leadership positions, because "they disagreed with WAMM's decision to remain in the anti-war Coalition [a decision not noted in the article] and to selectively endorse Coalition protests." Some disagreed with the decision to stay with the Coalition, because they believed the marches were tending toward violence; others were unhappy with what they saw as class differences within WAMM's leadership; still others doubted WAMM's ability to lead in such a charged atmosphere.

The Project weighed in on protest endorsement, too. After meeting with the core committee, Marv signed a letter from the Coalition leadership to the young anarchists, stating, "Your testosterone fit at the recruitment office on Lake Street has not furthered the cause of uniting people against the war… You are also endangering the lives of other people by the response you provoke."

Marv threw in his lot with WAMM demonstrators who marched to Senator Durenberger's office at 6th and Hennepin to urge the senator to oppose military aid to the Contras. The three hundred marchers then walked south to Peavey Plaza for a rally, without incident.

Meanwhile, the fifth and last large demonstration organized by the Coalition gathered at the Federal Building. The National Lawyer's Guild–Minnesota sent a team of legal witnesses with video cameras to monitor and document the event. After a brief rally, six hundred demonstrators marched in a serpentine route through the streets of downtown Minneapolis, avoiding any confrontation with the police.

The Honeywell Project and its affinity groups met to determine a position for endorsing future Coalition demonstrations; they decided not to work with groups who used violence, property destruction, or confrontational tactics, naming RABL and the Backroom Anarchists. Marv spoke about following David Dellinger's advice (reprinted from *Z Magazine* to the Project's *Circulator*) to "draw sustenance from some kind of beloved community," and engage in "various methods of conflict resolution (breaking down the barriers that separate us, overcoming the efforts of provocateurs)." He began work with the MN Peace and Justice Coalition to host a "Unity" forum for all local peace groups, which would be held the following winter.

In the course of the year support for protests at Honeywell ebbed, though the question of the effectiveness of civil disobedience was still hotly debated. Some advocated direct action, others found the entire discussion "too symbolic," and others still questioned whether the effectiveness of an action could even be judged in the short term.

Marv's position? "The main virtue of the Project is its endurance. There are intergroup conflicts about strategy and tactics, conflicts between young and old members, between men and women. I get burnt out from time to time—then I talk to a therapist or I go fishing. We're always worried about money; we live on $5 and $10 that people send to us. … I've lived right on the edge as other organizers in the peace and justice movement do. It's hard but it keeps me honest."

21

The Project goes into MIST

In the fall of 1988, we held a grand celebration of the Honeywell Project's work from 1968 to 1988. Marv invited author Grace Paley and David Dellinger to speak and to bestow awards on peacemakers who had made significant contributions to the Project. Artist Gregory McDaniels designed award certificates for a dozen activists.

Despite the ceremony and the celebratory ambience, the focus, as always, was to be Honeywell and its deadly business. Just before the event, Marv was in Los Angeles visiting friends and drumming up support for the next round of actions. When a radio interviewer asked what the Project had accomplished after twenty years, Marv responded, "So why are you even talking to me?" Meaning, across the country people wanted to know about this work.

At the time of the anniversary, local protest groups were anguished about another Central American country that had come within the sights of U.S. intervention—El Salvador. In early 1988, the right-wing ARENA party won control of El Salvador's National Assembly, precipitating a civil war. Although the U.S. Senate tried to cut back military aid to El Salvador, a death-bed message from President Duarte blocked the peace initiative, and U.S. weapons and military aid continued to be directed to that war-torn country. Marv pointed out in an anniversary letter, "We can't forget that recent evidence shows indiscriminate use of cluster bombs—Honeywell bombs—in the vicious air war in El Salvador." He knew the solidarity groups already had their hands full but wanted to continue making the link between weapons profit and foreign policy.

The centerpiece of the three-day event was an action at Honeywell headquarters during which eighty-five protestors risked arrest by scaling the fence as Grace Paley and Emile d'Antonio cheered them on. (Paley had read the night before, d'Antonio was to appear at a showing that evening of *In the King of Prussia*.)

Tony Bouza was smiling, said Craig Cox of *City Pages*, anticipating a "civilized" performance by Erica's friends, and remarked that Erica herself would "no doubt throw her body across a nuclear reactor" to make her point. Cox quoted a number of Project supporters, including Marv, Ken Tilsen, Don Olson, and coordinator Sue Ann Martinson, who said that the company and the government *each* had responsibility for "murder and mayhem." But Cox also asked the question whom "these people were trying to reach besides themselves. Would somebody in the fourplex on Park and 28th catch the 15-second blip" on the news? Would they make the connection between military expenditures and bus fare and begin to think badly about their corporate neighbor across the street?" He concluded: "Probably not."

The arrests went off peaceably and feature pieces in the print media followed. *Minneapolis Tribune* devoted a front-page *Variety* section feature to the Project, with photos of Marv and present and past protests. Marv explained cluster bombs as he unwrapped another of his personal bombs—the type of weapon wreaking havoc in Israel and El Salvador. "They carry as many as 500 of these 'bomblets' … in canisters under the wings of the Phantom A-6 night bombers. When the pilot presses a button, the 'mother' container opens in the air, the 'daughter' bombs explode. They jump up about belt high and steel ball bearings spray out at 2,200 feet per second." He opened his album of photos showing the effects of these lethal projectiles on human flesh in Vietnam and Laos—a scarified child's face, shattered limbs, a whole torso pockmarked. "And Honeywell says, 'We just make them.'" Company spokesperson Kathy Tunheim claimed the "conventional antitank and antisubmarine weapons" accounted for perhaps 20 percent of Honeywell's revenue but was careful to say the weapons represented 7,500 jobs.

The paper called the company *Goliath*, but emphasized, "*David* is very patient." Yes, he was. "It's persistence," said Marv, "that makes social change. The early labor organizers persisted over many years to shorten the work week and abolish child labor. Same with the women's movement and civil rights. If the peace movement had not grown and persisted, the Vietnam War would have gone on and more lives would have been lost." Historian and professor Mulford Q. Sibley agreed: The Project was tenacious, and Marv exemplified the "dedication and faithfulness to the principle of nonviolent resistance." The "David without a sling" had the last words in the feature, "When we put our bodies in the way, when we sit at the door, people step over us and they symbolize the company stepping over human life. Knowing what we know, how can we live with dignity, unless we involve ourselves?"

Marv and his staff were gratified; they'd taken time to honor the work and the people who had given so much. Even when the media had backed off coverage of protests, the community showed its support in attending events and providing financial support. Marv vowed that the Project would continue protesting, it members would continue to be arrested and jailed, until the group's goals were met: "A stop to research, development and production of conventional and nuclear weapons systems, and peace conversion with no loss of jobs."

Just before the anniversary celebration I finished my own last stint in jail for the Project. It was a good thing, too—good to be 'out.' Life was full of family matters. My older son was in his senior year at Gustavus Adolphus University in St. Peter, Minnesota, a Lutheran school of sound academic reputation and progressive, though somewhat staid politics. Carl would graduate in the spring, and when I phoned, he no longer had to shout down the dorm hallway, "Keep it quiet, would you? Mom's calling from the slammer!" Carl had been part of a Mother's Day action in 1985, on his eighteenth birthday, and knew the cost of taking a stand, but I think he enjoyed the "crazy mom" aura, too.

In those same months during the winter of 1988-89, my younger son Paul was raising funds at South High to finance a student exchange trip to the Soviet Union he would be taking with ten other young men from his Russian class.

Who would have thought that in the summer of that year, Ronald Reagan and Mikhail Gorbachev would consent to ease Cold War tensions by wrestling with details of disarmament treaties that had been on hold since the early 1980s? Although regional conflicts were still a source of disagreement, said President Reagan, "Our differences continue to recede. ... Mr. Gorbachev and I agreed that there must be peaceful solutions to these conflicts. ...The Soviet decision to withdraw from Afghanistan is significant, and ... leads to an approach to other regional problems. Our discussions also dealt with Cambodia, Angola, Ethiopia, the Middle East and the Persian Gulf, and Central America."

Most significant from the peace movement point of view was that the leaders seemed to be looking to their *people* for help. The idea of having cultural exchanges was furthered, particularly among the young. "General Secretary Gorbachev and I have worked to build a relationship of greater trust ... We both recognize that one way to do that is to improve understanding between our two countries through broader people-to-people contacts ... We agreed to expand our student exchange programs, with a goal of allowing hundreds, and eventually thousands, of Soviet and American high school students to study in each other's classrooms." For the first time in Cold War history, high school students would stay in citizens' homes.

South High in Minneapolis (my son Paul's school), was picked for a pilot program along with a school in Belarus. Lilia, a young woman studying to be an elementary school teacher, would stay with us for a month and Paul would stay with her family in Minsk.

Well into the funding plans, there was a bit of a problem, at least as far as I was concerned. The Honeywell Foundation was giving a grant of $600 to each student for the trip. A crisis of conscience: Could we accept that money? I talked with women at WAMM, who thought a gracious acceptance was perfectly fine, and I talked with Marv, who laughed. He said Honeywell owed us. "Owe me? They don't even know me!" I thought. Or know the kids still picking up cluster bombs as toys in Vietnam and Thailand. Marv thought I should take the money but say something about Honeywell.

At the next parents/students meeting, I raised my hand and told them (most knew) of my ex-con status and my discomfort at accepting money from our nemesis. I said I thought everyone else might in good conscience take Honeywell's donation—it was for a peace project—but that I preferred to pay the $600 portion myself. A few of the kids grinned, a few groaned; most of the parents, and Paul, looked stricken. "Don't worry," the funding coordinator assured us, "we'll work it out." She called me that same night, with word that the students had another funding source, a local milling corporation that would cover the difference. Corporate interlock? I wondered but didn't ask. There are many roads to peace, I muttered, and she agreed.

During Lilia's sojourn with us in February, I brought her over to the Meridel LeSueur Center to meet Marv, who greeted her at the door like an old friend; his father Louie was from Minsk, he told her. Just then, she caught sight of a poster on the wall. "Oh!" she said excitedly, "Leonard Peltier! Do you know him?"

"A little. My God, 99% of the people who walk in here, peace people, don't recognize who that is. And you come halfway around the world...."

Shy now, she told him that her class had studied political prisoners, oh, and that there *was* a peace movement in Minsk. "Carol and I have been political prisoners," he responded, "But not so famous as Leonard, not for so long." Lilia glanced at me, puzzled. Her teacher hadn't told her. "What did you do?"

In the Project office, Marv tried to explain the anti-weapons campaign. He displayed his gray, ugly cluster bomb and told her about Honeywell's products and profits. She hadn't heard about Honeywell and was too uncomfortable to study the frayed pictures of Vietnamese injured by cluster bombs; that war was so long ago.

I worked with Marv at the Meridel Lesueur Center from 1988 to 1991, for the Minnesota Peace and Justice Coalition. Honeywell Project and WAMM were keystones of the Coalition, which prided itself on being one of the longest-lived multi-issue coalitions in the nation. MPJC's strength, in contrast to the Honeywell Project, was that it was a collection not of individuals but of groups, small and large, including congregations or church committees; solidarity, women's, and peace groups; and chapters of national policy organizations like the United Nations Association, Fellowship of Reconciliation, World Federalists, and Women's International League for Peace and Freedom. Monthly meetings of MPJC were open, as were meetings of the representative board. Each group paid dues on a two-tiered scale.

The Coalition's primary tasks were to prevent scheduling conflicts and to facilitate communication between groups via a bimonthly newsletter and calendar. That was my responsibility, and I loved being the peace and justice reporter/promoter for my corner of the earth.

My colleague Ginger Ehrman and Marv were old friends and confidants. Marv had recommended me for the job, Ginger said—maybe to keep me in the peace fold once my younger son was off to college—and free-lance editing jobs were scarce. I wasn't an organizer but I was involved in the multiple issues that were pulling so many of my friends in too many directions. I was pleased that the work was focused on pulling groups together. For the Project and local peace groups, the conflicts between pacifists, anarchists, and the liberation struggles in Central America were difficult to discuss, let alone solve.

Those years "between wars"—after the Cold War but before the hot wars, proxy wars, and mid-East and African conflicts of more recent times had erupted—seemed to be a time of growth and deepening of local peace and justice organizations. Focuses shifted between international, national, and local justice issues. Questions about civil disobedience and its place in justice struggles continued to be debated. The early 1990s was a time of relative stability for Marv, as friendships helped support him financially and personally.

During the late 1980s and early 90s Marv entered into a relationship with a woman named Nancy Peterson. They became lovers. A petite, vivacious woman, she brought out Marv's tender and ebullient side. She was a decorator and designer and tried for years to "organize" his living arrangements as she saw him organize meetings, events, rallies, and people. For weeks at a time Marv's apartment would glow with freshened furnishings and polished hardwood floors, before the dust, foot traffic, papers, and cigarette ashes again held sway.

Nancy accompanied him to events and helped with Marv's parties, though demonstrations and arrests were not her métier. Memorably, she spoke at a pre-action rally in the late 90s, when they were no longer lovers, saying, "Marv has his faults, but," pausing for the concurring laughter, "at heart, he is the kindest, most generous man I've known." They remain friends.

In the late 80s, when various activist groups struggled with the court system and with one another, attorney Ken Tilsen circulated a major position paper on civil disobedience. Marv deemed it extremely important to the "protest culture" in the state, and felt we could not afford to ignore it.

In a speech given before Friends for a Non-Violent World in January 1987, Tilsen outlined his experiences as a lawyer defending blacks in civil rights struggles, antiwar activists, American Indians at Wounded Knee, and farmers protesting power lines (and suing Honeywell and the FBI). He had serious reservations about the efficacy of civil disobedience as it was practiced in the late 1980s.

"My view is very simple," Tilsen said. "I measure every activity by its effectiveness in achieving change in actions of our government, change in society, and growth in the movement for change—not necessarily in that order."

When black students occupied the University of Minnesota's Morrill Hall in 1969, Tilsen said, they demanded a change in specific racist policies, and they achieved that change; when Native Americans confronted the FBI at Wounded Knee, they intended to end a reign of terror on the reservation, and they ended it. Labor and farm workers banded together to change specific policies: they had an immediate goal while being intimately connected to a broader concern. Those were the two essential principles—a clear, obtainable goal and an intrinsic connection with broad community concerns. But Tilsen had come to the tentative conclusion that the actions of protest groups who merely brought attention to themselves were likely to be counterproductive, no matter how moral, sincere, or valid their concern.

Marv agreed that activists had to make common cause with poor and disenfranchised communities, and he believed that the Honeywell Project and other nonviolent campaigns he had led had done so. But mass organizing was fraught with difficulties, chief among them sustainability. He was never worried, as peace groups sometimes chafed, that African Americans, Native Americans, immigrants, and other members of disenfranchised communities did not sign up to join a particular protest. "We have to join them," he said, "be where they are—if they ask us to."

Friendships with Native American activists, especially the Belle-courts and other AIM members, were especially important. When racial violence erupted over native fishing rights it was Marv who introduced the Minnesota Peace and Justice Coalition to tribal members from the Lac du Flambeau Anishinaabe. The issue seemed somewhat removed from MPJC and Project concerns and was certainly removed from our understanding. We had to learn some history and a new language for addressing racial tensions in the region. In the process we gained allies, Native groups who had been there for peace coalitions earlier, the American Indian Movement and Women of All Red Nations; and a new organization focusing on treaty rights, Honor Our Neighbors' Origins and Rights. HONOR representatives came to the LeSueur Center to help us understand their history and the implications of their current struggle.

Wisconsin and Minnesota Ojibwe (Anishinaabe) had signed treaties in which they ceded their lands to the federal government at several times between 1837 and 1854. In these treaties, the tribes retained the right to hunt, fish, and gather wild rice and maple sap on the ceded lands. But over the next century various Wisconsin court decisions granted the state the authority to limit Indian hunting and gathering practices to reservations. Ojibwe were finally able to exercise their off-reservation rights when the U.S. Court of Appeals for the Seventh Circuit said Wisconsin could not regulate fishing on reservations and, more important, that treaties guaranteed the Anishinaabe the right to hunt and fish *off* their reservations. The U.S. Supreme Court upheld this decision.

As small groups began spearfishing on rivers and lakes outside the reservations over the next few years, angry whites in northern Wisconsin mounted anti-treaty campaigns in response. A few public figures like former Vikings coach Bud Grant lent their influence to lobbying and media efforts; and a growing sector of disgruntled protestors undertook more dangerous activities, organizing rallies and disruptive actions at boat landings where native spearfishers were harvesting. The harassment and racial provocations escalated; a favored technique was noise, including ear-splitting whistles. The federal Department of Natural Resources sent monitors but they were stretched thin at late spring, the time of the walleye harvest.

Vernon Bellecourt, a native woman from Wisconsin, and a man we knew only as Bear spoke at the LeSueur Center to a collection of about forty MPJC representatives that included members of peace groups, congregational advocates, and environmentalists. Their proposal was that MPJC send trained witnesses as native people attempted to exercise their fishing rights. When someone mentioned the name Witness for Nonviolence, Marv perked up his ears.

"We know your group has the ability to do this," Bellecourt said, "and we need you to stand with us."

Marv was eager, but he could see the worry on some faces. "As I look around, I see, and you'll notice, too, Vernon, that most of us are pacifist palefaces," pausing for the nervous laughter, "and we're not used to protesting protestors."

"Exactly," said Vernon, responding to the first objection, "We want non-Indians of good will to be a buffer, to come to the boat landings and simply witness. To be silent witnesses between the PARR and STA groups and the fishers." Protect American Rights and Resources was the largest of the groups culled from disgruntled sports fishers and property owners; when they had information about a walleye harvest, they showed up in numbers to try to disrupt the spearing. STA (Stop Treaty Abuse) was the most militant and organized some of the largest and most violent protests at boat landings.

For Marv, the issue of our involvement in the controversy was simpler than legalities or traditional alliances: "We should do it because it's a justice issue. Besides, they asked us."

We would be given directions and a time to show up. It would be at night, late April to early May, around a particular public boat landing to be named. It would probably be cold. Marv wasn't able to go that first spring but persuaded Project organizer David Bernstein, an Easterner, to represent the office. Bea Swanson, Anishinaabe grandmother, and environmental activist Susu Jeffrey rode with David and I.

The lake chosen was on the Lac du Flambeau reservation where my family used to vacation during summers in the 1950s. I had idyllic memories of pine forests, clear blue lakes, and long July afternoons of paddling in the shallows or watching a lethargic bobber. David was less enthralled with the north woods scene, more familiar with the East and West Coasts—"civilized" country. As we drove past mile after mile of Wisconsin pines and spruce he commented often on the "bleak" landscape.

We'd met previously with Bea when we learned about the mercury contamination in Wisconsin lakes. Marv was an avid fisherman and loved the north woods, where Gerty's family had a cabin. He might have been able to allay the sportsmen's fears—he would have tried, anyway.

"Yes, you'd tell them, Marv," Bea laughed.

We asked Bea why the tribes wanted to exercise their fishing rights now, and didn't the protestors know about the mercury?

Yes and no, she told us. The Great Lakes Indian Fish and Wildlife Commission had started, but only this year, a public-awareness campaign. "People are eating smaller fish and we tell them to vary them, especially the walleye, with other species," she said. "And pregnant and nursing mothers have to be especially careful." As to why they would fish, "It's complicated. It ties in to who we are, who the People are."

Bea was a gentle spirit, proud of her Native heritage, and a feminist Christian who combined the traditions in a powerful way. She was a leader in the peace community, an effective counterpoint to male voices like Marv's and the Bellecourts'.

In early May a glaze of ice is likely to form on northern lakes overnight, which the boats would skin as they set out to the spawning sites. I was disappointed as our carpool neared the lake; the landscape was not as I remembered from my family's vacations. The rolling fields were studded with farms and small towns rather than deep forest. It was mile after mile of following a string of taillights past brief illuminations of snow patches and yard lights.

Just after midnight, our caravan pulled into a roadside parking lot, the last in a line of about fifty cars. We hiked a wooded path to the sound of catcalls and whistles, still well before the fishers were due to arrive. David, Susu, and I walked with Bea down a national forest side road, following the faint circles our flashlights cast on the sand. She had no light, but carried her drum to send the spearers softly out with its heartbeat.

The faint piping I'd been hearing for some time swelled to a whistling cacophony as we entered a deciduous grove near shore.

"It's the peepers, spring frogs. That's good luck."

The mating frogs ceased their singing when her drum and others began, as though honoring the human heartbeat. For whatever reason, that midnight was the most peaceful the landing had seen since the fishing controversy began. STA had fewer representatives and the harvest was good. On the way home, we stopped our car to climb an incline to the edge of a clearing. Even David was impressed. The northern lights, a rare sight in the Twin Cities, spread their dazzling scarves across the skies as they must have years ago when Marv and other Project members met on a Wisconsin hill to retreat and dream of a national campaign.

We were not to witness again in Wisconsin. That same week, Wisconsin Federal Judge Barbara Crabb issued a temporary injunction against protesters who engaged in disruptive behavior at boat landings. She made the injunction permanent in 1992.

About that time, as George Bush assumed the presidency, support for many peace groups, including the Honeywell Project, began to dwindle drastically. Yet the new president gave every indication that he would continue Reagan's militarized, intervention-driven policy, which in his view had driven the Soviets to their knees and made the world safer for democracies.

The Project debated closing its office in the Meridel LeSueur Center, as it could no longer sustain salaried employees or pay the rent. As the Soviet Union disintegrated and the Cold War came to an end, activists spoke openly about a Peace Dividend—what did it mean, how could it be reified? Some from Women Against Military Madness wondered (albeit only briefly) whether their very name was relevant in the new geopolitical climate.

Economic realities were not so bright for the Honeywell Corporation, either. During 1986-1988 Honeywell experienced net losses and rumors circulated that the company was vulnerable to a hostile takeover. To satisfy stockholders, Honeywell planned to restructure, selling off portions of the weapons empire. More damaging to its local image, Honeywell laid off 4,000 employees, at least a quarter of them in the Twin Cities. In 1988, Honeywell was discovered to have cost overruns in a number of defense contracts, some of them carryovers from Unisys, resulting in a net loss of $434.9 million for the year. A general slowdown in defense contracts combined with Pentagon waste-reduction measures made for a difficult defense business climate.

Finally, in late September 1990, the management announced the spin-off of its military and marine systems business into an independent company, named Alliant TechSystems Inc. For each four shares of Honeywell stock, the company's shareholders would receive one share in the new, free-standing military company. For the management, the decision made good business sense.

Marv had a different take. When Honeywell couldn't sell its Defense Division in 1990, it created Alliant TechSystems, "bastard offspring of Honeywell. ... Over 22 years [the Honeywell Project] created a worldwide movement to pressure Honeywell management to stop making cluster bombs, land mines and guidance systems for long- and short-range nuclear missiles. So after 2,200 arrests, and nearly 100 trials, Honeywell reduced its dependence on weapons systems. We were—thousands of us—a major factor in the decision."

He could take credit for more than convincing activists to risk a temporary loss of freedom. With the help of Marv's friends, national figures from the Vietnam/civil rights era, the Honeywell Project helped form a local ethos of resistance and sacrifice for the common good. For many, the activism of the eighties led to changes of careers, relationships, and perspectives. And for Marv, the "time" done was a lifetime.

Whether or not the media reported the actions or trials, he considered the education campaigns successful. Minnesota maintained the political "peace posture" that made the state an exemplar around the country. Reports from inside the company confirmed that the protests were a constant topic of discussion; Honeywell management took definite steps to repair its public image, instituting a charitable foundation in the mid-eighties that financed Phillips neighborhood developments and ventures. "They co-opted the moral high ground," Marv insisted, "in addressing poverty issues here. But we still name it for what it is, the knife in the heart of the neighborhood."

Other peace groups, notably Minnesota Jobs with Peace, were picking up on the slogan "peace conversion with no loss of jobs," the third or fourth goal named in every Project protest. Jobs with Peace issued the report "Military Production and the Minnesota Economy," showing the effects of Pentagon spending on the work force and advocating funding to retrain employees.

PAMM groups decided to broaden their focus. They would engage in other conversion efforts and examine other Twin Cities military-industrial corporations such as FMC, which had established a headquarters near the University of Minnesota. The university itself gained lucrative defense contracts in the early 1990s, collaborating with FMC on a high-tech research-and-development contract with the Department of Defense.

FMC, although it began business as a "food systems" chemical company, was the primary contractor for the Bradley tank, a cumbersome personnel carrier that was lauded as the best at "defeating enemy tanks and other fighting vehicles while moving at high speeds in any kind of weather." As the Cold War ended, FMC's defense division declined and competition from a cheaper Russian tank, combined with Defense Department cutbacks, foreshadowed FMC's exit. Early in 1994, the company created United Defense, a joint venture with Harsco Corporation's Combat Systems, to control its defense unit.

From 1987 to 1990, PAMM groups attached to the Honeywell Project vigiled weekly at FMC following the Honeywell model, and held larger demonstrations on religious holidays, often with small groups risking arrest. The demonstrations took place at FMC's company headquarters in Fridley and also at its new facility in downtown Minneapolis near Washington Avenue and Interstate 35W. The city considered the new FMC offices a cornerstore of its "technology corridor," and had provided tax-increment financing for the building. FMC executives, in turn (according to business writer Dave Peters) were cultivating community leaders in an effort to become more visible and competitive with Honeywell for Defense Department business. Company executives admitted that its higher profile also made it a likely target for those in the Twin Cities who objected to the presence of military work, and that the possibility of protests was always a part of its analysis.

"Some people have no shame," said Marilyn Mason, one of the ten or so core members of the Citizens FMC (Fight Military Contractors) Committee who were veterans of protests against Honeywell. Others included Marv, Moira Moga, Mary Lou Ott, Deb Bancroft, Sue Ann Martinson, Marjorie Wunder, Marilyn, and me. On occasion, members of the Progressive Students Organization from the University of Minnesota would join us. A memorable Star Wars Campaign introduced the idea of carrying tattered, perforated umbrellas, mocking the sort of shield that the Strategic Defense Initiative provided against potential nuclear attacks.

The Project continued to monitor war-related operations that remained under the purview of Honeywell, including navigation systems and guidance gyroscopes. As we considered our next actions—did the Alliant TechSystems spin-off mean the Project would move protest operations to Hopkins?—Marv watched the business pages. But the attention of peace movement activists was also turning in another direction—Iraq.

On August 6, 1990 (Hiroshima Day), four days after Iraq's invasion of Kuwait, U.S. pressure on the U.N. Security Council brought about passage of Resolution 661, comprehensive sanctions on Iraq. "The whole international community thought this was going to be a temporary thing," Marv said, "but the movement was getting ready for serious action." On January 15, 1991 the Security Council endorsed a U.S.-led air war that destroyed much of Iraq's civilian infrastructure. Part of the administration's case for war was that an Iraqi force was threatening to attack Saudi Arabia. "The first Gulf War, as well as the current one," Marv emphasized, "was preceded by lies."

Citing top-secret satellite images, Pentagon officials claimed that 250,000 Iraqi troops and 1,500 tanks were massing on the border, threatening "our" oil supplier. "It was a pretty serious fib," said Jean Heller, the *St. Petersburg Times* journalist who broke the story. The *Times* acquired two commercial Soviet satellite images of the same area, taken at the same time. No Iraqi troops were visible near the Saudi border.

As American forces prepared to oust Iraqi forces from Kuwait during the fall and early winter, we were busy in the Honeywell and WAMM offices preparing mailings, phoning, and summoning support for antiwar vigils. Marv insisted that we should keep pointing at Honeywell corporation, because Honeywell's navigation systems for fighter jets would be used on the battlefield and cluster bombs were in the pipeline.

Mothers were worried about the draft returning. Neither of my sons had refused draft registration; registration was recommended if not required for males seeking college loans or scholarships. I persuaded Carl and Paul to file forms with the Central Committee for Conscientious Objection, hoping the forms could establish a clear paper trail for C.O. status, should that be necessary. They didn't think a draft was likely, but I was still Mom, even if they considered me a little obsessive about the country's growing enthusiasm for war. I had other worries: My brother Denny was in the Air Force and my husband Ken's son-in-law Larry was a helicopter pilot in the National Guard. We didn't know when they'd be deployed but we knew the destination.

In December 1990, reporter Steve Wilson prepared a story for *Inside Edition*, a television news program. Wilson intended to focus on Honeywell's and other war contractors' sub rosa sales to overseas clients. Wilson and a camera crew dropped in to the WAMM office in mid-December to film our preparations for a protest. They'd asked to talk to activists who had friends or family in the service, and there I was. Wilson told us that he would be interviewing Honeywell executives about Honeywell's weapons in the hands of Saddam Hussein. Could those weapons be used against our troops in Iraq? The weapons were called fuel-air explosives, Wilson said, sort of a "poor man's nuclear bomb... like a gas oven filling with gas and then having a lighted match tossed in."

Then he turned on the mike and asked me, "And when you hear that some of this technology comes from virtually down the street, how do you feel?" Watching the images years later, I see my grimace and wonder that words came out at all: "I've been close to this issue, as I told you, arrested at Honeywell, ... it's hard. It's just another twist of that knife in my heart." The camera swings to a family picture of Denny, wife Willa, little daughter Lindsay. We asked when the segment would be aired; Steve couldn't give us an exact date, but he thought it would be mid-January.

In a few short weeks—January 16, 1991, to be precise—the show was broadcast, but not in every market. I was not to see it that day. Around suppertime on the 16th, we had news of the first air strikes against Baghdad. Tears were still running down my cheeks when the phone rang. It was my brother Bob, in Indiana.

No, he hadn't heard anything more about our brother Denny, except that he was in Riyadh. But that wasn't why Bob called. An hour earlier, my eight-year-old nephew Jason had seen a trailer for *Inside Edition*, and yelled that Aunt Carol was going to be on! He taped the show; Bob said they'd make a copy and send it along.

On January 17, 1991, the peace movement was on the streets again, on freeway entrances, and at Peavey Plaza. "WAMM and some of us had already been holding signs against troop deployment since August," Marv remembered, "Since January, there was at least one protest every week over the first Gulf War all through downtown. Once I got to the Federal Building and Don [retired professor Don Irish] was standing by himself with a sign; but sometimes there were several hundred people. The media hardly touched the story!"

After several weeks of intensive air attacks on Iraqi cities, the land offensive began on 24 February. The war ended in what journalist Edward Herman dubbed the "highway of death" and a "turkey shoot"; a "completely helpless army in retreat from Kuwait was mercilessly slaughtered, by weapons of doubtful legality, such as fuel air bombs." President Bush declared victory on February 28. Kuwait was "liberated," though Saddam Hussein remained in power.

Just as the war ended, my brother Bob's package arrived. We watched the tape and heard the Honeywell executives' version of events. Honeywell technicians had crafted a three-hundred-page document on fuel-air technology, but they'd objected to the assignment, they said, thinking there was something "malodorous" about an intent to sell it; and they had omitted any description that would not be available elsewhere. A Honeywell public relations spokesperson concurred; nothing was in the report that couldn't be found in other places. She did evade

Antiwar rally, 1991. (Photo by Mark Jensen.)

questions about a sale combining the document with "ring-laser gyro" technology, reportedly sold to a Swiss company that was a front for Saddam Hussein. Steve Wilson concluded the segment with the statement that Honeywell was not alone; twenty-two U.S. defense companies had sold military technology to Iraq in the previous decade.

I called Marv to come and watch the tape. I reminded him that the war had pre-empted *Inside Edition* from the scheduled showing in Minneapolis (10:30 pm, on WCCO, after the news). A special news report on the attack went on and on instead, phosphorescent green and yellow explosions ripping into moonlike landscapes.

Marv thought the Twin Cities should see more of what Honeywell had been up to, and called WCCO. WCCO said they didn't get the "feed," and that they couldn't get a feed now, it was gone; it would be expensive to broadcast now. "We have a copy," Marv said, "and we think this is an important story for your viewers, here, in Minneapolis."

"You have an agenda," said the WCCO voice.

"Damn straight," Marv said, and promised to bring it to the studio.

We did; Marv took it up to a viewing room. He brought the tape back after half an hour. The format wasn't "suitable"—at any rate, the show never aired in the Twin Cities, except in my living room and church basements.

Minnesota Daily, September 27, 1991 (by Molly Guthrey): "As of October, the 23-year-old Honeywell Project will be gone. Through the years, thousands of people with the group have persistently and peacefully protested the corporation's production of military hardware. Many went to jail."

"*Persistence,*" Marv read, rattling the *Daily* as we sat outside the LeSueur Center at a picnic table, preparing to bid the office good-bye, "Yeah, that's a good word. The *Strib* used it too. They'll find out we won't leave them alone." A dozen or so of us were formalizing a new organization at a pizza-and-packing party. The new group, the Midwest Institute for Social Transformation (MIST), was to be a training ground for activists and resisters, too. Marv said, "We're not going to stop protesting but we're broadening our perspective."

MIST's mission was to help people who intended to spend their lives as workers for peace and justice. An institute with dedicated teachers and an educational goal, we thought, would be taken seriously and gain respect. Marv would use his contacts to continue the infusion of radical, transformative ideas to the Twin Cities. He would bring in politicized artists who could catch the hearts of youth. With Marv's deep experience in organizing, we'd engage partners among movements and organizations such as unions, farm advocates, and human services.

"Davidov believes that what the people in Minnesota need," said Guthrey in her *Daily* article, "is information about a variety of issues." Courses would enlighten students on such issues as people's law, people's medicine, "accuracy in the media for progressives" and "theater games for radicals." The *Daily* quoted Marty Roth and David Noble, university professors who had agreed to be advisors to MIST, to the effect that such an institute would meet important needs in the community. Traditional higher learning institutions did not ("*could* not," said Marv) carry courses that would bring about social change.

"We have an agenda," Marv said, remembering the WCCO call. "There are all sorts of problems the capitalist system won't address. We will."

22

Coalitions and Victories

The religious affinity groups so active in the 1980s and 90s proved themselves willing and able to put their bodies on the line—but for how long? And where? Weapons could be made and were being made elsewhere. New wars, arms build-ups and terrorist activity were never in short supply. The enemy shifted shape, forms of repression changed, campaigns stalled, and victories were scarce.

But there *were* victories. Marv's next campaign was one. It involved Martin Goff, a union organizer for the Hotel and Restaurant Employees (H.E.R.E.) Union Local 17, who had been pumping Marv for his ideas about nonviolent resistance, wondering if such pressures could work in labor disputes.

Goff's union was seeking to represent union members in major Minneapolis hotels—the cleaners and service workers who did the unseen low-wage jobs that kept visitors to the Twin Cities comfortable. Many of the workers were people of color or recent immigrants; most worked for an hourly wage and many of them worked more than one job; a large percentage were women. Martin knew that participation in any kind of public campaign would be difficult for these workers, dependent as they were on low wages. In fact, many of them had lost their jobs when the Normandy Hotel owner in downtown Minneapolis closed it for renovation and refused to rehire union members when it reopened. The owner, Tom Noble, stated he wanted a more upscale image for the hotel to compete with others downtown. (Noble had sold the building in 1985 then bought it back in 1990 for a fraction of the price.)

"He said he wanted to 'remove the lingering taint of a failed business'!" Goff fumed. "He's putting the blame on workers who have been there ten, twenty years, some of them working every holiday. Obviously, because they're union."

For Marv, organizing around a labor justice issue seemed like a golden opportunity for several reasons. Labor offered a history and a righteous cause that could lance the boil of capitalist oppression; other progressive forces in the community would support the cause; it was a local battle, intimately connected to broad concerns; and the battle was winnable, especially if mainstream media picked up the story. The cause would fulfill Ken Tilsen's mandate that the goal be specific and immediate: gains for the local union, jobs for the employees.

Union members had been picketing in shifts throughout the fall of 1991 and on into the winter, marching from 7 a.m. to 5 p.m., and maximizing their numbers at afternoon check-in times. They received small amounts of union benefits and the compliments of local politicians who declared they wouldn't patronize the hotel until the owner settled. But the picketers had been there for months.

Goff filled us in. "We've been on the picket line since early summer, with all kinds of unions, community groups, and religious groups lending support. When the AFL-CIO had their convention last month, Bernard Brommer gave a really strong pitch to the delegates, and we had dozens walking the line with us! That was really the peak. Every day we get support, buses always honk—it gives us a lift."

Marv asked if he wanted people from the Movement to organize shifts. Goff shook his head, "It's time to escalate. We've been talking about civil disobedience among the union staff and the executive board has weighed in. Seriously. I mean, these guys and women, we're like family. People donate food, cook for each other, support each other, but we're hurting. The other day, somebody in management talked to one of the staff; he said, like it's a joke: 'It's going to be a long, cold winter!' Noble doesn't care!"

"What about the Labor Relations Board—you contacted them, right?" Marv asked.

"Back in August. Noble refused to negotiate. We filed an age discrimination suit with the Minneapolis Civil Rights Department, because the new hires are all young. We're using all the tools. We've studied the events of the 20s and 30s, looking at how they supported each other."

"Like the 1934 Minneapolis truckers' strike, setting up meals!" I chimed in. My husband Ken could remember the strike. His dad was president of Yellow Cab when the cabs helped on deliveries and shuttles; drivers helped deliver groceries to the strikers' families.

"Yes, exactly. We know the hotel is only one workplace, but like the truckers' union, this struggle is kind of a baseline. If we lose this battle, we lose a lot. Noble is sure we'll dwindle away. He thinks he can outlast us. Of course he never thought it would last *this* long. "

"Your board's considered the risks, it sounds like," Marv said. "I don't mean just personal, like being arrested, though I always tell people, if you can't do the time...."

"Don't do the crime. We know. We're coming to you because you know how to do it. Jaye [Jaye Rykunyk, president of H.E.R.E. Local 17] is asking you to do a nonviolence training for civil disobedience."

In the course of the subsequent meeting, Marv outlined a plan to increase the numbers and the visibility of the union picketers. "You all know what's happening next month in downtown Minneapolis!" Everyone nodded: Super Bowl XXVI was coming, a rare wintry venue. We hadn't really paid much attention, since the Vikings were out of it. But the implications were clear for hotels.

"We'll organize, get some of our experienced people with the union—whoever can take the risk. We can get a good-sized group to sit in; it doesn't have to be huge, but we want to fill the lobby."

Of the hundred people who had lost their jobs, seventy were women—waitresses, front desk checkers, behind-the-scenes cleaners and maids: hospitality crews. "We've got to have gender balance doing the training," Marv said, gazing at each one of us. By pure luck, I was the only one of the other gender in the room.

Marty nodded. "Jaye will help out, but we could use your perspective."

"We'll do a circle, you know, everybody talks. Tell them your experience, what you do, why you do it."

"About nonviolence? I don't know ... "

"You don't have to be philosophical," Marv said, already preparing my talk, "just talk from your heart, tell them who you are, a writer, a family woman."

"Actually, I do know something about cleaning …" I began; Marty Goff laughed, assuming I meant my house. "Ken and I work for an elder care program, keeping people in their houses. They need help with cleaning, lawns and gardens, that kind of thing."

"Oh," Marv said, sounding unimpressed with my working class credentials, "How's the pay?" It was my turn to laugh, "Not great, it's a nonprofit." I agreed to help with the training and MIST officially joined the union's campaign.

Not long afterward, filmmakers at University of Minnesota Labor Education Services began to record key aspects of the struggle. A documentary *A Line in the Sand: The Struggle at the Hotel Normandy, 1991-92* highlighted interviews with Local 17 workers, picketers marching in all sorts of weather, including the famous Halloween blizzard (during which 31 inches fell in some parts of the city), and the sit-in. Normandy worker Doug Hill remembered, "There were days 12 degrees below zero, maybe lower. That storm, when even the buses couldn't get through, we were there picketing. We crossed a real psychological barrier with management then. They knew we weren't going away."

Mindful of our allies, the week before the Super Bowl, Marv brought Goff to the NFL headquarters where AIM was picketing, protesting racist mascots (Chiefs and Redskins) to talk to Vernon and Clyde Bellecourt. The pair agreed to participate and speak at the Normandy sit-in.

January 24, 1992: A temporary office has been set up in a construction pod two blocks from the hotel. Union staff and organizers check off names, answer phones, and give instructions to small groups who file out to cheers and handshakes. The camera catches Goff pacing, shouting encouragement, asking for reports from the "site." Putting down the phone, Anne Theurer (union organizer) says, "Someone was just calling from the coffee shop. People are sitting down, unobtrusive." Marv asks someone, "I go now?" Team leaders assign picketers to specific locations and entrances.

In the hotel lobby, people in parkas or heavy sweaters drift inside and begin to make themselves comfortable on the floor; the camera pans to faces, conversations, and tense or startled expressions. In a strong voice, an organizer announces to a red-faced manager, "We are here in solidarity with Normandy workers who have been wrongfully denied employment!" The scene shifts repeatedly, to Clyde Bellecourt on a bullhorn, Marv on the floor chatting with a circle of young people. There are snatches of songs: "Whose side are you on?" "Solidarity forever," and verses improvised to fit today's issue. A pizza is delivered. Marv instructs us, "When the cops come to arrest you, get up and walk out with them. Don't make them carry you. Cops get sore backs, too." Finally, the manager gives us the warning of impending arrest. Behind him wait a double line of embarrassed police ("They're union," Marv explains), and the lieutenant implores, "You have 15 minutes, we don't want to have to arrest you." Off camera, a high-pitched voice (perhaps a Sister of St. Joseph) replies: "You're going to have to!"

The workers were rehired. On the very day of the NLRB hearing, February 11, 1992, as the judge sat preparing for a trial, the union signed off on a settlement. "The paradox is that the union not only survived," union secretary-treasurer Dan Kuschke said, "but was stronger in the eyes of the public, and the employer."

All charges stemming from the arrests were dropped. Most moving was the testimony of a young worker who admitted to being terrified at the sit-in, but "if we gave up, the union people in the 1920s and 30s would have suffered for nothing. My dad told me he was proud of me, for standing up for what I believed. He fought to make this a union town and we fought to keep it!"

Marv's leadership in the Midwest Institute for Social Transformation brought a temporary hiatus to his antiwar/antiweapons protests. MIST's emphasis was on education for social change, promoting change through "programs and actions based on the principles of radical nonviolence and self-determination."

"We're bringing the Highlander model, in a modest way, to Minnesota and the Midwest," Marv explained. He had read about Highlander Folk School in Tennessee and Myles Horton, the school's founder. Highlander was controversial (right-wing groups labeled the school "communist") because it taught leadership skills to blacks and whites in defiance of segregation laws. Its literacy program focused on persuading blacks to register to vote.

MIST, like Highlander, intended to work closely with labor unions, antipoverty organizations, and human rights groups. In the first brochure, we named Local 17's campaign at the Normandy as the premier example of a successful action using principles of nonviolence. Marv's choice of advisory board members highlighted the institute's dedication to education for nonviolent social change. These "national sponsors" included Daniel and Philip Berrigan, Noam Chomsky, Dave Dellinger, Herb Kohl, Winona LaDuke, Meridel LeSueur, Grace Paley, Margaret Randall, Barbara Smith, Gerald Vizenor, Harvey Wasserman, and Howard Zinn. Marv was in regular touch with most of these visionary figures, who contributed to or were featured in MIST's programs.

"Our first program, in October 1991, featured Herb Kohl, progressive educator and advisory board member, with poetry by Roy McBride and music by Phyllis Goldin and Wanda Brown." In 1992 MIST sponsored activities with Sandy Levinson, director of the New York-based Center for Cuban Studies. Marv retained an interest in Cuba and its revolutionary socialism; he sponsored group trips on his own or with other organizations to challenge the travel ban. One such trip was with Dr. Patch Adams (who later came to Minneapolis for a MIST event). The group visited hospitals, AIDS wards, cultural centers, and a food production coop, and they also met some of the hundreds of Russian child victims of Chernobyl treated by Cuban doctors.

In the fall of 1992, the board organized a four-day retreat with Dave Dellinger and his wife Elizabeth Peterson. During the next spring, Marv organized a book tour for Dellinger's autobiography *From Yale to Jail: the Life Story of a Moral Dissenter.* The two visited thirty cities, bringing the message of active, revolutionary nonviolence to both students and mainstream audiences. Marv had many opportunities to share his own story and trade examples of activism around the nation.

Another MIST emphasis was corporate actions affecting the environment. For example, they supported the Mdewakanton Sioux community in its attempt to stop the nuclear waste dump at Prairie Island. MIST was a small but significant voice in the Prairie Island Coalition against Nuclear Storage (PICANS), thanks to Marv's friendship and working relationships with AIM and George Crocker.

Prairie Island, home to Prairie Island Mdewatkanton Dakota, is situated about as close as a community can be to a nuclear plant. Two 580 megawatt reactors border the community, sitting a few hundred yards from homes, businesses, and childcare centers. When the plant was being planned and built in the early 1960s, the tribe was told it was getting a "steam generator." Only after many questions was the tribe finally told that the steam would be heated by nuclear reactions.

"According to George," Marv told the MIST board, "all the Indian community *got* was a swing set. George has been watching energy issues since the power line days, and he thinks this is the time for organized action."

The plant was advertised as a safe and efficient source of energy but within the decade it faced a familiar problem—what to do with the waste. In 1990 Northern States Power Company (NSP) revealed plans to store it outdoors in 48 steel casks, though it could propose no safe process to unload these non-transportable casks. "It's the worst kind of environmental racism," Marv said. "Nobody wants to live downriver from radioactive waste—for God's sake, they built the plant in a flood plain—we should all be terrified! And they built it two blocks from the tribal community, from a little children's playground!"

Marv's interest was, as always, corporate profiteering at the expense of poor and minority communities, though in this case, environmental concerns were paramount: he wanted to stop our state's bad energy habits and promote renewable resources.

In early 1993, new MIST half-time staff member Kris Pranke traveled to Washington, DC for Hazel O'Leary's confirmation hearing as new Secretary of Energy. With others from Minnesota, she persuaded Paul Wellstone to raise questions about Prairie Island during the hearing. She also represented MIST in bringing nuclear waste storage at Prairie Island to the attention of the *New York Times*.

MIST used our list of activists to publicize the Prairie Island Coalition's findings and to organize demonstrations at Prairie Island and at NSP's headquarters in downtown Minneapolis. Board members and volunteers were involved when PICANS intervened in NSP's lawsuit against Westinghouse over leaking nuclear steam generator tubes. One of Crocker's worries was that "reactors like Prairie Island have thousands of steam generator tubes that could rupture at any time. If this happens, radioactive water in the core will boil; radioactive steam will be vented; steam will force water out of the core; and without cooling water, the core will melt ... the industry doesn't know what to do to prevent it."

Sometimes the task of sifting through files and technical reports takes as much commitment as standing in a demonstration: MIST's Ken Masters and Bruce Drew spent many hours reviewing nuclear industry documents, and PICANS secured copies of more than sixty thousand pages. In 1994 the legislature and NSP finally reached a compromise. NSP was granted an extension of on-site storage while giving the tribe a legal say in the issue. The Westinghouse suit was settled out-of-court in April of 1996.

Since that time, the issue has not disappeared. The Prairie Island reactor (and also the reactor further upstream in Monticello, Minnesota) is currently being relicensed for 20-year extensions, even as "reactor parts age and deteriorate and are modified to run hotter and at higher pressures," according to Crocker. Marv likes to point out to policymakers and corporate profiteers, "Anything is cheap if you don't pay the costs!"

In the mid-1990s MIST worked on another aspect of the nuclear issue in supporting Catholic Worker protests of a U.S. Navy communications site near Clam Lake, Wisconsin. The site transmitted signals at extremely low frequency (ELF)—the only kind that can be picked up by deep-water submarines. They are generally used simply to tell a submarine to surface, where a more detailed message can be received.

Friends Mike Miles, Barbara Cass, John LaForge, and Barbara Katt founded the intentional community of Catholic Workers called Anathoth not far from Luck, Wisconsin (named for the town where the prophet Jeremiah bought a field to signify that the people would return from exile). Anathoth was a working farm, an environmental center, and a direct action site. The four were all veteran peace activists, and they had come to the conclusion that the ELF transmission system was a trigger for nuclear first-strike capabilities. They protested at the Clam Lake site, were tried, and went to jail. Each year in spring and fall, dozens of Twin Cities activists, including Marv, also caravanned to the

Wisconsin site for protests or civil disobedience actions.

In the *St. Paul Pioneer Press* (January 1993), Mike Miles asserted that ELF's nuclear submarines were effectively outmoded by international agreements. "As the world order has changed— the Soviet Union is gone and the Warsaw Pact is gone, along with their military threat—ELF and the Trident submarine fleet are not needed." Furthermore, they were expensive (each submarine was about $2 billion and $14.5 million a year to run the stations).

MIST and Anathoth activists worked closely on a number of campaigns in the 1990s, both in Wisconsin and in the Twin Cities. MIST also sponsored retreats at the farm to promote community-based nonviolent resistance to war systems while using the farm itself as model of moral, sustainable living. Presenters such as Phil Berrigan and Elizabeth McAlister (antinuclear activists, founders of Jonah House) led the retreats and helped the community enlist activists to take part in vigils and civil disobedience.

Anathoth remains a model for peace and environmental activists, and Marv's class on active nonviolence at St. Thomas brings students to the farm at least once a year.

MIST continued its educational focus throughout the 1990s, sponsoring events and speakers on a variety of policy and justice topics. But corporate profiteering from weapons of mass destruction was never far from Marv's mind. He had announced when Alliant began its operations in 1990 that the company would also fall under the scrutiny of the Project, and he kept tabs on its weapons contracts. As news of Alliant's Pentagon contracts became more widespread, the MIST board started talking about having a presence at Alliant.

Alliant's contracts for the Iraq war (and sales to other countries, like Israel) included 120 mm uranium core antitank shells, 30 mm bullets for the A-10 Warthog and Apache helicopters, and other ordnance, including the Adam land mine. These weapons systems were about to make headlines. When Reverend Jim Ketcham of Church World Service and community development organizer Dave Gagne approached Marv with news that the International Committee to Ban Land Mines was taking a close look at Alliant production, he was ready to move.

23

Peace Prizes

The International Campaign to Ban Landmines (ICBL) in 1995 formally identified Alliant TechSystems as *the* major U.S. producer of land mines. After talking with community organizers Dave Gagne and Jim Ketcham about Alliant, Marv met with Handicap International's Susan Walker, who had recently moved to the Twin Cities to be near an aging parent. Susan had worked in Southeast Asia from 1979 to 1994 as director of the American Refugee Committee and regional director for Handicap International. As a manager of programs for physically disabled persons in Thailand, Vietnam, Laos, and Cambodia, she came into contact with thousands of men, women, and children who had lost limbs to land mines.

"I can't do this anymore," she finally decided. Resolving to follow the lead of those who addressed the causes rather than the effects of war, she became a co-founder, along with Dave, Jim, and Marv, of the Minnesota Campaign to Ban Landmines, with a particular focus on Alliant TechSystems. MIST became a regular presence at Alliant's corporate headquarters in Hopkins, a first-ring suburb west of Minneapolis, and later at its headquarters in Edina and then Eden Prairie, drawing public attention to the types of things Alliant manufactured—bombs and land-mines—and the devastating and indiscriminate effects those products had on civilian populations.

From 1969 to 1992 the United States exported more than five million antipersonnel land mines to more than thirty countries including Afghanistan, Angola, Cambodia, Iraq, Laos, Lebanon, Mozambique, Nicaragua, Rwanda, Somalia, and Vietnam. Because unexploded mines continue to wreak havoc among civilian populations for decades after a conflict has ended, they fit the definition of indiscriminate weapons. The majority of victims are farmers, ordinary citizens, and children. When the land mine ban campaign began, an average of seventy people were dying each day because of mines in different parts of the world. Millions more lived in fear as they walked to their work or school and every day risked their lives to plant crops.

At the end of his term, President Clinton said that one of his greatest regrets was that he could not sign the Mine Ban Treaty, because the United States relied on them for the security of its troops abroad. Marv is unsympathetic to such "liberal" regrets from ex-presidents or retired CEOs. "Making millions from murder, or enabling the profiteers with a murderous policy—as every U.S. president from Kennedy on has done—is more than regrettable. It is shameful. It is unforgivable."

Early in 1996, Marv wrote in our MIST newsletter, "A few things are obvious to me. As Leonard Cohen sings: 'Everybody knows, the rich get richer. The poor get poorer...' Mass layoffs, early retirement, and deep cuts in income create profound insecurity and anxiety that bludgeon the poor and middle class...at the same time, corporate profits soar. 'Everybody knows' the income gap between average workers and the corporate elite is now 180 to 1. So what solutions do the leaders of both parties suggest? The answer: Nothing serious."

No one in that election season, he fumed, talked "about the bloated military budget, which siphons 270 billion dollars into a subsidy for high-tech industry and corporate welfare for the already rich and powerful. War contractors steal from the taxpayers!" In the same issue of our newsletter *MIST Rising*, he made the announcement that we would confront Alliant: "We're Ba-ack!", warning that the "Largest Landmines Producer Should Expect Large Turnout" on May 7, 1996.

Responding in advance to Alliant's likely defense of its products— that U.S. mines were "smart mines" that would hit precise targets— Marv wrote, "This argument would be ridiculous if it were not so evil. Land mines by their nature are indiscriminate; their targets are predominantly civilians; they are a weapon of terrorism. They cannot be accident proof... other countries do not want to give up their 'inferior,' more cheaply made mines as long as the United States has mines. It is totally unacceptable for management to be making profits off the murder of children and peasants." We were not going to have that in our state, and we would "put our bodies in the way of this obscenity."

We were back: to major movement events, rallies, publicity, and even large trials. Meetings of the MIST board over the next months ended with Marv pumping his fist, "We're rolling!" With the help of the local board, Marv provided the texts of occasional event- or action-linked newsletters; I edited and produced them.

On May 6, 1996, we kicked off the new Minnesota Campaign to Ban Land Mines with a rally featuring Howard Zinn, Dan Berrigan, Susan Walker, and Ed Miles, a leader of Vietnam Veterans of America who lost his legs in Vietnam. The band from Anathoth played at the rally, which pumped people up for the action the next day at Alliant TechSystem's headquarters in Hopkins.

That first land mines protest at Alliant brought out about two hundred people. Susan Walker and Jim Ketcham had contacted Alliant management several times in the previous weeks requesting a meeting but had received no response. Nevertheless, we took the responsibility to meet with the company's security team, Marv explaining the group's intentions and nonviolent philosophy. We invited Alliant management to attend the meeting—they sent a public relations representative. We also contacted the Hopkins police department.

The May 7 rally and march to the doors of the long, low building on 2nd Street was peaceful; we blockaded doors for an hour or two, and Hopkins police, though in evidence, made no arrests. "It has never been our intent to prevent any of the demonstrations or demonstrators to gather and express their opinions," said Alliant public affairs director Rod Bitz, in a rare interview for local press, adding that the land mines were smart mines and had a self-destruct mechanism.

For the first couple of years of the Landmines Campaign, Alliant spokespeople freely admitted that Alliant was a land mine manufacturer, indeed, the largest in the United States. This position changed as nationwide and international publicity grew and public pressure for an international ban brought an unwelcome spotlight to the corner of 2nd Street and Van Buren, Hopkins.

Over the next year, anti-weapons protest activity intensified, with weekly vigils once again interspersed with actions on significant dates and mass rallies and civil disobedience at least twice a year. But the campaign also had its lighter moments. Marv had a maxim that "We're not a one-party group!" Especially in tough times, we found or invented occasions to celebrate. For Marv's sixty-fifth birthday, MIST held a major gala in September 1996 at the Dakota Bar and Grill. "Roasters" included Robert Bly, Dick Bancroft, Char Madigan, comedienne Colleen Kruse, poet Carol Connolly, and musician Michael Hauser.

Besides renewed engagement in weapons issues, MIST continued to address problems of disenfranchised people. For example, we sponsored a workshop on Battered Women on October 19, 1996, featuring Sharon Rice Vaughan, Char Madigan, Evan Stark, and Dr. Ann Flitcraft. Sharon, Char and Evan had been with the Honeywell Project in the early days, and during that time their eyes had been opened to the effects of militarism. They all went on to pursue careers in "works of mercy, not works of war," as our signs proclaimed. Sharon began the first battered women's shelter in the United States. Char was a founder and first director of St. Joseph's/HOPE Community in Minneapolis. And Evan and Ann also did pioneering work in the area of countering violence against women in New Haven, Connecticut.

The 1996 Welfare Reform legislation gave Marv opportunities to contrast corporate wealth—particularly Alliant's—with the desperate conditions of poor and powerless people everywhere, even in our own neighborhoods. "In my opinion," he said, "President Clinton and a majority of Congress, Republican and Democrats, voted to bash poor children and immigrants in the most oppressive public policy this administration has engineered so far. At the same time they continue to bless the Corporate Reich with welfare. And it is beyond the imagination of any mainline media source to even mention this." But we would broadcast it in every publication, flyer, and event MIST planned, continuing to draw the connections between poverty, U.S. militarism, and the corporate greed fueling it.

A few days after the conference on battered women, MIST sponsored a program at the University of Minnesota featuring Phil Berrigan and Liz McAlister, who also joined us the next day at a demonstration at Alliant. At that event we inaugurated the practice of bringing shoes, crutches, and prostheses to actions or vigils and leaving them behind when we left as graphic symbols of a land mine's effect. Bridget Macdonald, interviewed on Amy Goodman's show "Democracy Now," reported, "We leave one crutch and a shoe and maybe a sign there reminding them what land mines do. I know my garage and my trunk have tons of crutches in them… I can't go on a trip cause I have no space for a suitcase! People say my trunk looks like I've been to Fatima and back!"

Alliant management was weary of reporters' questions. The company's policy of allowing demonstrators to gather and express their opinions stiffened. At the October 1996 action, thirty-nine people were arrested for trespassing.

Immediately following the October action, Berrigan and McAlister facilitated a retreat at Anathoth farm, on "Spirituality and Resistance." Marv encouraged us to read Berrigan's autobiography, *Fighting the Lamb's War*, to give examples and help us overcome the pressures and frustrations of an activist life. In their presence and teaching, the couple was a living book for us. Phil Berrigan, one of the originators of the Plowshares Movement, spoke passionately about the suffering and evil of war, naming the countries and people affected by the devastation that Honeywell/Alliant weapons wrought. His wife, Elizabeth, was an exemplar of a feminist partner and educator. She managed Jonah House, an intentional community that, like Anathoth, nurtured activists.

Over the winter of 1996-97, seventeen trespassers prepared for trial. (Twenty-two others decided to plead "no contest" and were fined fifty dollars.) Marv suggested that we contact Peter Thompson, a lawyer sympathetic to the peace movement, for advice on legal avenues to follow. Marv needed help devising a long-term strategy that would bring together the local impact of small groups offering themselves for arrest and the international attention that land mines had begun to receive. If he could do that, media attention would follow.

Honeywell Project veterans remembered that we had read aloud the Nuremberg Principles in Honeywell's lobby, and been scoffed at as a result: "The crazies are trying to argue international law!" Mostly, judges wouldn't allow that sort of defense. Honeywell Project defendants John Brechon, Mark Wernick, and others, had won an important concession in the 1983 *Brechon* decision, when a judge ruled that defendants could offer evidence as to their personal reasons for trespassing.

Throughout the Honeywell trials individuals testified as to their moral position but there were few references to international law; nor would judges allow such inflammatory material as pictures of wounded children. We also understood that we'd have a better chance of presenting our reasons before a judge if we did it without lawyers (pro se) because lawyers had to operate within well-established but colorless protocols that granted little scope for an activist's passion or moral conviction.

Peter Thompson and Sarah Aho, a staff member with the law firm, reviewed the numerous Honeywell trials and identified within the Minnesota trespass statute the legal basis for our defense: that we did *not* trespass "without claim of right." Minnesota trespass law allowed people to enter someone's property *if they had a right to do so under a law, rule, or statute.* In the Alliant defense, we would base our "claim of right" on international law.

The legal system seemed to be stacked in favor of the weapons corporations and militaristic policy. But as Marv observed at the November 13, 1996 bench trial after the first arrest at Alliant, "The Holocaust was legal. Slavery was legal. The production and threatened use of nuclear weapons is supported by laws, as is the production of antipersonnel weapons that kill and maim farmers and children indiscriminately. Any morally, spiritually, politically alive person must *break* that kind of law, and we will go back again and again to do it at Alliant."

Marv's was the first of several statements at our sentencing. Others continued with the "one-minute" statements Judge Poston requested, outlining their personal reasons for barring the doors at Alliant. Moira Moga stated, "My son works [for a Catholic mission] in Angola, so heavily mined that there are more mines than people. He has told me about the great suffering and starvation in that beautiful agricultural land, because they can't work the fields." Barb Mishler said, "I am the director of a Minneapolis Loaves and Fishes program, where we serve about four hundred people a night, about a hundred and fifty of them children. When I see a hundred and fifty hungry children a night, I want my tax dollars going to support *them*, not to a producer of weapons that blow apart children around the world." Ken Masters emphasized the duties of a citizen in a representative democracy. "I worked this past election on voter registration, convinced of the value of that work, even though less than half of the registered voters finally went to the polls. But as I see my beloved country go down the path of imperialism and militarism, I know I have a duty to confront those who profit by [those systems], to stand up to weapons makers like Alliant." One man bent down to unlace and remove his boot, placing it on the podium and saying, "This shoe speaks for itself."

A program for the Ban Landmine Campaign at St. Stephen's Church in Minneapolis.

Numbers at the vigils continued to grow as the ban campaign gained publicity and the world moved closer to a treaty banning mines. More than forty nations had agreed to a ban by late 1996; the U.S. was not among them. Susan Walker initiated a "Ban Bus" tour around the nation, bringing land mine survivors to dozens of communities to share their stories. Activist Ariel Brugger began a 1,300-mile cross-country walk in October 1996 from Alliant to Washington, D.C., to bring to the public's attention U.S. export of anti-personnel land mines. Members of Congress supported the treaty, especially Sen. Patrick Leahy (D-VT), who called for a ban in the production of all U.S. anti-personnel land mines including those with self-destruct devices: "People who talk about 'smart' land mines should ask themselves if a smart land mine can distinguish between an innocent child and a soldier? I call on all U.S. manufacturers to get out of the business."

In Minneapolis, MIST planned for the next months' actions, holding seminars on international law and its relevance to weapons makers for anyone who was interested. Marv enlisted poet Robert Bly to headline an evening rally in April 1997 and to write something for the MIST newsletter. Thinking of others who might be inspired to join this new international cause, Bly wrote a "Call to Action, special invitation to the Men's Movement." "One task of mature men is to protect children," he wrote. "I want to invite men… to join us on April 24 in an action of civil disobedience at Alliant TechSystems in Hopkins. Your presence among the number of people who are protesting land mines is important, whether or not you choose to be arrested."

On April 24, 1997 three hundred people assembled in Alliant's parking lot for brief speeches from Marv, Bly, Susan Walker, and others. Quaker Michael Bischoff shared his perspective as a first-time protestor at the site; he was uncomfortable with the scene and had qualms about being arrested: "Marv asked us to form a single-file line and get with our 'affinity group,' people we knew well who would stay together and support each other.…" Since Bischoff didn't know anyone present that well, he wandered up and down the line, looking for a place that felt right. When the key organizers were arrested, "the crowd lost some of its focus and momentum. … Others proceeded around the building, dropping off some people at each door. It was rather anti-climactic.

"As the police took each person away, the crowd would cheer.… The applause turned me off. My choice of whether or not to get arrested felt, at the time, like a private and sobering one. The crowd's encouragement reminded me of a high school pep assembly, and that didn't fit with my motivations." Nevertheless, Mike remained, and "hearing the clear focus on voicing challenge to land mines, I was reminded that this morning was about more than the way I felt and more than an interesting dance between some polite protesters and some friendly police." He decided to risk arrest. "I stepped in front of the employees' entrance at Alliant. … the shiver I'd had for the past hour subsided. I knew I was in the right place."

Mike and seventy-eight others, including many on the MIST board, came to trial in the third week of September 1997, just as representatives from more than ninety countries were meeting in Oslo to work out the final wording on the Land Mine Treaty. Peter Thompson and a partner represented nine of us who planned to testify, and we, in turn, represented the seventy others charged. During the Honeywell years it had been common to have a consolidated trial in which all agreed to abide by the verdict given those who testified, but it was uncommon to have such a large group trial.

Nothing about the trial was "business as usual," from jury selection, which began September 22, 1997, to Judge Nordby's post-trial remarks to the defendants. As Doug Grow wrote in the Minneapolis *Star Tribune*, "From Day 1 of jury selection, [juror] Connie Sproles knew she was in for an unusual experience. She was one of about 20 Hennepin County residents who were led into a courtroom jammed with 79 defendants Monday, including some of Minnesota's best-known repeat offenders. 'We didn't know what the trial was going to be about,' Sproles said of that first day. 'I looked out over the courtroom and saw all those people with white hair and I wondered, What could these old people have done?'"

We tried to balance the age, gender, and perspectives of the testifiers, but Steve Sato, an activist from Chicago, may have been the only one without white hair. Through a quirky set of circumstances he was the one who saved the day.

Peter had briefed us on the language we should use in claiming a right to be on Alliant's premises, but advised us to speak freely of our moral reasons for protesting land mines. In the Memorandum to the Court (in support of proposed jury instruction), he summarized: *Defendants' theory of defense is that they acted pursuant to a bona fide claim of right, believing they had permission to be upon the premises of Alliant Tech pursuant to statute, rule, regulation or other law.* The prosecutor, Hopkins city attorney Wynn Curtiss, strove to convince the jury that neither Alliant nor the law gave us permission to be there.

Curtiss was a quiet, gently humorous young lawyer who at one point told the jury, "This is not exactly what I had in mind—prosecuting nuns." Curtiss and Peter Thompson were a matched set in appearance, both tall, lanky, bandbox neat and "suited up," except that Peter in the final day of argument wore suspenders, lengthening his lean frame and evoking a northern Atticus Finch.

Peter cited customary international law, the Hague Convention, and Geneva Conventions, informally called "the Rules of War," which prohibited indiscriminate weapons and targeting civilians. He said that the jury would benefit from a definition of the term "statute, rule or regulation," the crux of the defendants' theory of defense. Laws would include "treaties and customary international law." He cited Article VI(2) of the United States Constitution, which provides that … "all Treaties made, or which shall be made, under the Authority of the United States, shall be the supreme Law of the Land; and the Judges in every state shall be bound thereby."

One after another, the defendants duly referred to international law before they spoke of their specific motivation. Curtiss zeroed in on Marguerite Corcoran, a sixty-seven-year-old Sister of St. Joseph of Carondelet, who spoke of meeting "a boy from El Salvador who had crawled over a land mine while working in a field. The explosion left him blind, blew off his arms, and killed his younger brother. He came to Minnesota to learn whether specialists could restore his sight. They could not."

Wynn questioned her understanding of international law and how it applied to her actions. He handed her a hefty document from the Geneva conventions and asked her to locate the passages that allowed her to trespass. Silently waiting for her to thumb through the papers, Wynn blushed and tried to suppress amusement. Thompson objected, and she was allowed to leave the witness stand to find the relevant passages.

Witness Steve Clemens, warehouse manager for Twin Cities Habitat for Humanity, had studied international law as a student and activist for more than twenty years. He and his family had been members of Koinonia Farm in Georgia, an intentional, interracial Christian community based on principles of nonviolence and shared goods. Steve gave a clear explanation of international law—that general principles evolve over years into explicit treaties (such as the evolving ban on land mines). He was passionate about the validity of our legal argument. To Steve, the "permission" clause in the Minnesota trespass statute was more than a hook on which to hang a slim defense: "We're responsible as individuals for treating each other with certain basic rights," he said. "The U.N. in its charter adopted the Nuremberg Principles, which clearly state that we *each* have a responsibility to prevent crimes against humanity. Just following orders does not justify contributing to or passively witnessing these crimes."

Jane Macdonald, the youngest of the four Macdonald sisters who are Sisters of St. Joseph of Carondelet, gave one of the closing statements on Thursday, September 25. After asking permission of Judge Nordby, she lit a candle, saying, "It is better to bring light to the world than to curse the darkness. We usually make decisions in the courtroom from the neck up. I'm asking you to use your heart and the rest of your body. We obeyed the spirit of the law and didn't act with criminal intent." She spoke about Desmond Tutu, who had sent his blessing; at that point the judge stopped her. The reference was "new evidence" that she could *not* present in a closing statement. She then sang the song that was a staple of Alliant vigils: "Take away the land mines, what we need is to ban mines, ... an eye for an eye leaves us all blind...."

The jury was unable to arrive at a decision that day, and the next morning it remained deadlocked. We waited out the deliberations in the courthouse basement cafeteria. Defendants who could take time off dropped by, joining the testifiers and witnesses. Marv arrived, excitedly holding up the morning's Minneapolis *Star Tribune*. He carried it from table to table, pointing to an article about the Campaign to Ban Landmines. It had been nominated for the Nobel Peace Prize! "Unbelievable!" he said, "I wonder if the jury noticed this." Should the ICBL win, we had a part in that victory and could hold our heads high. "Not that we didn't before!" Marv said, insisting, not for the last time, "We're the most active group in the Ban Land Mines Campaign!"

Around 1:00 pm, the jury returned to the courtroom. It took about an hour to round up the defendants who had stayed in the courthouse—some had been obliged to return to work, and only the nine representative defendants were required to be present. We took our seats, waiting for the jury's entrance. Would any of them meet our eyes? They wouldn't—a bad sign.

The lawyers had agreed that if any one of us were found not guilty, all must be dismissed. But I didn't realize until the last name was read that the verdict rested on one testimony. "The prosecution, defense and judge had agreed to drop misdemeanor charges against everyone who blocked the doors of Alliant TechSystems in Hopkins April 24 if the jury found even *one* not guilty. The defendants—nuns, students, a poet and others—seemed shell-shocked as the judge read guilty verdicts against eight of the nine who testified." Then the judge read Steve Sato's name, and intoned, "Not guilty." Expressionless, he quickly dismissed the case against us and ordered everyone out of the court-room except the defendants and their lawyers.

We could not seem to react with appropriate celebration. Under Judge Nordby's glare, we whispered as our supporters left, speculating about the jury's choice. I wondered if they had confused Sato with Steve Clemens, who had been so persuasive in explaining international law. I was later told that the jury was reassured about Steve Sato's lack of criminal intent when he said he probably *wouldn't* protest at the Alliant CEO's home. Wynn Curtiss had insistently questioned defendants on the limits of protest, attempting to undermine the "reasonableness" of linking international law to trespass. In his closing statement, Curtiss argued that a not guilty verdict in such a case would be "the nose of the camel under the tent."

Judge Nordby silenced the whispered speculation and launched into a tirade against the defendants, our supporters, and particularly our lawyers. We had abused his time and the legal system. He emphatically discouraged us from using international law to justify ourselves, and excoriated the lawyers for arguing it as a defense in a trespass case.

Stone-faced, Peter made a mild reply. The rest of us filed out, embarrassed by the scolding. But our heads were high and our hearts were on fire for the next time we would try it.

We'd been embarrassed, too, earlier in the year when Alliant announced that it was not making anti-personnel land mines. Our publicity around the April action had emphasized Alliant as the U.S. largest land mines producer. Richard Schwartz, Alliant's CEO, had written Human Rights Watch in August of 1996 to say that since Desert Storm, production of "self destruct, self-deactivating mines has been limited to replenishing inventories used during that conflict, and we anticipate no future production of ... [such] mines. The Pentagon has requested Alliant to reconfigure the Volcano land mine system solely to an antitank capacity."

A representative of Human Rights Watch, present for the April evening rally, told Marv that the only thing that may have changed was the terminology—the company had *completed* a contract for one type of mine but would not refuse Pentagon contracts for others. Human Rights Campaign reported that "Alliant does a brisk business in land mines. It raked in $350 million in land-mine sales between 1985 and 1995. ... Together, Alliant and its subsidiary Accudyne 'hold a prominent role in that particular hall of shame,'" said Cooper, land-mine researcher for the Arms Project of Human Rights Watch.

According to an Army letter to Minnesota Representative Jim Ramstad, Accudyne and Alliant had contracts to produce the Volcano [an antitank mine] through July 1999. But Rod Bitz, who handles public relations for Accudyne, says the company had been making the 'brains' of the land mines, and stopped in May 1997. Furthermore, Cooper said, Alliant was "the most vocal opponent of an anti-personnel land-mine ban," lobbying Congress intensely against Leahy's mine-export moratorium.

Our protest of Alliant's posture was difficult to explain to many ban supporters who had been called to civil disobedience. An activist who had invited a clergyman was furious. "This man came because he thought Alliant made land mines! He was upset! What am I going to tell him?"

"You tell him," Marv said, "that seventeen U.S. companies, Alliant the first and the largest, *rejected in writing* Human Rights Watch's appeal to forego any future production of antipersonnel mine parts." The campaign continued to focus its "stigmatization" publicity on Alliant, but protesting future possible weapons was a harder argument to make.

Alliant CEO Richard Schwartz wrote: "The International Campaign to Ban Landmines has served an invaluable role in shedding light on a terrible problem that must be addressed" (letter to Human Rights Watch) but insisted that his company's land mines were not to blame. "It is irresponsible to imply in any way that companies such as Alliant TechSystems have contributed to the world's land mine problems. To do so wrongly maligns responsible U.S. citizens."

Two weeks later, on October 10, 1997, the Nobel Peace Prize announcement came: The International Campaign to Ban Landmines and its coordinator Jody Williams had won. The media again paid attention, though not to us. One exception was Amy Goodman of *Democracy Now*, a public radio show dubbed "the exception to the rulers." Goodman interviewed Marv, Sister Bridget Macdonald, and

Barbara Pratt, who was arrested with her daughter, because the day of the protest was Take Your Daughter to Work Day.

Marv began his interview with a quote from comedian Paul Krassner about MIST's origins: "I thought you said you were *PIST!*" He recounted the first civil disobedience action at Alliant and who had been involved: "Howard Zinn, Dan Berrigan, Ed Miles. That was sixteen months ago. Sister Char Madigan suggested we do a weekly vigil, every Wednesday, which we had done at Honeywell. Then we go out to breakfast together." As always in interviews, he needed to "go back" to explain the history of Honeywell as it morphed into Alliant, emphasizing the Project's constant vigilance. When Honeywell announced in 1989 that they wanted to sell their weapons division, "we felt we were one serious part of that decision." Asked about the effect of his protests over the years, he continued, "one effect—going back to the Honeywell years—when a new CEO came, this was in the 80s, he was asked, What are you going to do about Honeywell Project, constantly at headquarters? See, that's where we demonstrate, not at the manufacturing plant, where the line workers are. It's always at the *corporate office*, because the main culpability stands with management! The CEO said, 'I found morale at corporate headquarters *so low*, abysmally low, because of the anti-Honeywell activity. Our way of dealing with that was to increase Honeywell foundation corporate giving to the community'—That's only one aspect, I could say more, but we'll run out of time!"

On December 4, 1997, 122 nations signed the Ban Land Mines treaty in Ottawa, Canada. Burkina Faso became the fortieth country to ratify the agreement, and in March 1999 the treaty became binding under international law and did so more quickly than any treaty of its kind in history. Jody Williams, in her acceptance speech for the Nobel Peace Prize, acknowledged the work of all groups that were part of the International Campaign. "And the real prize is the treaty. What we are most proud of is the treaty. It would be foolish to say we that we are not deeply honored by being awarded the Nobel Peace Prize. ... But the receipt of the Nobel Peace Prize is recognition of the accomplishment of this campaign. ... Together, we have set a precedent. Together, we have changed history."

Marv agrees, adding, once again, "*We* were the most active group."

24

Revolutionary America

The United States has not yet signed the land mines treaty, nor did the Bush administration show any interest in the International Cluster Bombs Treaty. When 111 governments signed that treaty on May 28, 2008, the BBC laconically reported: "The Pentagon stood firm, saying: 'While the United States shares the humanitarian concerns of those in Dublin, cluster munitions have demonstrated military utility, and their elimination from US stockpiles would put the lives of our soldiers and those of our coalition partners at risk.'"

The land mines ban campaign continued at Alliant through the 1990s. The new language, calling for Alliant to reverse its position on mines (and *all* indiscriminate weapons), was persuasive to activists if not the company. The vigil circle grew over the next two years to include young people that Marv drew in from his classes and talks.

In the fall of 1998, Marv and the vigil circle planned to step up the pressure on management by holding *two* consecutive days of protest. We added a call for Alliant to cease developing the Objective Individual Combat Weapon (a weapon that promised to "shoot around corners") and delivery systems for the First Strike Trident II Nuclear Missiles. We also recommended that it explore meaningful peace conversion. Sixty-six people were arrested over the course of the two-day protest.

In an attempt to forestall the second day of protest, police picked up three of the local leaders (Marv, Tom Bottolene, and Bill Barnett) and Duluth Catholic Worker Joel Kilgour. They were held at the St. Louis Park Police station for 36 hours, at the request of the Hopkins City Attorney Wynn Curtiss.

"I didn't know he had that power," Marv mused. "Well, he was going to help us. People stepped up." A hundred or so protestors turned up the second day and the action went on as planned. The four were released after demonstrations were over on 8 October.

Marv continued to teach Active Nonviolence courses in Peace Studies departments which drew more students to the anti-weapons movement. "There's a hunger out there for some kind of truth and some kind of meaning," he said. "I found that students didn't know a thing about the history of dissent in America." In classrooms at Carleton, St. Cloud State University, and St. Thomas University, and on the streets, he gave them examples of what it means to confront oppressive systems nonviolently. "I say to students, 'What's your morality? What's your spirituality? What's your philosophy? Why don't you live it?' You got to live this stuff wherever you can. ... We can change lives."

He loved working with people whose motivations stemmed from spiritual beliefs, sisters like the McDonalds, Char Madigan, and Rita Foster, who remained the core of Alliant and antiwar vigils. For all the plain, scathing talk about war profiteers and the government that enabled them, much of his most deeply felt, pointed admonition is rooted in spirituality.

"People are always asking me, why are people smiling when they're getting busted for making social change, or against war, or for peace? And the answer is, for a few minutes, privately and publicly we're one person! We're acting out our deepest personal, political, humanitarian insights. And that makes you a whole person!"

About the four Sisters Macdonald, on the front lines of the Twin Cities' protest community since Honeywell days, he is laudatory: "They're all like Irish elves; They're youthful and have an interior life. They're powerful women who went through a great transformation and liberated themselves." Cheryl Reed of *City Pages* interviewed Marv and the four at breakfast after an Alliant action in 1999: Besides the protests at Honeywell and Alliant, "the four sisters ... participated in 'die-ins' in front of the Pentagon, marched into the U.S. Army's School of the Americas in Fort Benning, Georgia, and even staked out the steps of the St. Paul Cathedral. And they've never backed down, even when their beliefs publicly pitted them against family members and their own church."

Music at AlliantTech was part of the Ban Landmines Campaign.

As land mines faded from the public consciousness, MIST shifted emphasis to cluster bombs, nuclear components, and depleted uranium weapons. In each case, we identified the weapons as indiscriminate, which put them in violation of international law.

Tom Bottolene and his partner Pepperwolf were active members of MIST and essential to communications. Tom initiated a web site, *Circlevision*, and Pepperwolf published a weekly update for the vigil circle protesting at Alliant TechSystems. The group at Alliant became known as Alliant Action, continuing to have small presences each Wednesday morning at corporate headquarters as the company moved its headquarters from Hopkins to Edina and more recently, to a brand new headquarters building on Flying Cloud Drive in Eden Prairie.

MIST sponsored several conferences, including a major multi-issue three-day event in 1999 that featured anti-war and anti-weapons work, among other topics.

But as the 1990s drew to a close, internecine struggles reappeared once again. Marv struggled to accept other leadership in anti-weapons work, differing volubly over matters of policy and techniques of organizing. His main complaint of Alliant Action's vigil and civil disobedience actions was, "They're satisfied to stay small! You can't build a mass movement if everybody knows everybody!"

In the spring of 1999, we held the first "surprise!" protest at Alliant. Marv was reluctant to use the strategy, which entailed a demonstration for which neither police nor media nor the company itself had been given prior warning, but other activists were frustrated with declining mainstream interest and were eager to try something new to disquiet the company. After blocking several doors for two hours, twenty-eight activists waited serenely for arrest. Charges were subsequently reduced to a petty misdemeanor which limited defendants to a bench trial by a judge. The judge listened politely to the defendants' stories, found all guilty, and fined each $25.00.

During the greater part of 1999, the MIST board, working in coalition with Alliant Action, planned a mass action for fall that would bring a conference called "Committing to Peace" to a climax. Marv lined up a stellar list of speakers and panel participants including Tony Avirgan, Vernon and Clyde Bellecourt, Medea Benjamin, the Berrigan brothers and Phil's children Frida and Jerry Berrigan, Robert Bly, George Crocker, Sam Day, David Dellinger, Amy Goodman, Kathy Kelly, Staughton Lynd, Elizabeth Martinez, Chuck McDew, Jack Nelson Pallmeyer, Grace Paley, Elizabeth Peterson, Utah Phillips, Margaret Randall, Norman Solomon, Harvey Wasserman, and Lizz Winstead, along with a score of regional activists, legislators, journalists, musicians and writers. It was hoped that with such a line-up, the conference would draw nationwide attention.

Yet fundraising for the conference was difficult, since we wanted to keep the costs of registration low enough to entice students. Marv was energized and tireless in calling old friends, writing letters, and talking everywhere throughout the spring and summer, and with advanced registrations we were able to meet a bare-bones budget. Planning meetings were often tense, and long. Sparks flew, most often between Marv and Tom Bottolene, over money, personal styles, language, and establishing precisely what sort of conference the group was planning.

One major flashpoint was the name of the conference itself. Tom, a graphic artist, had designed and produced brochures, a logo, and a website advertising the event under the name Committing to Peace; Marv insisted that it be called Committing to Peace *and Justice*. One of the MIST speakers had critiqued our materials for the lack of the word "justice," emphasizing that among oppressed populations, the omission would be obvious. Tom pointed out that changing names would raise difficult and expensive logistical problems. Marv stormed out of that meeting.

The second glaring issue was whether Sara Jane Olson, who was in town pending her trial, should be invited. During the 1970s Olson (formerly Kathleen Ann Soliah) was a member of the Symbionese Liberation Army, a radical group seeking to bring revolution to the U.S. and end poverty and oppression. The Army styled itself after South American urban guerilla movements, and like the Black Panthers, it sponsored assistance programs but also adopted militaristic tactics. Several members of the group were convicted of robbery and murder, and Soliah was alleged to have planted pipe bombs under a police car. She went underground, living under the alias Sara Jane Olson for decades before she was discovered in 1999. (In 2001, under a plea bargain, she pled guilty to two counts of "possessing explosives with intent to murder." Her attempt to recant her plea failed.)

The feelings of the MIST planners were mixed. Several in the group supported Sara's inclusion, characterizing her as a "good citizen" during her time underground, and now a political prisoner. Tom was adamant that she should not appear. Marv was furious that Tom would convict her before a jury heard the case. In the end, Sara Olson did greet the conference at the gala dinner, though she spoke only briefly and could say nothing about her case.

The conference itself was a great success, drawing more than eight hundred people, many of whom were students from Midwestern colleges. On the final day of the four-day event, sixty-five people were arrested for blocking the doors at Alliant's headquarters.

As the millennium turned, the vigil group at Alliant grew smaller although no less spirited. Marv was a vigorous voice but increasingly turned his attention to other campaigns and local issues. Early in 2000, MIST began researching an issue that did not focus on weapons. The new topic was sustainability and the food supply, and the group had a nearby firm—grain giant Cargill—upon which to focus its attention.

Marv met with Mark Ritchie, then president of the Institute for Agriculture and Trade Policy, and obtained a thick file of articles about the company. We learned that Cargill was the largest privately owned company in the world; that it controlled 40 to 45 percent of the world's grain; and that it formed, with Monsanto, an interdependent cluster of operations controlling all aspects of the production of certain foods, a model known as a "food chain."

Marv proposed making connections with other groups working in this field such as the World Trade Organization protesters, GrainRAGE, religious organizations, unionists, and farmers, to develop a project to address the many issues involved in corporate control of agriculture.

The previous November Marv had attended the large-scale protests in Seattle during the WTO Ministerial Conference, which was to be the launch of a new millennial round of trade negotiations. The anti-globalization movement in the United States was reaching a peak, and the "battle of Seattle" was generally thought to be a model of organized mass nonviolent protest.

Before MIST was able to do much studying, young people of the anti-globalization group GrainRAGE made headlines by closing Cargill headquarters for two hours: "Before employees arrived ..., Grain-RAGE members in white biohazard suits and respirators blocked the road into the Cargill compound with cars and their bodies."

Marv was gleeful because this was his kind of action—an organized protest against a local company that had massive effects on the environment, poor peasants and farmers, and ordinary people around the globe. The issue resonated with justice organizations both locally and nationally. Similar actions were taking place in other nations against corporate agribusiness, such as Indian farmers' burning genetically engineered cotton and British activists' trashing test crops.

At the February MIST meeting, Marv proposed that we form a nucleus to build a new Twin Cities coalition of radical peace and justice groups, including environmental groups. Why shouldn't these causes and their supporters be brought together? He drafted an invitational letter to go out within the week. As usual, he was thinking large. Groups could pay dues and have representation on the MIST board. Individual members could pay a smaller amount in return for a newsletter. Besides,

Rita McDonald, Marguerite Corcoran, Brigit McDonald and Jane McDonald perform at a fund-raiser.

he said, we had to recruit new members for the board.

That was most certainly true: attendance at meetings was minimal. Tom and Pepper had not been coming since the 1999 conference, so the half dozen of us who regularly attended board meetings were stretched to the breaking point.

Board member Kyle Makarios, a union representative for our friends the Hotel and Restaurant Employees local, proposed a mediation session to rebuild relationships with Alliant Action. Those at the Alliant Wednesday morning vigil were not sure how effective mediation would be but finally agreed. A psychologist friend, Deb Clemmensen, facilitated a meeting that brought grievances into the open and went a long way to restoring friendships, especially between Pepper, Tom, and Marv.

MIST played a small part in the burgeoning "anti-GME" movement. Long-time antiwar protestors had difficulty shifting their focus from weapons to environmental issues, while advocates for nonviolence were concerned about tactics that pushed the edges of resistance. In late summer 2000, Minneapolis police arrested eighty-one people during a march protesting the International Society for Animal Genetics conference. The *St. Paul Pioneer Press* reported that "most of the clashes occurred as police used pepper spray and struck protesters who tried to break through police lines... police [said] that they tried to allow protesters to get their message across but had to prevent them from disrupting downtown Minneapolis."

Marv was involved in discussions about Cargill, but did not participate in planning or nonviolence training for this march. He had other concerns. In May, he was diagnosed with prostate cancer and opted for surgery. MIST board member and nursing student Mary Ellen Clark, who lived with Marv at the time, "nobly took care of me after prostate surgery." He made a good recovery, and was soon out on the streets again for a Hotel and Restaurant Employees Union demonstration.

Hotel and Restaurant Employees Union (H.E.R.E.) Local 17 members had been walking the picket lines again. An influx of immigrants had swelled membership and their organizing success at the Normandy had encouraged initiatives for better wages, healthcare and workplace dignity that garnered national attention. MIST board members Martin Goff and Kyle Makarios kept us informed of the new struggles and we joined Local 17 to march with Jesse Jackson.

In mid-October, a celebration of Marv's life was held at the First Unitarian Church on Mount Curve Drive in Minneapolis. The proceeds were to go to Marv himself, because, as Bob Lamb, Mel Duncan, and Polly Mann wrote in a newsletter announcing the event, "from the 1950s through the present, Davidov has supported his civil rights and antiwar activism on minimal income. In Marv's activist career there were no 401(k) plans, stock options, severance packages, or even a minimum-wage guarantee."

Every pew at the church was packed that night. Even the balcony was standing room only. There were certainly more people present than at most Alliant demonstrations. There were tributes, a slide show, splendid music and entertainment by two great comedians, Susan Vass and Merrilyn Belgum. "The peace community does know how to organize a party!" Marv laughed, "I didn't have to do a thing."

Despite multiple health issues including the cancer recovery, diabetes, and a broken ankle (suffered after a misstep from a curb in New York) Marv was ready to march again. On November 1, 2000, Alliant Action held a "Day of the Dead" procession from downtown Hopkins to Alliant's facility. We had often speculated that its suburban neighbors had little idea what was happening at Alliant; we thought that this solemn, highly visual procession might arouse interest in the heart of Hopkins. On a cool, sunny Wednesday morning, there seemed to be few spectators in downtown Hopkins and even fewer on the residential streets leading to Alliant. In fact, scarcely a car passed us and the only sound was the distant hum of traffic from Highway 169 a few blocks away.

In white masks or whiteface, mourners carried flowers or signs representing the destruction Alliant devices were causing. Marv was one of about a hundred marchers who concluded the ceremony by spreading ashes at the main entrance. By agreement, there was no civil disobedience (I planted a mass of iris bulbs in the employee park, but no one seemed to mind).

A second procession took place the next spring, called "Farewell to Arms (in Hopkins)" because Alliant was moving its facility to Edina. Twelve people were arrested while attempting to block the main entrance, though the City of Hopkins declined to press charges. According to Circlevision.org, that brought the number of arrests since 1996 to 404.

In midsummer 2001, Alliant Action and MIST, with the help of international researchers, began a campaign to sharpen public awareness of depleted uranium (DU) weapons. Locally, Nukewatch's John LaForge and Mike Miles, based at Anathoth farm, provided research and information. Marv initiated a new organization, inviting membership among MIST, Minnesota Vets for Peace, Nukewatch, and Alliant Action. In memory of Phil Berrigan, the new group would be called the Phillip Berrigan Depleted Uranium Coalition. In the months before his death, Berrigan had been speaking out about the weapon; he and three others from the Plowshares movement were jailed in March after damaging an A-10 Warthog aircraft. During the Persian Gulf War A-10s had fired 940,000 depleted uranium rounds, and this was considered a likely cause of Gulf War Syndrome.

We wanted to learn more about the munitions, where they had

been used and, especially, what health effects had been documented. In August 2001, the coalition brought in Dr. Doug Rokke, then Director of the U.S. Army Depleted Uranium Project. A depleted uranium poisoning casualty himself, Rokke was dedicated to obtaining medical care for all DU affected individuals and to environmental remediation. He spoke about his findings of massive contamination and the Army's reluctance to stop using the weapon or deal with the aftermath.

It has often been said that the world changed on the day when terrorists piloted aircraft into the Pentagon and the World Trade center in New York City in September 2001, sending thousands of office workers and visitors to their deaths. The tenor of protests also changed on that day. On September 12, Wednesday vigilers were present as usual at Alliant, but wearing black or white to symbolize our mourning, carrying candles, and standing in silence—unlike our typical verbal sharing and singing. "We wanted to carry the message of standing in opposition to all violent solutions," said Char Madigan, including the appalling attack of the previous day. Alliant issued a statement expressing outrage that we would protest at all.

Two month later, on November 7, 2001, the theme of the mass protest was "Who Profits? Who Dies?" and sixteen were arrested as they attempted to plant warning flags at Alliant's new facility. On March 25, 2002, all but one of the sixteen were convicted and sentenced to ten days of community service or seven days in jail. On Monday, May 20, six peace activists entered jail, Char Madigan, CSJ, Rita Foster, CSJ, Mary Ellen Halverson, Rita Steinhagen, CSJ, Steve Clemens, and Tom Bottolene.

Also in 2002, Jack Silberman released the documentary *Bombies,* highlighting cluster munitions, with a great deal of footage on the Honeywell Project and Marv's work against the weapons that had devastated Southeast Asia. Marv had been in contact with Silberman during the making of the film and kept us informed about its progress. The film's title, a term that was unfamiliar to most of us at the time, refers to a bomblet that is released in mid-air from a cluster bomb, but fails to explode, thus presenting extreme hazard to anyone who passes nearby even months or years later. Between 1964 and 1973, the United

States dropped two and a half million tons of bombs on tiny Laos, and a good percentage of them became bombies. The film was a powerful piece that Jack succeeded in having televised on PBS.

In April Marv joined a busload of Minnesotans at a three-day multi-issue peace rally in Washington, DC, including a "Rally for Palestinian Rights." He gave a lengthy report on the three-day event in our MIST newsletter. He wrote: "The Palestinian cause became the dominant theme Saturday, although I did see many signs opposing a possible U.S. invasion of Iraq. I could not help thinking, one day 10-20 million Americans will take to the streets after a general strike, and topple capitalism. This day reflected the growing justice and peace movement in our country and gave hope for the future."

On the second day of the rally a thousand people demonstrated near the World Bank and then joined a larger mass near the Washington Monument for events featuring music and impassioned discussion about the policy of the United States toward Colombia. At seven the next morning two thousand people gathered for a disciplined nonviolent march against that policy. "There were no incidents until we reached the Russell Senate Building, where people held a rally and police began to circle the group. "... As people left the building area toward the streets again, police blocked the way ... Every fourth cop wore a Seattle-style 'Star Wars' body armor and plastic helmet masks, carrying long batons and readying pepper spray. Kids under 10 in our group were screaming in fear, looking at these menacing figures."

Such ugly incidents notwithstanding, the three-day event left Marv with the impression that progressive Americans were coming together once again to advocate for peace on many fronts.

During the next few years Marv remained involved in a variety of issues, taught, and traveled several times a year to marches and conferences; MIST and the Alliant Action vigil groups continued to focus on depleted uranium weapons. Over time Alliant has manufactured more than sixteen million depleted uranium shells carrying a toxic, radioactive substance that burns spontaneously on impact and disperses a toxic radioactive dust into the air, soil and groundwater, where its effects will linger for decades. The U.S. has been spreading this radioactive waste in Iraq, Afghanistan, Bosnia, Kosovo, and at testing ranges around the world.

As Marv editorialized in the *Pulse*, a Twin Cities alternative newspaper, "Since the first Gulf War, incidents of cancer, leukemia and kidney disease among Iraqi children are sky-high. ... The Pentagon refuses to conduct a large-scale epidemiological study on returning veterans. Neither Honeywell nor Alliant Tech Systems bothered to do a health study of the workers who built the millions of DU shells at the Arden Hills plant. Government and corporate management do not give a shit for veterans or for workers. We do! ... The U.S. military consumes bullets big time, and not only the U.S. military. Alliant sells all over the world. They can sell to both sides in a conflict. War and war preparation are profitable for them."

Wednesdays became busy for peace activists, with morning vigils at Alliant and evenings spent with signs on the Lake Street/Marshall Avenue bridge over the Mississippi. In 1999, bridge vigils began in solidarity with Yugoslavian citizens who stood protesting the NATO bombings of Belgrade bridges; the vigils changed focus as U.S. and Great Britain bombings *continued* in Iraq. With the ongoing devastation of Iraqi infrastructure (water, electricity, transportation) and the lack of medicines and food, UNICEF reported that as many as five thousand children under five were dying per month of epidemic dysentery, gastroenteritis, and even cholera and typhoid. Chronic malnutrition left children vulnerable to pneumonia, bronchitis, and other infections.

Marie and John Braun, retired psychologists and WAMM members, led the evening vigils. Marv made it part of his weekly routine, even when many took a break during the blustery winter months. Anywhere from a dozen to several hundred demonstrators (when an anniversary or a body-count milestone arrived) held signs and signaled peace to passing rush hour drivers. The signs changed along with conditions on the ground, at first emphasizing the sanctions and the renewed bombings of Iraq, then the Iraq war and later occupation.

Marie Braun insisted, as early as the winter of 2001 when the war in Afghanistan was underway, that Bush was going to "go after" Iraq. Marv agreed. Some of us couldn't see it. Wasn't the U.S. already invested in attacking Afghanistan to pursue Bin Laden? The September 11 terrorists had no link to Iraq, which was already devastated by bombing and sanctions. How many more signs could we hold on the windy bridge without being hydroplaned down the Mississippi?

Yet CBS News reports later confirmed Marie and Marv's intuition. "...barely five hours after Flight 77 plowed into the Pentagon, Defense Secretary Rumsfeld was telling aides to come up with plans for striking Iraq—even though there was no evidence linking Saddam Hussein to the attacks."

Unlike the Vietnam War protests, which began small and swelled over years, it seemed that world opinion was going to be massively against the invasion of Iraq from the get-go. On February 15 and 16, 2003, between six and ten million people took part in protests throughout the world. The rally in Rome that day drew nearly three million people and was listed in the 2004 *Guinness Book of World Records* as the largest anti-war rally in history. But nothing, not even Congress, stopped the march toward war.

In December 2002, several Twin Cities activists made the first of several visits to Iraq, touring hospitals and other sites. They brought back reports and photographs from Iraqi physicians, documenting the effects of uranium weapons. Similar information soon became more widely available on the Internet. For many of us, what conscience compelled us to testify was harrowing. The images of birth defects linked to depleted uranium munitions were heartbreaking. Yet the mainstream media wasn't covering the story or that of the escalating rates of cancer in southern Iraq and among returning soldiers.

Therefore, the following April the Phil Berrigan Depleted Uranium Coalition sponsored another action—a citizens weapons inspection—at Alliant Tech to protest the manufacture of such weapons and to draw attention to their devastating effects on Iraqi civilians, returning veterans, Alliant workers, and people who lived around the Arden Hills production site and the Elk River test zone. Many of the protesters were arrested as usual, but on October 17 the defendants secured a significant court victory when twenty-eight people (including Marv) were found not guilty of trespass, on the basis of the international law.

The verdict heartened us, although only progressive and antinuclear publications mentioned the trial. "It's great to win," Marv said, "but we've got a lot of work to do!"

And on the personal level, times were tough. In the February 2004 MIST newsletter, Marv revealed: "Once again I am broke, but not broken. I [will] do adjunct teaching at St. Thomas Justice and Peace Studies Department, one class in fall, one in spring. Some small speaking fees, minimal Social Security, and MIST money as director keep me going. ... Right now, I must make a choice of paying association dues for my apartment or buying food. ... constantly living on the edge, which I have done for 51 years."

A fundraising concert with David Rovics and comedy with "Attila the Stockbroker" kept Marv afloat through the summer as we stepped up the pace of actions at Alliant. All across the country, civil resistance to war was regaining strength, as the Bush administration's miscalculations, mismanagement, and deliberate misrepresentations about the Iraq war kept the peace movement on the streets.

That year Tom Bottolene and Pepperwolf assembled a document entitled "Employee Liabilities of Weapon Manufacturers Under International Law" and plotted a series of actions to deliver the information to Alliant's management. On July 14, 2004, Bill Barnett, Pepperwolf, and Tom walked into the company's lobby and asked to see Admiral Paul David Miller, the corporation's chairman, with the intention of delivering the document to one of four corporate officers. When they were told none was available, they offered to make an appointment to see any of the four. The security officer told them the only way to make an appointment was by phone. Pepperwolf took out her cell phone and dialed Alliant's number. The receptionist, facing her, refused to connect her to anyone, and the three were arrested.

Other groups of from three to five people followed the same strategy over the next few weeks, carrying "the book" and asking for a meeting, refusing to leave until they had secured one. (No one was given an appointment.) My group included John and Marie Braun, Steve Clemens and John Maus. During that time Marv worked on media friends to carry stories about Alliant and depleted uranium. He hit on the idea of bringing representatives from the Phil Berrigan DU Coalition to the *Star Tribune* offices to meet with his friend Gary Gilson, an editor who was also a director of the Minnesota News Council. He thought Gilson could influence investigative reporters to do a substantial piece on DU.

We prepared a packet of materials, scientific studies, and a copy of the "Employee Liabilities of Weapon Manufacturers" document. Gilson was sympathetic, but local media response was almost nil.

In December 2004, I came to trial with friends Marie and John Braun and Steve Clemens; Marv was in the courtroom. As in the Honeywell days, he showed up for every trial, because "I want to support my friends. Second, hearing the truth keeps me sane."

"The verdict ... raises the question of who is responsible for the enforcement of International Law," Steve Clemens wrote later, "when ATK publicly admits it has manufactured depleted uranium weapons." Before 2000, the ATK website had boasted about their manufacture of weapons with depleted uranium penetrators, but after the group publicly raised concerns about the weapons, all references to it were removed and the words 'kinetic energy' replaced 'depleted uranium.'

Steve was eloquent in presenting the "evidence" of international law, now bolstered at the United Nations. Dr. Karen Parker had testified before the U.N. Commission on Human Rights that depleted uranium weapons clearly fail four tests, any one of which would make the weapon illegal: 1) Weapons must be limited to the field of battle—territorial test. 2) Weapons must not continue to kill long after a war has ended. 3) Weapons must not be unduly inhumane—the cancers, birth defects, and genetic damage linked to the inhalation or ingestion of radioactive DU particles impact both combatants and civilians. 4) Weapons may not cause long-term damage to the natural environment.

Steve, Marie and John Braun and John Maus had visited children's wards in Baghdad, and carried home direct information about the contamination. We did not introduce into evidence any pictures of cancers, birth defects, and genetic damage, but my co-defendants provided medical articles and testimony to what they had seen and heard in the Iraqi hospitals. Although John Maus died of liver cancer three months before the trial, we carried his message as best we could. We presented our defense as accurately and thoroughly as we could, knowing that the jury had to reach its verdict based on the "reasonableness" of our belief that we were upholding law.

I testified last. My brother and son-in-law were servicemen in the first Gulf war. I was less than collected, though; I could not control my tears as I said that my relatives were "older" soldiers who had already had their children. Birth defects weren't likely in their cases—but that I was so sorry for those young men and women veterans, Iraqis, and the yet-to-be-born children who were still at risk.

"I'm such a baby," I wailed to Marv after it was all over. He consoled me: "I get tears on the stand, too. But you know Alliant is the one making the poison—they should be crying. The jury got it."

The jury deliberated for several hours, but they were in by the end of the day. It's strange, I thought, as I watched the jury's faces, hoping they were thinking hard about the hard testimonies, "getting it," while they wrestled with a fine legal point. It seemed so desperately important that they understand. Our trespass cases weren't likely to have terrible consequences or to stop the weapons, but winning the hearts of the jurors meant something.

The jury entered, unsmiling but watching us intently as their foreperson handed over the verdict. The judge read it, first warning the audience against "unwarranted noise or demonstration." Not guilty—sweetest negative in the language. We joined our friends in quiet jubilation in the hallway.

In the meantime, John LaForge and several others were on trial upstairs and we rushed up to their courtroom to catch the end of the testimony. The next day, their verdict came in: Not guilty. LaForge celebrated "the end of a losing streak" after twenty-five years of protesting.

Our actions were having an effect on management, though not the one we wanted. They wouldn't change their deadly product; they couldn't stop our insistence on international law; so they changed the local law. In March 2005, acting on the advice of Alliant's legal department and the city attorney, the Edina City Council passed a new trespass ordinance. In the Honeywell years, it was the purview of the prosecutor to reduce charges from a misdemeanor to a petty misdemeanor; in Edina, the *charge* was now written into the law. For a petty misdemeanor, a defendant would be entitled only to a bench trial (in front of a judge), not before a jury of peers. In addition, the new ordinance removed the phrase "claim of right" as a defense against a trespass charge.

On appeal, in February 2007, the Minnesota State Court of Appeals ruled the ordinance was legally passed. It remains to be seen whether Eden Prairie, Alliant Tech's new home, will enact a similar law. In the meantime, the actions continue.

In 2006, Marv began a Minnesota chapter of the national War Resisters' League, with the idea of sponsoring a conference on weapons profiteering. We invited Joanne Sheehan, chair of War Resisters International, to meet with organizers in Minnesota. The conference, to be called "For Justice and Peace: Stop the Merchants of Death!" would be the kickoff to a national/international network of groups resisting the production of nuclear weapons, conventional weapons, and uranium munitions.

The new network was to meet twice a year, and when political situations called for action, they were to act. "Let's say the Nevada Desert Experience Against Nukes calls for an action, then those in the network who can make it, go there and participate with them," Marv said in an interview for *Pulse*, "If you can't make it, you select a site, here it could be at the Federal Building, and the same day they're doing their action, worldwide, we act."

MIST never formally dissolved, but Marv's letters and political action took new forms from 2006 on. MIST's members joined antiwar activities as the Iraq war dragged on, or focused on other peace or political campaigns. Our newsletter became an occasional "Memo from Marv," a peace movement report. He continued to critique anti-weapons/antiwar organizing when it did not attract great numbers (such as to the Alliant site): "When the turnout for demonstrations at Alliant is small, media make us look silly and management has said, 'they do the protest of the day and drink their café latté.' The public relations guy calls the protest 'a non-event.'" He stressed that the potential was great for stronger participation: Minnesota had an intimate connection with Iraq in the persons of "returning veterans, soldiers currently serving, and weapons systems … made at Alliant." He was convinced that the large conference-rally-nonviolent action scenario would generate most attention: "Media will come when we have numbers."

The Merchants of Death conference on September 29, 2006, featured music (Utah Phillips, the Prince Myshkins, the Singing Sisters), comedy (Paul Krassner), and speakers Winona LaDuke, Vernon Bellecourt, Medea Benjamin, Frida Berrigan—and, of course, Marv. On Saturday evening, September 30, we held a Honeywell Project/Alliant Action reunion, inviting old friends from the Project's early and latter days for sessions of storytelling. People came from nearby and around the country, such as Sharon Driscoll, a union electrician and organizer; Mark Paquette, a Honeywell engineer who saw the light; Sharon Rice Vaughan, who started one of the first battered women's shelters; Barbara Mishler, who has been active in food programs for impoverished people for twenty years; Sarah Martin, an early member of WAMM; and Evan Stark, initiator of the Project and currently an expert on issues assisting battered women. On Monday, October 2, to honor Gandhi's birthday, conference attendees joined Alliant Action in nonviolent civil disobedience at Alliant Tech. Marv asked Edina police at the scene to turn around "and arrest Dan Murphy, the CEO for War Crimes." The police made seventy-eight arrests, though Murphy wasn't among them.

The four-day event broke even. Meanwhile, Congress voted $70 billion in supplemental money to the war budget: "Not one single senator voted against it. It shows how simply going to Congress is not the issue anymore."

"Of course we have to keep the pressure on Congress," Marv reflected. "But everybody knows the saying, 'Follow the money!' These Merchants of Death contribute *massive* amounts to candidates and there's this revolving door between the Department of Defense, legislators, and these companies."

In a interview with *Pulse* before the action, he said, "[Historians] Howard Zinn, Edward Galeano, and others have called for a serious movement to abolish war. This [conference] is one serious part of it."

But Marv couldn't help being disappointed with media coverage. Despite the organizing, the numbers, and the publicity, Twin Cities journalists showed little interest. "Eight people locally, and four at War Resisters' League in New York, worked ten months to pull it off. We now have a network of groups resisting The Merchants of Death, which we will expand internationally to coordinate and integrate our movement," he wrote. "For the first time in 24 years, the Minneapolis *Star Tribune* did not cover a sizeable arrest. Editor Dennis McGrath told me, 'When cops ticket and release it is like jaywalking—routine.' Yes, production of indiscriminate weapons like cluster bombs, which Israel used in Lebanon the last two days of the war, is routine—they are routinely used to murder children!'"

For the last four years, Marv has taken time out from organizing, traveling, teaching, and protesting to undergo kidney dialysis three times a week for about three hours. (This "time out" is not absolute, he reminds me, because he frequently enlists the medical staff to listen to his class analysis of political systems while his blood is being refreshed.) His rapport with the medical people is generally good. In his first hospitalization for kidney failure, he was astounded when two attending nurses separately came up to him and told him they were "honored" to be part of his medical team. He says it's happening every month or so: someone will come to thank him for what he's done.

"Gerty used to say, 'What's going to happen in your old age?' and 'I don't have any grandchildren!' Well, that's true. It's frightening sometimes. I don't have any money.... But then someone thanks me, and I'm so profoundly grateful for that. My life has meant something, it's been worth it!"

March 27, 2008. Five years of war. Four thousand United States soldiers dead, close to a hundred thousand Iraqi citizens killed since the March 2003 invasion. We are heading over to the University of Minnesota to support some grandmothers who are joining students risking arrest at recruiters' offices on campus.

"Sometimes we win," Marv insists, "and sometimes history overtakes us." Near a mall just off Washington Avenue, Marv is outside the National Guard recruiters office, waiting with a few dozen demonstrators. Of the hundreds who have marched, these await the outcome of a confrontation between police and the grandmothers who are part of the Anti-War Committee protest. Other student clusters are chained to locked doors and traffic signs at recruiters' offices down the street. Marv introduces me as a "radical grandmother" to two fresh-faced

St. Thomas students, Erin and Amy. "This is great!" he crows, "hundreds of students, and cops all over campus!" Police in cars, on foot, blocking streets and doorways, police in vans, on bikes, on horses. I admire the bikes and the horses. "Green cops," Marv concurs. "And look, *integrated* cops."

But I am close to weeping from anxiety. I've come from the upstairs office where two policemen were kneeling on a struggling young woman, while other Anti-War Committee members were pounding vigorously on a plate glass window. Just as I left, the grannies peace brigade (Deb, Sarah, Maura, and Mary—all veterans of the Honeywell days) were being lined up for arrest. My four brave friends were beginning to hate the scene. I have $400 of their bail money and Maura's keys, phone number, and a description of her car. I can't find Sue Ann Martinson, who is my support team and ride. I've been winding around the police, my ear glued to a cell phone.

The police have allowed me to stay upstairs with the grannies until the car conversation was completed. Now I am afraid they've swept up Sue Ann. I circle the building once more and find her talking to police at the side door. They've brought everyone out, she says, including our friends, and taken them to a National Guard Center on Central and Broadway. After more delay getting straight information, we learn that they will be ticketed but released without bail (what we call "catch and release"). We get directions and set out to fetch them.

Coverage of the protest, which involved hundreds of students and several dozen police, was scant. "It's beyond disgraceful," Marv fumed, the next day. "The *Strib* had nothing, zero. I didn't see anything on the network news." Two days later, the university paper, *The Daily*, had a feature article.

Two years ago several of us (grandmothers) invaded the University campus Marines recruiters office and sat in. We announced we'd stay until we were allowed to enlist: we wanted to replace young men and women trapped by the "stop-loss" program. When the police came, they declined to arrest us: a clever lieutenant negotiated with the recruiters to let us fill out applications. Our rejection letters turned up in a couple of weeks.

Today the grandmothers were going to try again to 'enlist,' but the recruiters locked the door. Minnesota Public Radio had the story two days later, reporting on their web site: "Police say they arrested two dozen people at an anti-war rally on the University of Minnesota campus. Those arrested blocked the entrance to a National Guard recruiting office near campus." That was a bit strong, I thought, since the only people actually blocking the locked second floor office were the police.

Marv judged the protest a success from an organizer's standpoint—good attendance, energetic and coordinated action, high visibility—but he referred to the local media coverage as "disgusting."

Ten months later (January 13, 2009), there was no media coverage of the Minneapolis trial, a rare trespass trial by jury. But in an email to the grannies brigade, Sarah exulted: "Seven were found not guilty today of trespass at the army guard recruiting station in the stadium village mall on the u campus ... our judge allowed just enough of the claim of right defense to give the jury some legal windows to not convict us. yahooo!"

As Marv reminds us, we have to be creative, we have to be persistent. He persists, marching, teaching, speaking at peace venues and to everyone around him, including doctors, nurses, and technicians at dialysis. In an interview before the 2008 Republican National Convention, a reporter asked about the thrust of his activism over the last fifty years, and now. He said: "Many things. I call myself a revolutionary, a nonviolent revolutionary. And it can't just be foreign policy. It has to be the environment, it has to be relating to working people, to blacks, to Indians, Chicanos, women's struggles, gay-lesbian struggles... and so wherever there is decent struggle, I show up, as a troop. Not to lead everything, I couldn't possibly. Nonviolence has to be *revolutionary* or it's irrelevant." Asked for his advice to protestors at the RNC, about whom local media seemed nervous, he insisted, "People doing it, the young people, old people, are thinking it through. Strategize, build serious coalitions, which people *are* doing. Do it with nonviolence, be disciplined, go ahead and be disruptive, but be disciplined. Be nonviolent."

Peace awards given for serious labor over a lifetime are few and far between. But one such expression of gratitude was the 2007 Chomsky Award, given by the Justice Studies Association, for Marv's

Marv in class at St. Thomas University, March 31, 2009. (Photo by Michael Bayly)

work dedicated to non-violence, equality and social justice.

"Marv has 53 years of activism under his belt and has been arrested some 51 times for nonviolent civil disobedience, for which he's served a total of six months in jail. ... Noam Chomsky has said, 'He has committed himself with a kind of dedication that has rarely been matched to reversing the drift toward global destruction, and his work has been extremely effective.'"

These days, Marv's most treasured awards are the faces of students and their comments in journals:

"Every student in his or her own way says in journals, 'To get it from books or films is great. But to hear from someone who was a Rider and who has never quit is awesome.' ... I get to relive these experiences and work with young people who develop their own world view, their ethics, politics, morality, and spirituality—unique to them but informed also by those who came before. Every serious thing we do will count eventually. Don't despair. No one thought the Civil Rights movement had a chance.... If someone had told you in 1970, 'The Berlin Wall will come down. Mass nonviolent peace movements will topple all the Stalinist governments of Eastern Europe. The U.S.-backed leader of the Philippines, Fernando Marcos, will likewise leave. Nelson Mandela, after twenty-seven years in prison, will be president of South Africa. The Soviet Union will collapse'—if someone had told you these things, you would have said, 'Take him away!' Mass nonviolent movements that were grass roots and bottom up have forced social change in America and around the world."

Political commentators wrestling with the darkness of the last decade, wondering how to analyze the global economic meltdown, endless 'terror' wars, and environmental ravages, are hard put to suggest solutions. Few of them look to the history and honorable traditions of active nonviolence, from civil rights to human rights movements that speak from the streets, jail cells, classrooms and board rooms, vigils in line and online.

Marv is lucky. He has been able to seize the moment and the movements. He has been an inspiration to many—so that when the Power says "You can't do that!" we know how to answer. He can look into the faces of his students and see a future that gives him hope. He has always had the integrity of a man speaking his deepest truth in the places and to the powers that don't want to hear it.

A Note of Thanks from Marv

Thank you…To the medical men who took care of me pro bono. I tried to save the world. They gave me loving care. I could never have done what I did without them: Dr. Charles Fisher, for 36 years of dental care, who along with his wife LaVon became dear friends and comrades; Dr. Sam Scher, psychologist; Dr Ron Groat, psychiatrist; Dr. Peter Dorson; Tom Sengupta at Schneider Drug, pharmacist, gave me medicine for years. Tom is a public philosopher on the many fronts of social change, holding special hot stove discussions in his drug store. To my kidney doctors Tom Davin, Kim Thielen, Jamie Gitter; my dialysis technicians Chris, Erin, Janeen, Kelsey, Kim, Jessica, and Ashley, all of whom stuck me right and listened, respected what I did and brought joy and laughter into the clinic. Nurses Jimmy, Erica, Celeste, Debbie in the office, Karen, nutritionist, and Bev at Park Ave, an enlightened social worker. To the Abbott transplant team led by Dr. Mark Odlund.

I must mention Bob Lamb, friend, comrade, life long activist, confidant for almost forty years; Carol Connolly, poet laureate of St. Paul… we talked endlessly about our lives and made delicious satire of friends and the ironies of life. Ed Felien, publisher of *Pulse* and *Southside Pride*… Ed and I just look at each other and break into laughter. Carol Hogard, his wife, studied nonviolence with me and was an artful teacher.

I thank Polly Mann and Marianne Hamilton, founders of Women Against Military Madness, elders who inspired me and generations of women and men with their grace, endurance, and class; Charlie and Irving Bloss; Joe and Linda Muldoon, for wonderful dinner parties.

Sharon Rice Vaughn, Sara Driscoll, Cinder Boxrud, and Evan Stark were in on the founding years of the Honeywell Project and kept up the friendships while following their own creative careers. Sharon started one of the early battered women's shelters and became known world wide; Cinder is an excellent eye surgeon; Sara, a lesbian-feminist-electrician and body worker. Evan is an expert on battered women and a fine teacher, partnering with his wife Dr. Ann Flitcraft.

Bill Tilton, Frank Kroncke, Chuck Turchick, Don Olson, Mike Therriault, Brad Benecke and Pete Simmons of the Minnesota Eight Draft Raiders did noble work, trying to save the lives of Vietnamese and Americans.

I am thankful for poker partner Scott Cramer of Northern Sun Merchandising; Berkeley's Dr. Neal Blumenfeld, psychiatrist and radical activist. He lost his lovely wife Leesee in March. They both practiced clinically and were deeply enlightened radical activists.

Dave Dellinger introduced me to Father Dan and Phil Berrigan in 1965 at a Vietnam demonstration in front of the White House. Later I met Phil's wife Liz McAllister, and their three children, Frida, Jerry and Kate, and Jerry's wife Molly. I've always been inspired to push harder in my antiwar activism by the profound risks Phil and Dan and Liz took fighting nuclear weapons. I could always make Dan and Phil laugh with Jewish Mother stories and I eagerly read every book Dan wrote.

I thank Martha Boesing, friend and comrade of almost 50 years, feminist, playwright, singer, actor, practitioner of Zen; Vernon, his wife Janis, and brother Clyde Bellecourt, American Indian Movement founders in 1968. Vernon and I would talk frequently about the state of the movement by phone, always ending with the latest jokes. Vernon died suddenly in 2008 and I was profoundly touched to be named an honorary pallbearer. I always went to hear Winona LaDuke when she spoke her ecological wisdom or anything else. I thought of her as a worldwide figure true to her roots, an example to students everywhere.

Michael Birchard and Amy Danziezen, my first two student radicals of St. Cloud State 1992, together with Peace, Michael's wife, and Micah, Amy's husband, remain friends and activist comrades. Thanks to friends Bill Barnett, one of the most sensitive helping men in the movement; Marie and John Braun, exemplary activists and leaders of the Iraq anti-war movement; Maris Arnold, with me on the Canada to Cuba Walk.

I am privileged the past six years to co-teach Active Nonviolence in Justice and Peace studies at St. Thomas University, St. Paul, with Jack Nelson Pallmeyer, wonderful father of three daughters, fine husband to Sara, author, brilliant athlete, beloved teacher, activist. He would have made one of the best congressmen or senators in U.S. history, a spiritual prophet and stunning speaker. I want to thank the St. Thomas colleagues, especially Father David Smith, who had the courage to hire Jack and me in the Justice and Peace Studies Department, and went to Cuba with me—his first trip. He plays a mean fiddle. Our program works thanks to David's ground-breaking effort. Dr. Chris Toffolo, our former chair (removed in the banning of Bishop Desmond Tutu scandal)… a brilliant, compassionate teacher, wonderful, ethical chair. She was hired and named chair of the Justice Department at Northeastern Illinois University in Chicago. Thanks also to Mike Klein; Phil Stoltzfus; and

Father Gerald Schlabach, new chair.

Thanks to Tony Avirgan and Martha Honey, D.C. and world activists forever; to Michael Bayly, fine photographer and peace worker with the Catholic Pastoral Committee on Sexual Minorities; to Medea Benjamin, founder of Global Exchange and Code Pink—I went to Cuba seven times with Medea and Global Exchange. She is the finest citizen diplomat I know.

I'm grateful to Father Roy Bourgeois, founder of the School of the Americas Watch, which does the best nonviolence mass organizing in the United States. Roy lived in the Maryknoll House in Minneapolis and was a runner. Once, I saw him sitting near an inner city lake deep in thought; I asked, "What are you thinking?" he said, "About that army school at Ft. Benning, Georgia that trains Latin soldiers to repress their own people. I think I'll go there—see if we can do anything." Many years later thousands of people come every November to protest and try to close the school.

Thanks to our small chapter of the War Resisters League: Shane Bastien and his wife Lauren Muscoplat, wise beyond their youth, Lauren a Jewish radical activist teacher with a darling new baby; Cathy Statz, a nurse and wound expert who lost a sister in the Pentagon attack September 11; Joe Kling, professional St. Thomas student and subtle humorist; Bob Kolstad, a Lawyers Guild attorney on loan to the WRL for the Stop the Merchants of Death conference, bright, articulate, a morale-lifter along with his wife Kim and darling five-year-old Issabella (we bonded the first time we met); and Barbara Mishler, my neighbor in our co-op building, special loving friend and comrade. Barb and I have been close since 1980, along with her son Jesse; we always discuss the personal and political. When I'm ill Barbara is always there. She is a noble worker for over twenty years in Loaves and Fishes (providing meals to low-income people).

Thank you to Michael Pinsky, who looked at part of the original manuscript and said to put in the historical context of my campaigns, so that youth would know the background for these actions. Michael owns Bolerium Bookstore in San Francisco, which has the best collection of used books on radical politics I know about.

Thanks to Margaret Randall, writer, poet, revolutionary feminist. I met Margaret when she taught at Macalester in the 1980s. I read everything Margaret writes and honor her insights about the movement and the state of women in it worldwide. I'm grateful for Mel Duncan and Georgia Duncan, who raised foster children while being full-time activists. Mel is worthy of a Nobel Peace Prize for co-founding the Nonviolent PeaceForce. Both are the finest baseball fans on the planet.

Chris Kuhl did a history television piece on the Honeywell Project and became a lifelong friend; he was raised by single mother Cathy to have a social consciousness and a love of sport. Larry Long, troubadour, laughing friend, lover and teacher of folk music to children, in the vein of Pete Seeger—another special friend. JoAnn Sheehan, WRL leader is a comrade of decades—we think alike about the significance of organizing.

Thanks to all the people who have sent financial gifts over the years!

Friends who continue to influence me: George Crocker and Leah Foushee; Daniel Ellsberg; Father Hugo Montero; Mahmoud El Kati, honored African American elder who has invited me to speak on Civil Rights at Macalester; artist Mel Geary; Eric Etheridge (author of the recent book Breach of Peace); artist Jane Evershed; journalists Randy Furst, Nick Coleman, and Doug Grow; Los Angeles activists Marvin and Sherna Gluck; Sudie Hoffman, who hired me at St. Cloud State; Alan Hooper, faculty at the University of Minnesota and Viet Nam activist; elementary school teacher and activist Margaret Hinton; Moe and Charity Hirsch, friends and comrades who are among my most faithful supporters and advisors; Paul Krassner, Left comedian who never turns me down when I ask him to do his gut-breaking humor at a conference; Nancy Johnston, girlfriend of the 80s and fine social work professor at the U; Nancy Peterson, girlfriend and dear supporter of the 90s and now.

Friends and supporters past and present: singer and musician John Koerner and Utah Phillips; Jordan Kushner, Lawyers Guild lawyer of the younger generation carrying on in the radical tradition of Ken Tilsen, my "personal and political" pro bono lawyer, brothers David and Mark Tilsen who lived at Pine Ridge during important movement struggles there; brilliant and funny author Grace Paley, who was with us at Honeywell; poet Susu Jeffrey, Honeywell and Alliant Tech activist and Coldwater Spring protector. The Anathoth people: John LaForge, Barb Katt, Mike Miles and Barbara Cass, Bonnie Urfer. We continue to take our students each semester to Anathoth, a resistance community in Luck, Wisconsin where they built solar equipped houses, a garden, everything ecologically compatible—a high point of our classes.

Film Society founder and theater guru Al Milgrom—he brought a love of world film to thousands in Minnesota. The musicians who have entertained and inspired us, The Prince Myshkins. The Sisters of St. Joseph of Carondelet, especially the McDonald sisters, about whose humor and love in radical action I can't say enough. Old girlfriend Faye Powe. When I went to D.C. for demonstrations, I stayed with her. A Birmingham girl from a Southern working class family, she got a Ph.D. in Art History at the University of Minnesota. She died tragically in an accident in Germany in 2008. Peter Rachleff, labor historian at Macalester. WAMM leader Maura Sullivan, social work professor.

I love marching with the Chapter 27 Veterans for Peace at May Day to Powderhorn Park, and at Fort Benning, Georgia. No one talks with more authority against war. Thanks to Neil Sieling, old Northern Sun-Powerline comrade. A brilliant activist in the world of alternative national television, he lives in New York with his wife Lynn, who works on the Sundance channel there.

I'm grateful for the friendship of Susan Shaffer, radical DC lawyer who was instrumental in the Honeywell-FBI lawsuit and her husband Truman, former SNCC worker and retired judge; Lynn Shoemaker worked with me in the Los Angeles Resistance movement and later brought me to the University of Wisconsin-Whitewater for speaking; great poet and teacher Robert Bly, whom I've known since the 50s and who went to jail for the Honeywell Project. Eric Skoglund claims I brought him into the movement and changed his life. Sara Martin, nurse, activist, pours her life still into the movement through WAMM and the Antiwar Committee. Tomrat TaDemme, a comrade teacher at St. Cloud State. Adam Vincent, a former St. Thomas student who keeps in touch with me. Like others, he did not go for the money, but teaches. Anna Andahazy, also a former student, from the famous Andahazy ballet family – she is a dancer, dreamer, and activist. Thanks also to former students Chris Carroll, Nate Gray and, especially, Lisa Joy LoMurray who wrote and produced a documentary on my "life as an activist" (2007). Nate did the music. Thanks to Kathleen Ruona, multi-issue activist, and Mary Vaughn, with whom I went to Phil Berrigan's wake. Thanks to Steve Clemens, brilliant on international law, and all the faithful resisters at Alliant Tech. To all those in the MN antiwar movement who never give up and create the necessary coalitions to have an impact. And to all the WAMM members who have been my natural comrades exemplified by Mary Lou and Gene Ott and Mary and Jim White.

To my brother Jerry, fine civil servant, retired fireman who supported me and was a generous host to my friends at his St. Croix River cabin. And to Lorna Sullivan, Bruce Rubenstein, Bill Breer, friends during the Dinkytown Beat years, friends forever.

Thanks to Joel Weisberg, a close loving friend who with Mike Casper and Bob Tisdale got me my visiting lectureship at Carleton College during 1996 and 1997; Joel and Janet watch over me and we are politically on the same wavelength. Phil Willkie is a friend of 30 years and an eminent green activist. Phil and I agree completely on politics. We have both acted outside the Democratic party, and Phil has saved me more than a few times with his generosity.

I remember with thanks Diamond Dave Whitaker, out of the 50s—he is famous in the Bay area as a radio personality and radical hippie. Thank yous to Howard Zinn and Noam Chomsky for their friendship and incomparable services to the movement.

Thanks to teacher and civil rights activist Nina Zachary, who got me a Governor's Martin Luther King Award January 15, 2007. Profound thanks to the hotel workers and union activists during the Normandy Hotel campaign (1992); to my students at St. Thomas, St. Cloud State, Metro State and Carleton; to Fort Benning/School of the Americas activists, especially those who served time, like Tom Bottolene, Mary Vaughn and Sisters Betty McKenzie and Rita Steinhagen.

Rita and I were fishing buddies. Dick and Debbie Bancroft had given me a gift—I could fish any time in their canoe. When Rita died in 2006, I wrote for the *Pulse*: "If there were a million Ritas, there would be a nonviolent revolution; an end to racism, sexism and homophobia; worker and community control of all corporate power including media; abolition of prisons, a spiritually-based foreign policy, an end to torture, a cleaned-up environment, an end to war, and adequate time left for all to go fishing." The Bancrofts have been friends for many years. They have made me feel like a member of their family. Dick has been the selected photographer of the AIM Indian Movement.

To all our precious students at St. Thomas. They become people's lawyers, doctors, teachers. They work for nonprofits, they write well, listen carefully, laugh at our jokes, and live lives of commitment.

I wish to thank all of the people over many years who have sent gifts of money to supplement my small adjunct wages and social security. I could not have made it without you.

Carol Masters knows me through twenty-five years of activism and has been exemplary in her own direct action. Husband Ken is remembered by everyone for his gut-shaking humor and life-long commitment to social change. Great comrades.

My reform thoughts for the United States: a floor and ceiling on income. Have the Nonviolent PeaceForce train a U.S. nonviolent army. There should be worker and community control of the U.S. corporate structure, along with democratically owned and run national and local media. The education system, too, would be democratically managed. The U.S. empire should be dismantled, closing U.S. bases around the world. We need unilateral nuclear disarmament and the abolition of homelessness. We must cherish youth and honor elders, return stolen tribal lands, make reparations to black people for the crimes of slavery and racism. We must establish full civil liberties including the right of marriage to gays and lesbians. Finally, we must end corporate pollution and save our planet.

A Note on the Sources

Carol Masters has known Marv since 1983 and has worked with him since 1988, when she was assistant director of the Minnesota Peace and Justice Coalition. She interviewed him extensively while preparing for this book. She also interviewed other participants in the events described and spent a good deal of time examining private records at the Minnesota Historical Society and other libraries.

Those interested in learning more about the broader context of Marv's story might find the following works especially useful:

Ackerman, Peter and Jack DuVall, *A Force More Powerful, a century of nonviolent conflict.* (St. Martins Press, 2000).

Arsenault, Raymond, *Freedom Riders: 1961 and the Struggle for Racial Justice.* (Oxford University Press US, 2006).

Brockman, Vicky, "Social Movement Repertoires and Dynamics: A Study of the Honeywell Project and WAMM, PhD dissertation, University of Minnesota, 1998.

Deming, Barbara, *Prison Notes* (New York: Grossman Publishers, 1966).

LoMurray, Lisa Jo, "Marv, The Life of an Activist," (a documentary film) LoMurray produced this film while a student in the Justice and Peace Studies Department at St. Thomas University.

Losure, Mary, "Power Line Blues," TV series, Minnesota Public Radio.

Lynd, Staughton ed. *Nonviolence in America: a Documentary History,* (New York: Bobbs-Merrill, 1966).

Sharp, Gene, *The Politics of Nonviolent Action,* 3 volumes. (Boston: Porter Sargent Publishers, 1973).

Sibley, Mulford Quickert, *Pacifism, Socialism, Anarchism: which way to peace and justice?* (New York: War Resisters League, 1980).

Spector, Mordecai, *Twenty Years Toward Peace:* Honeywell Project History, 1968-1988 (Honeywell Project: Minneapolis, 1988).

Silberman, Jack, *Bombies,* (a documentary film).

PBS series, "Eyes on the Prize: The Limits of Nonviolence, 1962."

About the Author

Carol Masters' poetry and short fiction has been published in literary journals and anthologies. Her short story collection, *The Peace Terrorist* (New Rivers Press, 1994) received a Minnesota Voices award 1992 and was nominated for a Minnesota Book Award. She is the recipient of a Loft Mentor Series award, 1983; Loft-McKnight Fellowship 1990; and MN State Arts Board opportunity grant in 1996.